A Horizon of Kindly Light

A Horizon of Kindly Light

A Spirituality for Those with Questions

Jan Kerkhofs

SCM PRESS

Translated by John Bowden from the Dutch *Een Horizon van Teder Licht. Spiritualiteit voor zoekende mensen*, published 1997 by Uitgeverij Lannoo bv, Tielt.

© Uitgeverij Lannoo bv, Tielt 1997

Translation © John Bowden 1999

All rights reserved. No part of this publication may be reproduced, stored in a retrieval system, or transmitted, in any form or by any means, electronic, mechanical, photocopying or otherwise, without the prior permission of the publisher, SCM-Canterbury Press Ltd.

0 334 02743 8

First published 1999 by
SCM Press
9–17 St Albans Place London N1 0NX

SCM Press is a division of SCM-Canterbury Press Ltd.

Typeset by Regent Typesetting, London
Printed in Great Britain by
Biddles Ltd, Guildford and King's Lynn

For Lieve Allary

Contents

Introduction	1
1. In Search of the Light	4
Light in antiquity	6
Greece and Rome	10
Gnosticism	15
The Enlightenment	19
The defence of the light in literature	23
Even now no exceptional quest	33
2. The Light of Revelation	37
The 'glory' of the Lord	38
Paul	46
The Gospel of John	50
The Synoptic Gospels and Acts	59
The Book of Revelation	63
And yet . . .	64
3. Light in the Community of Faith	69
The first centuries	69
From Augustine to Ruusbroec	78
Augustine of Hippo	79
Dionysius the Areopagite	82
Icons	84

Churches as houses of light	89
The mystics	93
Francis of Assisi	93
The Divine Comedy	94
Hadewijch	98
John Ruusbroec	103
Julian of Norwich	108
Nicholas of Cusa, *The Vision of God*	109
John of the Cross	112
Teresa of Avila	115
Between the certainty of yesterday and the doubt of tomorrow: Blaise Pascal	116
The quest continues: the nineteenth and twentieth centuries	119
John Henry Cardinal Newman	119
Thérèse of Lisieux	124
Pierre Teilhard de Chardin	125
Dag Hammarskjöld	128
4. Through the Night	**132**
The threatening void	132
The mystery of evil	136
Jesus and evil	138
What about Jesus and the devil?	139
The strange longing for innocence	142
Veiled or absent light	150
5. Light, A Way to the Unnameable?	**162**
Experience	165
Religious experience and the experience of faith	170
Openness to God or to the void?	178

6. Towards a More Transparent Society — 190

- 'The people that walked in darkness . . .' (Isaiah 9.1) — 190
- The desire for harmony through honesty — 192
- Transparent government — 195
- A transparent economy — 199
- Transparent sexuality — 202
- Transparent dealings with life and death — 205
- Transparent churches — 207
- The 'holy remnant' (Isaiah 4.2–6) — 211

Notes — 215

Introduction

All children are born blind. Soon they see without knowing that they see. They experience the beginning of the creation story and distinguish light and darkness. The darkness makes them afraid. Only through a tender presence do they venture on the night of sleep. They experience the wonder of light when they see particles of dust dancing in a sunbeam and try to catch them.

Flowers, living colours, attract children. And soon they want to give a colourful bunch of them, which evokes the response of a father's and a mother's smile. Slowly nature becomes a book with thousands of kinds of light, including the bright chirruping of birds. Here older children have a foretaste of the inner light.[1] Light points almost irresistibly to something else. On a voyage through the Baltic Sea near Stockholm on Midsummer's Eve, the Swedish Deputy Chairman of the OECD broke off a conversation: 'Now I need to be quiet on deck for a while and enjoy this unique golden sky. I'm at home with it; that's my religion.'

The reflections in this book on one aspect of the human quest have many limitations. The white thread of consciousness, conscience and light can be replaced by the scarlet thread of pure vitality, the purple thread of much suffering or the black thread of a disillusioning nihilism. We all write about important things on the basis of quite personal experiences and equally unique interpretations and reinterpretations. These include some very important matters: the basic trust which we may or not have received as children in our upbringing; our relationship with nature, its silence, its noise and its violence; encounters with impressive though usually very ordinary people; the deep experience of love and tenderness. But just as impressive are the dismaying experience of the wickedness and treachery of our fellow human beings, their malice and their cowardice; our clash with the impotence of good and the triumphs of evil, sometimes subtly embodied in the ambiguity of leaders of all kinds, or in the anxious intolerance of the countless prisoners of every form of petty collective consciousness. For Christians, alongside the great suffering caused by the un-Christian nature of many faith communities, there is the unceasing attraction of the unique man Jesus of Nazareth, whose life, death and resurrection and whose message constantly keep breaking through time and history and continue to challenge waverers to keep on the path of discipleship. An undercurrent seems to go on giving meaning to the lives even of the many who have not (yet) seen him. Among them this undercurrent is characterized by a twofold nostalgia: for more liberation by more light – existential, scientific and ethical – and more tenderness. That nostalgia touches on the heart of existence. It comes over people and can grow in them as a call from elsewhere. Through that nostalgia they are both humanized and divinized.

It is still important to be able to 'listen to the light':[2] not only to the light of the conscience,[3] but more deeply to the light that is a dimension of existence. The symbol of light has been, and still is, a very important pointer to this dimension in almost all cultures. Of course symbols have several significances. Paul Tillich strongly emphasized that 'religious symbols are not stones which fall from heaven but are rooted in the totality of human experience',[4] and this experience always has a psychological and a cultural sociological determination. But, as M.Meslin rightly says, symbols are at the same time the most adequate expression of the self-manifestation of this constantly astonishing Other to human beings: 'they are the most suitable language for expressing the "ultimate reality".'[5]

The fundamental question remains: is there in and through the 'light' of consciousness, of the conscience, of revelation, an experience of another Light which conveys this distinctive light?

Is the light truly transparent to that other Light? Or does human existence just consist in being cast blind from darkness to night, without a horizon? In that case we could share the view of Rainer Maria Rilke:

> More than ever
> the things that one can truly experience move further away
> since what displaces and replaces them is activity without an image.

Others have treated the theme of light in their own way: L. Dupré,[6] H. Fortmann,[7] M. M. Davy.[8] However, their perspectives were different. This book does not set out to improve on these great authors, but rather to be attuned to the present-day world, which still continues to seek, and is more constrained by night.[9]

In his *The Four Quartets* T. S. Eliot has become the 'prophet on the dark mountain': seeing is just slightly better than not yet seeing. From the underground tunnel a ray of sunlight emerges; emptiness begins to reconnoitre the fullness, and 'the still point of a world which turns on itself' is reached. The old poet sees a horizon, a garden, where children laugh and everything comes home, fire and rose:

> And all shall be well and
> All manner of thing shall be well
> When the tongues of flame are in-folded
> Into the crowned knot of fire
> And the fire and the rose are one.

I

In Search of the Light

Symbols are part of everyday language. The sense of belonging to states, nations, ideologies, associations, schools and guilds is expressed by symbols: flags, monuments, badges, uniforms. Usually a symbol speaks volumes. The oldest symbols in all cultures are religious by nature.

L. Dupré rightly comments:

> Authentic religious symbols are essentially ontological, preceding any rational reflection. What we now call 'religious' symbolism has in fact grown out of the first attempt by human beings to structure reality. To begin with, all symbols belonged to the same existential sphere. Even today most people do not experience religious symbolism as the juxtaposition of two separate spheres in reality, the one religious and the other secular, as Western men and women usually do . . . Symbols come into being in a first fundamental reflection on experience of the world. Further reflection on this experience requires rational concepts. But these can never replace the primary expression.[1]

The symbolism of light occupies a central place in the religious bed-rock of the philosophical quest. Light conjures up many meanings. According to R. Pettazoni, light initially indicates the divine omniscience. The sun and moon are God's eyes. God sees everything all the time. One cannot escape God's gaze. Human beings stand naked and vulnerable before him, with no hiding place. According to Mircea Eliade, the sun and moon, with their cyclical rising and setting, at the same time indicate human transitoriness. The roots of the traditional, tellurian, worship of the moon, and the uranic worship of the sun, and along with this the symbolism of the polarity between woman (moon) and man (sun), are rooted in the cult of light. Light and life are of course closely interconnected. In the initiation into the Greek mysteries the marriage torch was a sign of new life. According to J. Mirsky,[2] Stonehenge, from the beginning of the Bronze Age (1800–1400 BC), marks the transition from the worship of Mother Earth, with the Stone Age fertility cult, to the sun cult, and above all the celebration of the winter solstice:

> The subterranean forms of cult, which together with the knowledge of agriculture and the taming of animals had come to Northern Europe from Mediterranean culture, now gave way to the gods from heaven.

Philologists think that the Latin word *deus* (god) comes from *divas* (bright sky), as in Sanskrit. Of course it is not surprising that in many religions light has a divine dimension. We need think only of the sun worship of the Inca Indians in the Andes or of the moon cult among the ancestors of Israel, who also had female deities. And I have personally watched the Muslim leaders in Chad announcing the end of Ramadan from the moment when they saw the fine crescent of the new moon appearing in the dark sky. Light preserves its prerogatives even in Islam, which is strictly monotheistic and aniconic.

Mircea Eliade, the expert *par excellence* in comparative religion, writes on the relationship between light and religion:

> It is important to emphasize that whatever the nature and intensity of the experience of light may be, it always evolves into a religious experience. In all the forms of the experience of light that we have cited [namely, transfiguring light, revealing light, annihilating light, etc.] we find a common denominator: they take human beings out of their profane universe or

their historical situation and transfer them into a qualitatively different universe which is a quite other world, transcendent and sacral. The structure of this sacral and transcendent universe differs from culture to culture, from religion to religion . . . However, one fact remains which seems to me to be fundamental: whatever the later ideological integration may be, the encounter with light brings about a break in the existence of the subject as a result of which this encounter reveals the world of the spirit, of the holy, or freedom, or discloses these more clearly than before – in a word, existence as a divine work of art, or the world hallowed by the presence of God.[3]

The symbolism of light is universal. We find it in ancient Egypt, in Iran, India, China, among the Greeks and Romans. Light can be both annihilating and liberating. Sudden spiritual illumination can be interpreted as wisdom or madness. Often it is compared with a flash of lightning, while the accompanying clap of thunder terrifies, as a *mysterium tremendum*. Those in ancient Siberia who were struck by lightning were thought to have been taken away by heaven, and afterwards their material remains were venerated as relics. Those who survived were regarded as transfigured shamans. Eliade gives similar examples from the Eskimos, the Australian Aborigines and from India.

Light in antiquity

We know how much ancient Egypt was characterized by the cult of light.[4] Re denotes both the sun and the sun god, and Aten the disc of the sun. Heliopolis, the city of the sun, was the most important sanctuary. It is the sun god who watches over truth and justice. Numerous hymns were dedicated to the sun. The most famous is that of Pharaoh Amenophis IV (1370–1352 BC). This Pharaoh ruled over an empire which extended from the Nubian desert to the Euphrates. During the first years of his reign he built a great temple at Karnak, dedicated to Aten. However, in the fourth year of his reign, he suddenly broke with his powerful clergy and founded a new capital in Middle Egypt, Akhetaten ('the horizon of the disc'), now El Amarna. He abolished all other cults and changed his name to Akhenaten ('the splendour of Aten'). His religious teaching was to last until his death, after which people returned to the previous cult. Akhenaten no longer gave a central place to the divinized sun, but to the effect of the sun, which permeates all creatures and divinizes them. He introduced a short phase of rationalization, individualization and internalization of religion, with at the same time a universalization as a result of the universal character of the experience of light.

Here is a short quotation from Akhenaten's famous hymn:

You shine out in beauty on the horizon of heaven,
living sun, the beginning of life.
When you have appeared on the eastern horizon,
you have filled every land with your perfection.
You are beautiful and great,
bright and high above every land;
your rays encompass the lands
to the very limit of all that you have made.
You are Re and reach to their limit
and restrain them for your beloved son.
Although you are far away,
your rays are on earth;
although you are in man's countenance,
no one knows your going.[5]

This involuntarily conjures up Goethe's poetic reflection:

Were the eye not attuned to the sun,
how could we look on the light?
If God's own power did not live in us,
how could the divine have carried us away?[6]

Ancient Persia was also familiar with the cult of the sun. Mithras, the god of kings and warriors, was visible in the sun. The central moment in the cult was the killing of the bull by Mithras; the world came into being from the dying bull. The bull was the white moon (the crescent its horns). The rising of the sun is the triumph of Mithras, and Mithras constantly kills the bull, which, from the time of the full moon, constantly disappears again.

This religion continued to live on in the Mithras mysteries of the Roman empire, above all from around 140 to 313. We know about this worship from archaeological material from all over the Roman empire. For the Romans it gave rise to a whole cosmic religion (with the zodiac, hence horoscopes), which played a great role in late antiquity.[7] Mithras also accompanies the souls to the hereafter, where he leads them up a ladder with seven steps to the pure light; at the same time he is also the vehicle for the most important non-Christian eschatology. The Mithras cult called for a brave life in the service of the god and for a fight against one's own passions. The initiated mystic had to set his gaze on eternity and orientate himself on the immutability of the vast starry heaven.

The Mithras mysteries responded to religious nostalgia with the comforting promise of the immortality of the soul and its bond with the deity. All this received a quasi-scientific support from the astronomy of the time. From the time of the emperor Constantine, who initially also followed the sun cult, the influence of the Mithras mysteries was to decline rapidly in the West under the influence of Christianity. This had already for some time purged itself of the sun cult and preferred the clarity of the word to the chaos of mythical accounts. The cult had a last revival under the emperor Julian (361–363), called the Apostate. He regarded the 'darkness' of Christianity – he thought that it was practised mainly by the poorer strata of the population – as an enemy and returned to the old worship of the emperor and the sun, the one god Helios, who was said to have founded Rome and given his benefits through the mediation of Apollo, Dionysius, Asclepios and Athene.[8]

The light mysticism in the Mediterranean basin was beyond

doubt subject to influences from Asia. Persian Zoroastrianism was marked by the tension between light and darkness. Many legends grew up around this. To give just one example: Zarathustra's radiance in his mother's womb during the last three days before his birth was said to have been so intense that the whole of his father's village was illuminated by it. Here too holiness is symbolized by luminescence. According to Plutarch, Zarathustra had accepted two gods, one of which was like the light, the other like the darkness. This doctrine – like the Mithras cult – influenced the later Manichaeism which was to attract the young Augustine so much.

Mircea Eliade gives a short synthesis of the complicated light mysticism which flourished all over ancient Asia. Thus the *Upanishads* in India say that the light which shines above the heavens, above all things, is the same light as that which shines in human beings. Light is identical to the immortality of the core of being. Perfect light is the pure light in which there is nothing but light, and in which one therefore no longer sees 'anything'. By the practice of yoga one comes to the light and liberates oneself for the absolute experience of light in which the deity reveals itself.

One example is the self-revelation of Krishna to Arjuna in Chapter 11 of the *Bhagavad-gita*. Here he appears in the form of fire.

> If the light of a thousand suns suddenly arose in the sky, that splendour might be compared to the radiance of the Supreme Spirit. That is how I see you – who ever saw you? – as fire, as the sun, blinding, incomprehensible. Without beginning, middle, or end; I behold your infinite power, the power of your innumerable arms. I see your eyes as the sun and the moon. And I see your face as a sacred fire that gives light and life to the whole universe in the splendour of a vast offering. Your vast form reaches the sky, burning with many colours, with wide open mouths, with vast flaming eyes. The flames of your mouths devour all the worlds.

In ancient India, flame and light symbolize the creation of the cosmos, indeed even the nature of the cosmos, precisely because the universe is seen as a free manifestation of the deity, in the last instance as its game.[9]

According to the tradition of Chinese Buddhism, five lights shine at the birth of each Buddha, and at his death a flame escapes from his body. And each Buddha can illuminate the whole of the universe with his eyelashes. The *Tibetan Book of the Dead* calls going into one's essential selfhood at death 'the pure truth', and commands: 'Be not anxious or oppressed, it is the splendour of your own true nature. Recognize it.' However, one can also reject that true nature and chose the murky light and then return to earth (here we think of reincarnation).

Greece and Rome

As is well known, light was also an important symbolic reality for the Greeks. The Greek word for light (*phos*) that we find in Homer seems to come from 'the appearance of the dawn'. Homer calls dying 'a parting from the light'. For him, light is the world of the gods, light is redemption and the redeemer is light. The woman is called 'the light of the house'.

Among the pre-Socratic philosophers, Parmenides sees the wise coming out of the night to the light of the truth. The Orphics see humanity coming to light through the mating of eros and chaos.

Here a short excursus on Plato and Neoplatonism is worthwhile because of the great influence that both these had on the later light metaphysics and theology. Plato (427–347 BC) was a pupil of Socrates, the founder of Greek philosophy.[10] He sees two great levels, that of the outside world which can be perceived with the senses, constantly changes and is subject to mortality, and that of the world of ideas, which remain, and of which the highest is the idea of the Good. Every soul is called to free itself for the world of ideas and the vision of it. When the soul is released from its union to the body, it is put in a position to return to the world whence it came. But this liberation is difficult, since most want to remain in apparent reality.

The idea is a model (paradigm) for the concrete on earth, which is only an incomplete depiction (*icon*) of it. Hence the notion of 'participation': things participate in the idea (later, in scholastic teaching, this becomes the 'analogy'). Everything concrete is relative and shifting. Only Being, to which the ideas belong, is abiding. However, the soul has seen these ideas from its previous incorporeal existence. This knowledge which has become latent during bodily life can again gradually be brought to consciousness from within. Plato sees the body as the tomb or prison of the soul. The wise man wants to be liberated from it; his soul is immortal and unborn. Plato never got away from this unavoidable dualism (see the myth of the winged chariot in the *Phaedrus*).[11]

The ideas are divine, and the highest idea is that of the Good. But Plato never calls this 'god' or 'gods', although it is divine. Nor does he give it any personal character. Insight (*nous*) is always the activity by which men can see the ideas; thus it is not the consciousness but conscious activity. Human beings are driven to the Good by a dynamism (*'eros'*). In this way they achieve their happiness (*eudaimonia*), a successful life. Those who are not in tune with this do evil to themselves (there is no mention of 'sin'). But Plato gives one sanction a mythical form: when after the death of the body the soul is again bound up with a body, any reincarnation thus brought about is governed by the moral state of the previous life, although on the way conversion is always possible. Every individual is solely responsible for his fortune or misfortune (*Republic* X):

> 'The responsibility lies with him who chooses; God is not responsible.'

The whole of a good and wise life consists in constantly turning to the Good, in which the soul more or less participates. This basic movement towards insight into the good supports the whole of reality.

There is no clear trace here of a metaphysic of light, but there will certainly be some side-effect, as is illustrated by the famous myth of the cave. In this myth, with which the seventh book of the *Republic* begins, Plato expresses the opposition between the world of true reality, that of the ideas, and the world of phenomena. This myth was later also to inspire the Christianity of the first centuries and was at the same time a threat because of the dualism which it expresses. Here is an extended summary of it. In his dialogue with Glaucon, Plato says:

> Imagine an underground cave with an opening that lets in the light extending along its entire length. In the cave are people who have had their legs and necks fettered from childhood so that they remain in the same spot. They can only see the objects in front of them. Behind them burns a fire and between the fire and the prisoners a narrow way runs, alongside which a low wall has been built, just as the exhibitors of puppet shows have partitions above which they show the puppets. The prisoners are like us. They can see only the shadows cast on the back wall of what moves there and, if they could speak, they would give the name of these objects to the shadows. They would think that there was no other reality outside these shadows. Now what would happen if one of these prisoners were released? He would look round, cramped and painfully. The light would hurt his eyes and he would not see any of the objects the shadows of which he had seen previously. If one were to ask him about them, he would assert that what he saw previously had more reality. If one were then to take him out of the cave into the sunlight, then very slowly he would see the real people and objects. Later he would enjoy the sunlight and recognize the seasons. If he were then to return to the cave, the darkness there would at first prevent him from seeing anything. If he were then to relate his experience to the prisoners, they would laugh at him and say, 'Anyone who wants to take us out of here will have to kill us.' Well, Glaucon, that is the human condition. The underground cave is the visible wortld.

The prisoner creeping towards the light is the soul that rises to the sphere of the invisible. Above that there is the idea of the good, which one observes only with great difficulty. In the visible world it gives the sun and in the ideal world it gives truth and insight. It is this idea which we must learn to know. It is the first cause of all that is beautiful and good in the universe. If one is to rule the state well, one must know it.[12]

After the explicit rationalism of Aristotle, which is alien to any dualism, and after the negative attitude of the Sceptics; after the Stoics with their special attention to ethics (Seneca), at the beginning of the Christian era many more religious thinkers returned to Platonism. The believing Jew Philo of Alexandria (c.30 BC–c. AD 50) tried to express the Old Testament teaching about God in Greek philosophical terms. The word that comes from God is seen as encompassing the world of ideas. From the created world one can come to know the Word and thence God. But truly to know God it is necessary to be given a vision by God, as happened to Abraham and Moses.

The most prominent Neoplatonist is beyond doubt Plotinus (205–270), who first lived in Alexandria and later above all in Rome. He derived the main features of his thought from Plato. In his teaching he refers to the inner experiences of his hearers: one achieves happiness only by transcending all that is external in order to achieve the simplicity of the good. Everything comes from a primal ground and returns to it, namely to the spirit (*nous*) in which the soul (*psyche*) participates. This soul is directed both towards higher things and to the body. However, even the spirit, with the multiplicity of the world of forms, is not the highest. The highest is the One (or the Good), which cannot be named or defined. Plotinus describes this as the radiance of the sun and the stars, as the appearance of an object illuminated in a mirror, as the flow from a spring. It is of the nature of this – impersonal – One to do this of necessity: through the gradual emanation towards Spirit, soul, matter, the One is still itself. The material world is the opposite of the One, in other words manifold, and in fact simply the absence of the One and the Good.

However, Plotinus, unlike the Gnostics, does not see the material world as wholly bad: it is as good as it can be. The soul became bad by forgetting its heavenly origin and losing itself in the material world, at least in its lower regions. The soul must return to its primal beauty through contemplation. It must again flee to the higher, so that, raised up by the urge of the divine eros, it forgets itself in ecstasy. The many elements which later turn up in philosophical and theological thought are contained in this philosophical attempt to understand the mystery of existence. Its influence on Eastern and Western philosophy was very great. Even the emperor Julian the Apostate drew from it the structure for his attempt to play off a renewed paganism against the Christians. And a militant anti-Christian Neoplatonism continued to be active in the Academy in Athens, until the emperor Justinian closed it in 529.

Here are some excerpts from Plotinus' work in which the motif of light is expressed. In the *Enneads*,[13] the relationship between body, soul and spirit is described like this:

> Thus there is in the Nature-Principle itself an ideal archetype of the beauty that is found in material forms and, of that archetype again, the still more beautiful archetype in soul, source of that in Nature. In the proficient soul this is brighter and of more advanced loveliness: adorning the soul and bringing to it a light from that greater light which is Beauty primally, its immediate presence sets the soul reflecting upon the quality of this prior, the archetype which has no such entries, and is present nowhere but remains in itself alone, and thus is not even to be called a reason-principle but is the creative source of the very first reason-principle which is the beauty to which soul serves as matter.

Then he describes the heaven of the gods and of the souls who came from there:

> For all is transparent, nothing dark, nothing resistant; every being is lucid to every other, in breadth and depth; light runs through light . . .

This alien world of light also embraces Zeus himself and the gods:

> This is why Zeus, although the oldest of the gods and their sovereign, advances first towards that vision, followed by gods and demigods, and such souls as are of strength to see. That Being appears before them from some unseen place and rising loftily over them pours its light upon all things, so that all gleams in its radiance; it upholds some beings, and they see; the lower are dazzled and turn away, unfit to gaze upon that sun . . .

Of course such language is perplexing for anyone living towards the end of the twentieth century, but it shows the groping for meaning through the symbols of light, as in the following quotation:

> Thus the Good is pure light, light that begets the Spirit without itself being quenched in this begetting, but remains like itself, while the Spirit is begotten by the fact that the Good exists. For if the Good were not thus, then the Spirit would not have been produced.[14]

Furthermore, Plotinus says that the Good does not itself think and that anyone who is united with it transcends any thought and even the Spirit. However, he himself recognizes that he does not see clearly.

Gnosticism

Meanwhile, during the rise of Christianity, the whole of the Mediterranean basin experienced the very powerful blossoming of new religion which has already been mentioned. This is usually summed up under the heading of Gnosticism, after the Greek word for knowledge, *gnosis*.

According to Hans Jonas, Gnosticism has a twofold source for its dualism: Hellenistic culture (with Neopythagoreanism and Neoplatonism) and the East, above all Persia. Others add a third source, Christianity: many Gnostics sought support in a – perverted – reading of the Gospel of John.

The success of the Gnostics was to a large degree due to the general situation which has already been sketched out, of a confusing quest for meaning and a religious revival, to some degree analogous to what is going on now in much of the Western world and also in Eastern Europe.

For us it is particularly important that the Gnostics distinguish our dark world from the heavenly world of light.[15] The dualism of the Gnostics saw the core of the human being as a spirit which had fallen into the human soul from the Light, a spark or pearl thrown into the darkness. In answer to the lament of this imprisoned light, the divine Light sends redemption from above to reunite the spark or pearl with itself, away from the dark cosmos. Gnosticism accepts two primal forces, those of light and darkness. Depending on the sub-system, which is packaged in much fantasy and mythology, the spark has to be 'redeemed' through irrational knowledge by means of a return to the Light. Those who do not succeed in this during their lifetimes are subject to a series of rebirths. Knowledge is attained through initiation. They liberate themselves from the cosmos: the kingdom of darkness and the fabrication of lower powers.

Two strands are developed in gnosticism: an ascetic strand (which condemns sexuality as bad) and a libertinistic nihilistic strand (which through its fatalism in fact rejects any personal responsibility and at the same time presents a closed androgyny, opposed to the split between male and female). Very soon, for example in the canonical letters attributed to John, action had to be taken against the Gnostic tendencies which had entered the young churches. We find a similar reaction in I Timothy 6.20–21:

O Timothy, guard what has been entrusted to you. Avoid the godless chatter and contradictions of what is falsely called knowledge (*gnosis*), for by professing it some have missed the mark as regards the faith.[16]

One example of prayer among the Gnostics should be sufficient here. According to an Apocryphon of John the disciples address the Redeemer as follows:

'Rabbi, reveal to us the mystery of the light of your Father, since we heard you say, "There is also a baptism of fire and there is also a baptism of the holy Spirit of light, and there is a spiritual anointing which leads souls to the treasure of light."' Jesus said to them: 'There is no mystery more excellent than this mystery about which you ask, for it will lead your souls to the light of lights, to the place of truth and goodness, to the place of the holy one of all holy ones, to the place which is neither female nor male, nor are there fires in that place but a constant and indescribable light.'[17]

Here we recognize the influence of light mysticism from Persia and Babylonia. It is also said to be perceptible in the teaching of the Essenes, as this can be read in the scrolls from Qumran by the Dead Sea. Ancient Gnosticism still seems to live on in Iraq among the small group of Mandaeans, which moreover is at the same time both anti-Jewish and anti-Christian (Manda is the Aramaic word for knowledge).

The strongest influence on Gnosticism came from the Babylonian prophet Mani (216–177), who emphasized the existence of a set of powers of evil and darkness and of a god of light, with sharp oppositions between god and the world, life and death, soul and body.[18] Mani regarded himself as the one who completed the teaching of Buddha, Zarathustra and Jesus. Although the church definitively suppressed Mani's teaching as a major current in the course of the fourth century, it keeps cropping up in sects which detach themselves from Christianity, like the Cathars ('the pure'), and present-day sects like that of the Sun Temple.

This did not prevent Manichaeism, in a quite radical way, from being the expression of a confrontation with the enigma of the existence of evil (we need only think of the Christian doctrine of 'original sin', which is still very obscure) that indicates a deep nostalgia for redemption. All this is aptly expressed in this Turkish Manichaean prayer:

> Now, our gracious Father, countless myriads of years have passed since we were separated from you. We long to behold your beloved, radiant, living face.[19]

It is not surprising that, above all in his youth, the greatest church father, Augustine (354–430), was strongly influenced by the pessimism and the fatalism of the Manichaeans. He never seems to have been freed from it completely, and this feature is handed down in a long tradition extending to the doctrine of predestination and Jansenism, with an abiding suspicion of what one would regard as a more optimistic authentic Christian humanism. Nominalism, too, even in its present-day forms,[20] has been coloured by it.

In his synthesis of Gnosticism down the ages,[21] S. van Wersch quite rightly sees a new Gnosticism in the New Age movement, though the pessimism is very much weakened. However, the initiates identify themselves with the divine and shining cosmos to such a degree that not much room is left for individual personal responsibility (even towards a personal God). The divine becomes immanent in the initiates, and the borderline with pantheism becomes blurred. Nor is it very surprising that here the doctrine of reincarnation is virulent, or that a new pessimism can soon come into being: individuals are simply a fleeting breath of air in a beautiful, closed cosmos, in which they are really imprisoned without a perspective, despite the wealth of symbols and new mythologies through which an abundance of esoteric literature tries to grasp the meaning of existence. Thus for quite a few people, what is supposed to be light becomes a new prison. They are imprisoned in an empty universe, with a fragile self-redemption as the only way out.[22]

Right up to the eve of the Renaissance, the whole of Europe was moulded by the all-embracing influence of Christianity. Moreover the quest for the light took place almost exclusively – apart from the Islamic part of Spain – under the influence of Christian faith. The next two chapters will investigate this. However, we must not forget that for great parts of northern and north-eastern Europe, pagan cults were of overwhelming importance until after the end of the tenth and eleventh centuries. And here the sun, heavenly bodies and seasons played a major role. A somewhat superficial or short-term Christianization meant that everyday pre-Christian religious views continued to remain stronger in a vague popular religion than elsewhere, coupled with little or no confession of the content of Christian faith (we might think of the 'celebration' of the winter and summer solstices).

The Enlightenment

After preparation for the new development in the fifteenth and sixteenth centuries (Nicholas of Cusa, Nicolai Copernicus and the great astronomers, Leonardo da Vinci and Giordano Bruno), towards the end of the seventeenth century a quite different approach to reality established itself with growing strength. Philosophy turned increasingly to the roots of human consciousness. Descartes (1596–1650) paved the way for Hegel and Kant, and was also already a long-term preparation for the phenomenologists and depth-psychologists. The natural sciences, which increasingly combined philosophy and physics, accelerated their investigation of the macrocosm (through astronomy) and the microcosm (through chemistry and biology), increasingly inspired by the doctrine of evolution. The difference between the 'superlunary' and the 'sublunary', heaven and earth, fell away. The world-view of Dante, laid out in spheres, disappeared. The earth, even the sun, was no longer the centre. The universe became an explosive movement of an endless mass of gigantic 'heavenly bodies'. All the former divinized symbols became objects for science. When Nicholas of Cusa still accepted God as a fixed point from which human beings, despite all their mobility, derive their fixed nature, God himself first shifted towards becoming a necessary principle for buttressing reason and then, having been depersonalized, disappeared by coming to coincide with the reality that can be perceived (Spinoza's *deus sive natura*).

Moreover it is not surprising that after Pascal with his suppressed awe ('What is a man, in infinity?'),[23] Voltaire himself goes further and in his last poem, at the same time his last letter, stoically communicates his hopelessness:

> Steadfastly I endure
> my long and sad existence,
> without the error of hope.[24]

However, before it reached that point, a large part of the Western European elite found itself in the grip of an all-embracing belief in progress. Astronomical observatories were built everywhere, and the Jesuit colleges had laboratories. P.Chaunu comments that 'the Europe of the Enlightenment continued to look at the heavens'.[25]

The way that had been taken led to an emphasis on immanence, with its endless possibilities, thanks to the technology and the increasingly refined organization of scientific research. The transcendent dimension was reduced to an aprioristic condition of the observable worlds within.[26] The description of this process fills whole libraries.

We shall not go more closely into it here, except to introduce a key word, the Enlightenment.

Although the French (*'les Lumières'*), the English ('Enlightenment') and the German (*'Aufklärung'*) components of this European event cannot be brought together under a common denominator, the basic view is the same: human beings are in a position gradually to get to know the whole of reality through scientific analyses. The God of revelation, to the degree that this word is accepted, moves completely into the inner chamber of the heart, although for most people he remains a kind of theoretical guarantee of the 'order' of scientific regularity.

In fact, apart from France in the eighteenth century with Voltaire (1694–1778) and Diderot (1713–1784), the vast majority in England and in the German-speaking world continued to combine 'religious' experience with the scientific approach, though always with a clear distinction between the two, until finally prayer and mysticism were brought under the heading of psychology. Above all at the time of Romanticism, cold scholarship was coupled with a pietistic current (we might think of Descartes, Newton, Locke, Leibniz, Rousseau and even to some degree of Kant). Auguste Comte (1798–1857), an exceptionally influential figure, made another attempt to win over the church (and the General of the Jesuits) to his view, regarding the conscience as the fruit of the collective consciousness. However, there was no question of any synthesis in which all facets of human nature are given their due, as was the case during the Middle Ages and even during the Renaissance. All that could be quantified was illuminated, but the old 'light' was largely quenched.

During this whole period of scientific progress the Protestant countries, with their greater tolerance, had a clear advantage over the Catholic countries, above all those around the Mediterranean.[27]

In the philosophical sphere it was Kant (1724–1804) who rounded off the eighteenth century and had an enormous and abiding influence as a result of his critical attitude towards any absolute knowledge. However, at the same time he revealed the limits of reason. G. W. F. Hegel (1770–1831) also tried to put Christianity in a rational context in a brilliant but closed synthesis. But his optimism came up against the criticism of the Dane Søren Kierkegaard (1813–1855), who pointed out the inadequacy of any one-sidedly rationalistic approach to reality and indicated the absurdity that is present everywhere in existence. Protesting against the way in which the church had been made middle-class, he turned towards an internalized Christianity. However, in the nineteenth century the process of secularization, which in the eighteenth century remained limited to an elite, increasingly broke through among the masses.

Still, it cannot be denied that the whole spiritual movement of the Enlightenment represented a tremendous contribution as a process of liberation from both political and ecclesiastical authoritarianism, if not obscurantism. At the same time we cannot lose sight of the fact that in this revolutionary period of the collective consciousness in art, mysticism and among the ordinary population, the motif of light in faith continued to have an influence on countless intellectuals, albeit against a weak theological background among both Catholics and Protestants (and of course throughout the Orthodox world). We need only think of the Baroque, and great artists like Rembrandt (1606–1669) and Georges de la Tour (1593–1652). Moreover the whole Bach family, including Johann Sebastian Bach (1685–1750), wrote sublime music in which the tones of another reality can clearly be heard, as in the many other brilliant composers of this time. Pietism – and later Romanticism[28] – opposed a one-sided rationalism that failed to understand the deep significance of the religious in human existence. A whole literature of piety, many hymns and powerful spiritual movements, find their origin here. Great representatives like John Wesley (1703–1791) and Emmanuel Swedenborg (1688–1772) exercised a deep influence in Protestant areas, the former in England as founder of the Methodists and in the United States, and Swedenborg in Scandinavia and also in North America.

Meanwhile theology in the eighteenth century and predominantly also in the nineteenth century was largely imprisoned in sterile schools intent on repetition, without daring to enter into dialogue with what was going on in the intellectual world of the great researchers.[29] The churches were flooded with cheap apologetic and devotional writings. And in the Catholic Church the few sound theologians were strictly held in check until the first decades of the twentieth century by a church authority which was characterized by fear of modernity.[30] We might think of Newman, Lagrange and later of Teilhard de Chardin, De Lubac, Chenu and Congar. The short period before the Second Vatican Council and the Council itself introduced a new era.

However, the longing for a second dimension to give more light in a life which was becoming flat did not die out. By way of example, let us listen to some great figures from literature who kept this consciousness alive. They stand out above the many who had no hope.

The defence of the light in literature

Nicolas Berdyaev calls Fyodor Michailovich Dostoievsky (1821–1881) a gnostic, albeit of a very special kind. He has seen something at the bottom of human consciousness, in its hellish and heavenly complexity.[31] So far no one has managed to synthesize the whole wealth of this utterly Russian genius. Dozens of authors have tried to explain his work in the most contradictory ways and to claim it as an argument for their own ideologies. It is certain that from the moment of his pardon on 22 December 1849, just before he was about to be executed, Dostoievsky began a difficult quest for the light. The son of a doctor and himself an engineer, he followed Gogol and opted for literature. His four years of forced labour in Siberia were decisive for his leaning towards ordinary Russian people. Just as decisive, however, was the fact that there was only one book in the camp: the Gospel.

Only from one perspective – which according to many writers is very important[32] – can we approach the man himself through his novels. Apocalyptic visions and the underworld of nihilism incessantly intersect. In the midst of the most ambiguous, passionate, even diabolical human relations sometimes a single nostalgia, a single eros emerges: in extreme dramas, the light of the crucified and risen Christ breaks through.[33] It develops from the confusion of the goodness and evil of tragically free human beings and at the same time becomes transparent in creation. The deepest, most devastating void can still be completely filled with sheer mercy, with God's tenderness, and thus can finally blossom in all-embracing harmony.

Two figures in Dostoievsky's novels express the primacy of the light: the innocent, apparently so naïve Prince Andrei Myshkin in

The Idiot, and Alyosha, the youngest of *The Brothers Karamazov*. Here Dostoievsky shows himself to be a great mystic, at the same with his feet firmly on the ground. With his Slavonic soul, but also as an epileptic, he had come to know the darkest abysses of the human psyche. And long before Nietzsche he was familiar with the challenge of nihilism. We read the following fragment in his journal:

> No single expression of atheism in Europe has been formulated so powerfully. Clearly it is not as a child that I believed in Christ, that I confessed faith. It is in the furnace of doubt that my Hosanna has arisen.

For the one who wrote 'Beauty shall save the world', beauty constantly had two faces, those of the Madonna and of Sodom. Few have described so consistently, contrary to all rationalism, the chaos of the challenges posed to the person seeking meaning by the suffering of the innocent, by animal vitalism, by encounter with the Satanic and the stark confrontation with absolute nothingness (we might think of *Letters from the Underworld*, *The Demon*, *Crime and Punishment*, and so on). But perhaps no one has drawn such a golden thread through them as the reader discovers in his works. Almost all his figures, apart from Myshkin and Alyosha, are a mixture of great darkness and a bit of light, and both these also express themselves psycho-somatically.

Dostoievsky had always felt in himself a dream of paradise. We hear him speaking, with his nostalgia and his experience as a prisoner in exile, when the psychologically sick Prince Myshkin, being looked after in Switzerland, describes his state of mind (in *The Idiot*):

> Before him was the brilliant sky, below the lake, and around, the bright horizon, stretching away into infinity. He looked a long time in agony. He remembered now how he had stretched out his arms towards that bright and limitless expanse of blue and had wept. What tormented him was that he was a complete stranger to all of this. What banquet was it,

what grand everlasting festival, to which he had long felt drawn, always – ever since he was a child, and which he could never join? Every morning the same bright sun rises; every morning there is a rainbow on the waterfall; every evening the highest snowcapped mountain, far, far away, on the very edge of the sky, glows with a purple flame; every tiny gnat buzzing round him in the hot sunshine plays its part in that chorus: it knows its place, it loves it and is happy; every blade of grass grows and is happy! Everything has its path, and everything knows its path; it departs with a song and it comes back with a song; only he knows nothing, understands nothing, neither men nor sounds, a stranger to everything and an outcast.

In a world of evil and violence, the experience of clarity and innocence is a strange sight on earth. Alyosha also had experienced that, but the encounter with Starets Zossima had taught him that the light is victorious. Soon after Dostoievsky, falsely accused of parricide, has been condemned to years of forced labour in Siberia, he says:

Yes, we shall be chained, we shall not be free. But then, in our deepest misery, we shall awaken anew to the joy without which man cannot live and God cannot exist. It is God who gives the joy; that is his great privilege. If God is driven from the earth we find him under the earth. Then there, under the ground, deep in the bowels of the earth, we shall raise a tragic song of praise to God who gives joy.

Like Albert Camus later, in *The Plague*, time and again Dostoievsky comes up against innocent suffering, above all the suffering of children. In guilt, the longing for the light of innocence breaks through. In his last and greatest novel, *The Brothers Karamazov*, this topic becomes a constant. The motto of the work is significant: 'Unless a grain of wheat falls into the earth and dies, it does not bring forth fruit' (John 12.24). All are to blame for the darkness of all, even the monk. Starets Zossima says of him:

But when he realizes . . . that's he's responsible to all men for all people and all things, for all human sins, universal and individual – only then will the aim of our seclusion be achieved. For you must know, beloved, that each one of us is beyond all question responsible for all men and all things on earth, not only because of the general transgressions of the world, but each one individually for all men and every single man on this earth.

And further on in the book Zossima says:

I predict that at the very moment when you see with abhorrence that despite all your efforts, not only have you failed to make any progress but even seem to be further away from your goal, at that moment you will suddenly reach your goal and will see clearly in your life the marvellous power of God, of the one who has constantly loved and guided you.

Dostoievsky repeatedly describes the suffering of innocent children, as though it is an obsession: a child whom a general throws to the dogs before its mother's eyes; a child beaten daily by its parents and at night shut up in a dark cupboard. Even the good girl Lisa confesses to Alyosha that she sometimes dreams of eating pineapple while before her eyes a four-year-old child is nailed to the wall and tortured to death. Ivan Karamazov refuses to believe in God because of the innocent suffering of a child. His brother Alyosha agrees with this, but then reacts by pointing to someone who can forgive everything, everyone and for all. For this Someone

. . . gave his innocent blood for all and for everything. You've forgotten him, but it is on him that the edifice is founded, and it is to him that they will cry aloud: 'You are just, O Lord, for your ways are revealed.'

Alyosha does not give a rational answer. He points to the life of Jesus, just as Starets Zossima refers to the faith of Job:

It is a great mystery of human life that suffering endured slowly gives way to silent, inner joy . . . and that our bitter tears will finally become tears of silent emotion and of a purification of the heart.

And in *A Raw Youth*, Dostoievsky makes the pilgrim Makar say: 'Love shines even after death.' In the same work Sonya teaches her son Arkadii: 'Christ, Arkashya, forgives all . . . Christ does not need anything from us and will shine even in the deepest darkness.' And we hear Starets Zossima say in his great farewell speech shortly before his death:

> Look at a child, at the sunset in God's world, at a blade of grass and how it grows; look into a pair of eyes which gaze at you and love you . . . Much remains hidden from us on earth, but in place of this, deep in our souls, God has placed a mysterious sense of a living bond between us and another world, an exalted, higher world. Moreover the roots of our thoughts and feelings are not here, but in other worlds . . .

Dostoievsky brings his whole literary work to an end with Alyosha's words:

> Certainly we shall rise again, certainly we shall see one another and shall tell one another gladly and joyfully all that has been.[34]

In the night of 27/28 January 1881 Dostoievsky felt that he was going to die. He asked his wife Anna Grigorievna to light a candle and bring him the Bible. From it he read Matthew 3.15: 'Let it be so now; for thus it is fitting for us to fulfil all righteousness.' Dostoievsky smiled to her: 'Do you hear that? "Let it be." That means that I'm going to die.' And that evening he did die. He was buried in the cemetery of the monastery of Alexander Nevsky. Thirty thousand people were present at his funeral.[35]

Dostoievsky had foreseen the flood of nihilism which swept over Russia after 1917. Solzhenitsyn has been affected by the hell of recent Russian history. In their experiences both found the beginning of an 'ethic of resurrection'.[36] Olivier Clément, a French atheist who converted to Orthodoxy, says in his book about Solzhenitsyn: 'It seems to me that through much darkness, clearly recognized, Solzhenitsyn has dedicated his work "to the light that is in us".'[37] Some fragments from his work can disclose this dimension.

In *Cancer Ward* Solzhenitsyn relates the musing of the old doctor D. T. Oreshchenkov. He had always insisted on having his own practice and did not treat the sick as numbers. He had just let a patient out and now he sank into a black rocking chair and sat there motionless for a long time.

> He had to take frequent rests nowadays. His body demanded this chance to recoup its strength and with the same urgency his inner self demanded silent contemplation free of external sounds, conversations, thought of work, free of everything that made him a doctor. Particularly after the death of his wife his inner unconscious had seemed to crave a pure transparency. It was just this sort of silent immobility, without planned or even fleeting thoughts, which gave him a sense of purity and fulfilment.
>
> At such moments an image of the whole meaning of existence – his own during the long past and the short future ahead, that of his late wife, of his young grand-daughter and of everyone in the world – was conjured up in his mind. At these times he did not see it as embodied in the work and activity which had occupied these people, which they believed was central to their lives, and by which they were known to others. The meaning of existence was to preserve untarnished, undisturbed and undistorted, the image of eternity which each person is born with – as far as possible.
>
> Like a silver moon in a calm, still pond.[38]

Here Solzhenitsyn is beyond doubt expressing his own experience, as where he makes the sick Oleg comfort the dying

Shulubin. Shulubin whispers: 'There's a fragment, isn't there? . . . Just a tiny fragment.' And Solzhenitsyn goes on:

> It was then it struck Oleg that Shulubin was not delirious, that he'd recognized him and was reminding him of their last conversation before the operation. He had said, 'Sometimes I feel quite distinctly that what is in me is not all of me. There's something else, sublime, quite indestructible, some tiny fragment of the universal spirit. Don't you feel that?'[39]

Earlier, this same Shulubin, during a conversation with his fellow-patient Vadim about science, had slowly answered with eyes closed his question 'What values would you call ethical?', 'Values which are directed towards the mutual illumination of the human spirit.' But according to Shulubin, science does not bring that about. For Solzhenitsyn there is only that wonderful inner light that brings liberation: in all his works the 'prison' is represented by the framework, the work camps, the cancer ward, 'science', 'the system'.

Elsewhere he shows clearly what the issue is. The imprisoned artist Kondrashov-Ivanov from *The First Circle* points out in Sharashka camp that human beings cannot be reduced to an element in 'the system'. He has to depict 'realistic' Soviet art. No one wanted to have a lofty painting, 'The Ravaged Oak'.

> The picture was of a lone oak tree, which by some mysterious force was growing on the outcrop of a bare cliff-face. A dangerous pathway led up the precipice towards the tree, carrying the eye of the viewer with it. The tree was gnarled and bent by the hurricanes which blew there. The strong sky behind the tree was a sky where the clouds never parted, the sun never shone. Destroyed by unceasing combat with the winds which constantly tried to uproot it from the cliff, this obstinate, angular tree with its broken, claw-like, twisted branches, had never given up the struggle and clung on to its precarious patch of ground over the abyss.[40]

After this a conversation begins with Nershin, a fellow prisoner. He insists that the circumstances of life, for example in the Gulag, determine his whole consciousness. The painter reacts vigorously:

> Man is invested from birth with a certain . . . essence. It is as it were the nucleus of his personality, his ego. The only question is – which determines which? Is man formed by life or does he, if he has a strong enough personality, shape life around him? . . . because he has something against which to measure himself. Because he can look at an image of perfection, which at rare moments manifests itself to his inward ego.

Then the painter shows Nershin a little canvas, 'a sketch of the greatest picture of my life', the veil of the Holy Grail the moment that Parsifal first sees the castle of the Holy Grail.[41]

> Dazed, wandering, he was looking into the middle distance, where the upper reaches of the sky were suffused with an orange-gold radiance which might have been from the sun or something else even more brilliant hidden from view by a castle. Its walls and turrets growing out of the ledges of the mountainside, visible also from below through the gap between the crags, between the ferns and the trees, rising to a needle-point at the top of the picture – indistinct in outline, as though woven from gently shimmering clouds, yet still vaguely discernible in all the details of its unearthly perfection, enveloped in a shining and lilac coloured aureole – stood the castle of the Holy Grail (258f.)

Solzhenitsyn's play *A Candle in the Wind*[42] has Luke 11.35, 'See then that the light that is in you is not darkness', as a motto. It was his intention to depict the moral problems of society in the developed countries, including Russia. The theme already becomes clear at the beginning of the play. It all takes place in a utopian settlement where Alex is 'in a little house at the edge of the enormous wilderness'. Mourik mocks Alex:

> *Alex*: ... At the edge of the settlement there wasn't even electricity.
> *Mourik:* No e-lec-tri-city? That sounds like the Stone Age. How do you get light, then?
> *Alex*: With a candle.
> *Mourik:* That could make you blind.
> *Alex*: Did Plato have a battery? Did Mozart have 220 volts? By the light of a candle your heart opens up. You go outside and the scent of wild grass borne by the wind comes to meet you! Great! And without electricity, when the moon rises over the wilderness –it's all bathed in moonlight. Surely you remember that from your childhood years?

Solzhenitsyn's whole work can be interpreted as one great accusation against a perverse and dehumanizing system which is built on lies and does not want to see the light. This is subtly expressed in some lines about the three daughters of the senior Major General Makarygin, the 'prosecutor' for cases which had to be developed in secret.

> His daughters' names were Danera, Datoma and Clara. As was the fashion in those days, Danera stood for DAughter of the New ERA and Datoma stood for DAughter of the TOiling MAsses. Clara was just Clara. No one in the family could remember whether her name was supposed to mean anything.[43]

The picture given by literature of the quest for light needs to be completed with two more poetic expressions. First the description of an experience of light felt as an icon of the divine. In his letters *From the Engadine*, the German Jesuit Peter Lippert, who counselled countless people between the two world wars, wrote:

> I have found a new gift for the eyes. I have discovered that sometimes I would like to caress the Lake of Silvaplana or the Lake of Sils with my eyes. Just as one lovingly caresses soft fine velvet with the fingers, so I would love to caress the surface of

the lake with my eyes, of course from afar . . . When I look at these lakes from a certain height, coloured with quite special hues, I experience something like this. I cast my eyes tenderly over their shining surface, glittering with an internal character and resting on depths filled with light. And a wave of tenderness engulfs me. What is it? A union with the beloved subject which only happens through the eyes? It is clearly a kind of sensuality, yet of the most perfect clarity. It is a completely selfless surrender, resting in the beloved. There one desires nothing and consumes nothing of it; one simply wants to do it good, one wants to caress it from a very long way away and only with the eyes.

Aren't we touching here on a point in the realm of sheer sensuality, in which the essence of spiritual, clear love glimmers through? At least symbolically, don't the senses have moments when they rise above themselves and reach further into the realm of the spirit, just as the soul also has moments when it wants to touch God, to caress him and – if this is not too strong – to stroke him with the finest threads of feeling that it can send out? And since this likeness of the clearest love occurs specifically in the sense of sight, one should be able to conjecture from this that the most purest cherishing, complete union with God in vision, comes about from an infinite distance and yet in a perfect union.[44]

From Dutch literature we might choose Hans Andreus (1926–1977). Although his work is also characterized by the link between love and death, from beginning to end he finds the strongest sensual experience in light. In his poetry he has a personal relationship to the light,[45] which has a redemptive function, though without becoming an object of religious mysticism. It remains limited to the poetry of a physical reality. Even when at a late stage he discovered his Jewish identity, he avoided being 'religious'. Time and again, with a deep melancholy which grew out of much personal suffering, he returns to a gentle redemptive eroticism. Healing, however, comes from the light: 'Only through the light can I get back to people.' Or, as we read in his *Last Poems*:

> Unimaginable nameless, you who
> are clothed and surrounded with so many names
> where no one knows or wants to know more,
> let me sometimes perceive that you are,
> not in a flash of insight, like lightning,
> but as a lightness breathing in me.

Another example, one of many, is the attractive poem from the collection *Around the Mouth of Light*.

> I love the light
> that undulates through the light
> with all its eyes open
>
> and that called me
> by my own name
> when sleepwalking I went
>
> on an earth which was strange to me
> no longer heard the voice
> of those who dwell in that light
>
> and resemble us as –
> if they look in a wavy mirror – children
>
> of such a clear reality
> that you sometimes even see
> around the oblique
>
> corner of time.

Even now no exceptional quest

The previous pages may give the impression that the quest for light is still an elitist one. However, it is possible and even probable that a large number of people in one way or another experience deep moments of 'illumination', but that they do not share these, find no words for them or neglect them.

Some investigations have been made into this, directly or indirectly. Thus the American sociologist Andrew Greeley has made a study of ecstasy which, he thinks, confirms that many more people than is usually assumed have mystical experiences in which light plays a role.[46] David Hay of the Alister Hardy Research Centre in Oxford takes the same line.[47]

Following a suggestion from Elisabeth Noelle-Newmann of the famous Allensbach Institute of Demoscopy, a question was inserted into the 1981 European Values Survey which ran: 'Have you ever had an experience of feeling deep inside you a strong spiritual power which seemed to you to arise from yourself?' Granted, this question was not about light as such, but in the context the answers are revealing. In Western Europe 81% answered no to this question and 12% yes; in the United States 72% as opposed to 24%. The highest percentage of yes answers for Western Europe came from Great Britain (19%) and the lowest from Denmark (2%). In fact this means that some tens of millions of people confirm that they have had such an experience. To the next question, whether this experience had changed their view of life, 12% answered 'very strongly', 16% 'strongly', 16% 'considerably', 20% 'a little' and 25% 'not at all' (in the United States 24%, 22%, 19%, 12% and 13% respectively). It is striking that there is virtually no difference between men and women in the answer to the first question. Nor is the difference between age-groups significant, though the oldest age-groups of women answered the second question more positively than the men. Nor are there differences between Catholics and Protestants. Those who call themselves 'religious' answered the first question more positively than those who said that they were not (16% to 7%). Religious practice similarly had only a limited influence. Whether the person was 'intellectual' or not was irrelevant.

Of course the significance of these facts for our study is limited. The link between particular experiences and the degree of religion emerges clearly when one compares Europe with the religious United States. However, this does not explain the fact that both in the less religious Great Britain (where 58% call themselves religious) and in the more religious Italy (with 83%), 78% declared that they had never had the experience mentioned in the first question.

This empirical material is ambiguous in many ways. However, it does not alter the fact that the age-old views which are so characteristic of all the great religions and of the quest of the human spirit for an experience of something other and greater reflect of a deep longing for liberation from an experience of being shut in. We need only think of the millions of candles which are lit every year by believers (and also by the superstitious). The ambiguity is expressed, sometimes disconcertingly, in a number of forms of new Gnosticism, characteristic of the New Age movement. Here there are dreams of a golden millennium which is apparently at the door and seems already to have broken in.

From the enormous number of publications, here is an example of how Christians can express the hope contained here, however naive the expression of it may be:

> At the present time an internal conflict is taking place at the highest level, both individually and globally. The old is perishing and the new wants to be born. Many people are already experiencing an expansion of consciousness, an internal revolution. We can work together to establish this consciousness in Europe, in Asia and America. Wherever people wake up, hope is born. It is a time of rising light. The darkness is no longer dark; we are at a turning point, on the way back to the light that is our home. Let us hope that we hear and follow this call home. The cry of the falcon finds an echo in my heart. Waking up is a deeply amazing, a marvellous event. The eggshell of creation breaks, and out creeps a powerful being with a gaze which surveys the whole world at a glance . . . At this moment the early light of the dawning day is spreading over the earth. The wraps have been on it long enough. The

New Age, the age of Aquarius, the time of Horus, of the sun of suns, has already begun, although most are still sleeping. But the bright day, mid-day, the zenith of the light is still far off and will not be here for several decades. However, some have been enlightened, for now already the rising sun is perceived by an increasing number of people.[48]

Here we have the language of Nietzsche, strongly diluted. How very different the words of his great opponent, the marginal Jew Jesus, sound!

2

The Light of Revelation

The three great religions of the 'Book', Judaism, Christianity and Islam, each emphasize that the ultimate meaning of human life comes as it were from outside. God gives us light to live our lives. At first sight this is in abrupt contrast to the whole scientific and philosophical quest: people try to discover lines of meaning by analysing a complex reality which is in process of development, and which includes the phenomenon of human consciousness. No answer is expected from outside here. There is no breakthrough 'from elsewhere' into a closed world. All must make their own way towards some perspective on the future. Men and women remain brave individuals who reject any 'outside light' as a mythical packaging of their existential anxiety.

However, whether the two approaches are so radically exclusive is an open question. Can there be no link between the quest 'from within' and being addressed 'from outside'? Isn't the quest supported by revelation, and doesn't revelation clarify the real heart of the quest? For those who follow the teaching of the 'book', in religious terms revelation precedes the solitary quest. Therefore I shall not begin with doubt and suspicion, but with a look at revelation, here limited to the Christian tradition as recorded in scripture.

For Israel, as for all peoples, light and fire were vital. Moreover, both were important religious symbols. But in contrast to many of its neighbours, Israel had no cult of the sun, the moon or light. Light is fundamentally good. The first thing that God did was to remove the primal darkness, when he said, 'Let there be light' (Gen. 1.3). And the Genesis story goes on: 'And there was light. And God saw that the light was good' (Gen. 1.4). But as fire, light is also dangerous. Moses ordered: 'You shall kindle no fire in all your habitations on the sabbath day' (Ex. 35.3). For Israel, light means life, salvation, truth and above all the omnipresent but invisible God.

The 'glory' of the Lord

The terminology of light is hardly worked out at all in the Old Testament. The Lord is not the light that can be experienced, but his presence shines through the people which is faithful to him. Isaiah describes the vision of the new Jerusalem like this:

> Arise, shine, for your light has come,
> and the glory of the Lord has risen upon you.
> For behold, darkness shall cover the earth,
> and thick darkness the peoples;
> but the Lord will arise upon you;
> and his glory will be seen upon you.
> And nations shall come to your light;
> and kings to the brightness of your rising (Isa. 60.1–3).

This vision is taken up later in the book of Revelation (21.9–27).

God's presence gives people insight into what they must do and guides their consciences:

> He made for them inclination, tongue and eyes;
> he gave them ears and a mind for thinking.
> He filled them with knowledge and understanding,
> and showed them good and evil.
> He set his eye upon their hearts,
> to show them the majesty of his works (Sirach 17.6–8).

God does not in fact seek the cult of light. He calls for the light of conscientious action:

> Your new moons and your appointed feasts
> my soul hates;
> they have become a burden to me,
> I am weary of bearing them.
> When you spread forth your hands,
> I will hide my eyes from you;
> even though you make many prayers,
> I will not listen;
> your hands are full of blood.
> Wash yourselves; make yourselves clean;
> remove the evil of your doings from before my eyes;
> cease to do evil,
> learn to do good;
> seek justice,
> correct oppression;
> defend the fatherless;
> plead for the widow (Isa. 1.14–17).

For only those who act like this are themselves bathed in light:

> If you take away from the midst of you the yoke,
> the pointing of the finger, and speaking wickedness,
> if you pour yourself out for the hungry
> and satisfy the desire of the afflicted,
> then shall your light rise in the darkness
> and your gloom be as the noonday (Isa. 58.9–10).

It is clear from these quotations that light is a symbol both of the consciousness and the conscience. Through both these, believers see what God requires of them. Moreover, 'Woe to those who call evil good and good evil, who put darkness for light and light for darkness' (Isa. 5.20).

Anyone who alienates Israel from itself and leads it into captivity is mocked as the false light which will never attain to the true light. Thus Isaiah taunts the king of Babylon:

> How you are fallen from heaven,
> O Day Star, son of Dawn . . .
> You said in your heart,
> I will ascend to heaven,
> above the stars of God I will set my throne on high . . .
> But now you are cast down to the realm of the dead,
> to the depths of the abyss (Isa. 14.12–15).

God is the one who constantly brings his people back to the light and directs it to the messianic perspective which opens up the whole future. He gives the people the hope that all will come right in the end; in other words, that history has meaning, despite the excess of night. Again Isaiah, who according to the New Testament strongly influenced Jesus and the first community, is most explicit here:

> The people who walked in darkness
> have seen a great light.
> Those who dwelt in a land of deep darkness,
> on them has light shined (Isa. 9.1–2).

Indeed, it is God who guides everywhere the blind who trust in him:

> And I will lead the blind in a way that they know not,
> in paths that they have not known, I will guide them.
> I will turn the darkness before them into light,
> the rough places into level ground.
> These are the things I will do,
> and I will not forsake them (Isa. 42.16).

This vision extends further than Israel, and takes on a universal dimension through the 'servant' whom the evangelists Matthew, Luke and John see as a prefiguration of Jesus.

> I am the Lord, I have called you in righteousness,
> I have taken you by the hand and kept you;
> I have given you as a covenant to the people,
> a light to the nations,
> to open the eyes that are blind,
> to bring out the prisoners from the dungeon,
> from the prison those who sit in darkness (Isa. 42.6–7).

It is this saving will that the 'servant' (i.e. the prophet) is to establish:

> It is too light a thing that you should be my servant
> to raise up the tribes of Jacob
> and to restore the preserved of Israel;
> I will give you as a light to the nations,
> that my salvation may reach to the end of the earth . . .
> I have kept you and given you . . .
> saying to the prisoners, 'Come forth,'
> to those who are in darkness, 'Appear' (Isa. 49.6, 8–9).

Then God will lighten all things when the exile is over:

> The sun shall be no more your light by day,
> nor for brightness shall the moon give light to you by night;
> but the Lord will be your everlasting light,
> and your God will be your glory.
> Your sun shall no more go down,
> nor your moon withdraw itself;
> for the Lord will be your everlasting light,
> and your days of mourning shall be ended (Isa. 60.19–20).[1]

The echo of this vision resounds later in the last two chapters of the Apocalypse, a synthesis of the whole revelation. In the meantime, however, the conflict between light and darkness continues, and the prophets make God deal harshly with those who remain in darkness and do not convert to him (cf. e.g. Amos 5.18–20):

> What will the day of the Lord be for you?
> It is darkness and not light;
> as if a man fled from a lion,
> and a bear met him;
> or went into the house
> and leaned with his hand against the wall,
> and a serpent bit him.
> The day of the Lord is darkness and not light,
> and gloom with no brightness in it.

Against this background, the significance of 'glorification', a central concept throughout scripture, can be clarified. 'Glory' (*kabod* in Hebrew, *doxa* in Greek, *gloria* or *claritas* in Latin), originally means emanation of power, riches, beauty, like the rays of the sun which are visible round the edges of a cloud. Therefore 'glory' is the characteristic of leaders like Abraham (Gen. 13.2) of kings like Solomon (I Kings 3.9–14). This property is attributed to God *par excellence*.[2]

The Old Testament gives an impressive example of this in connection with God's appearance to Moses. First of all there is the long narrative of the encounter between the two on Mount Sinai, where Moses receives the stone tablets containing the Law. Some quotations from the book of Exodus illustrate the important experience of God's 'glory':

> Then Moses went up on the mountain, and the cloud covered the mountain. The glory of the Lord settled on Mount Sinai, and the cloud covered it six days, and on the seventh day he called to Moses out of the midst of the cloud. Now the appearance of the glory of the Lord was like a devouring fire on the top of the mountain in the sight of the people of Israel. And Moses entered the cloud and went up on the mountain. And Moses was on the mountain forty days and forty nights (Ex. 24.15–18).

When Moses descended from the mountain and saw how the

Israelites had meantime made an idol, a golden calf, 'his anger burned hot, and he threw the tablets out of his hands and broke them at the foot of the mountain' (Ex. 32.29). After that he melted the image in the fire and had all the idolaters murdered by the Levites. Then he set up his tent outside the camp. When Moses was in the tent, the Lord's pillar of cloud descended on it. Then Moses asked the Lord whether his 'face' would go with him and the people. There follows the story of Moses' great request to see the 'Lord':

> Moses asked, 'I pray you, show me your glory.' And he said, 'I will make all my goodness pass before you, and will proclaim before you my name "the Lord"; and I will be gracious to whom I will be gracious, and will show mercy on whom I will show mercy. But,' he said, 'you cannot see my face; for no one can see my face and live.' And the Lord said, 'Behold, there is a place by me where you shall stand upon the rock, and while my glory passes by I will put you in a cleft of the rock, and I will cover you with my hand until I have passed by; then I will take away my hand, and you shall see my back; but my face shall not be seen' (Ex. 33.18–23).

The longing to see that face still lives on, but in a much more hesitant context. It is described in a very authentic way in a diary entry by Fridolin Stier, once professor of Old Testament in Tübingen, on 11 August 1972:

> One day to comment on one of the greatest scenes in the Old Testament, Exodus 33.17–23, in such a way that – finally – what it is about, namely the longing of the man Moses to see the glory, the face of God, speaks for itself. That means that the exchange consisting in dialogue, promises of protection and guidance is no longer enough for him. In him burns a longing for the full experience, the immediate perception of the reality of God. It continues to be denied him. He is put at the edge of the rock. God holds his hand before his eyes while his glory

passes – 'then I will take away my hand, and you shall see my back; but my face shall not be seen'. And that is the highest, the most extreme, the last that is granted to any theology, philosophy or science to see: God's back. Provided that they desire to see his face.[3]

To return to the Exodus story. After his encounter with God from behind, Moses cut two new tablets of stone on which 'the Lord wrote the words of the covenant, the ten commandments' (Ex. 34.28). After that the glory of the Lord was also reflected on Moses' face:

> When Moses came down from Mount Sinai, with the two tables of the testimony in his hand as he came down from the mountain, Moses did not know that the skin of his face shone because he had been talking with God. And when Aaron and all the people of Israel saw Moses, behold, the skin of his face shone, and they were afraid to come near him (Ex. 34.29–30).

Thereupon Moses put a veil on his face. He took this veil off his face only to speak with the Lord. He did not want to show the shining to the Israelites. Then the Israelites made the ark of the covenant according to the instructions which God gave to Moses. The ark was put in a tent with the documents of the covenant. The whole symbolized the abiding faith of God who goes with his people. The cloud by day and the fiery glow by night are signs of his presence (Ex. 40.36–38).

> Throughout all their journeys, whenever the cloud was taken up from over the tabernacle, the people of Israel would go onward; but if the cloud was not taken up, then they did not go onward till the day that it was taken up. For throughout all their journey the cloud of the Lord was upon the tabernacle by day, and fire was in it by night, in the sight of all the house of Israel.

Thus God, 'clothed in a garment of light' (Ps. 104.2), accompanies his people on the journey through the wilderness.

The power of the encounter of the Lord with Moses must long have made a deep impression on the Israelites. When the life of Moses ends with his death in the last chapter of Deuteronomy, it is summed up in one sentence: 'And there has not arisen a prophet since in Israel like Moses, whom the Lord knew face to face' (Deut. 34.10). The end refers back to the beginning, when the Lord called Moses to lead the people in his name and he had to use all kinds of arguments and signs to convince the reluctant Moses.

This first encounter with the Lord was also clothed in light and fire. On Mount Horeb the angel of the Lord had appeared to Moses 'in a flame of fire out of the midst of a bush' (Ex. 3.2). When out of curiosity Moses approached this bush which 'was burning, yet it was not consumed', God called him from the bush. Moses heard God without seeing him. And then the text continues: 'And Moses hid his face, for he was afraid to look at God' (Ex. 3.6). Although Deuteronomy says that Moses 'knew the Lord face to face', in reality this never happened. He heard and experienced the Lord, but never saw him, except sideways, as it were in the reflection of his shining presence. More than that is not in fact given to a human being, but the experience was so powerful for Moses that it continued to be handed down among his people as far as the New Testament (Matt. 17.3).

However, this experience did not stop a large proportion of the people constantly refusing to recognize the Lord. They doubted in his faithfulness, like those who questioned Job about his suffering: 'They say to me continually, "Where is your God?"' (Ps. 42.10). For those who believe, the Lord remains the one who is always faithful, and the rainbow in the heaven is a symbol of his covenant (Gen. 4.13).[4]

The 'glorious' God also appears in the Old Testament as a God of love, a tender God. The prophets, like Hosea and Amos, present him as a lover who does not betray his unfaithful partner. And the Song of Songs, which was later to inspire so many

Christian mystics, is a love song. Paul's own hymn to love (I Cor. 13) is wholly rooted in Jewish soil, as is Jesus' own constant use of the marriage feast as a symbol of the kingdom of God. Like the Lord in the Old Testament, in the New Testament Jesus appears as a horizon of kindly light.[5]

Although Jesus appears simply as a marginal Jew,[6] the New Testament transposes the whole of the Old Testament glory of God to his person. D. Mollat sums it up like this: 'The essential revelation of the New Testament concerns the link which is made between the "glory" and the person of Jesus.'[7]

Paul

This is expressed most clearly in Paul's Second Letter to the Corinthians (3.1–4,6). Paul compares his task with that of Moses: now Christ writes through Paul not on stone tablets, but with the spirit of the living God in the heart of living men and women. The glory of Moses 'fades in this surpassing splendour' (II Cor. 3.10). The veil which covered Moses remains for the 'Jews', 'when they read the old covenant, that same veil remains unlifted, because only through Christ is it taken away' (II Cor. 3.14). There then follows Paul's very concentrated view (II Cor. 3.16–18).

> But when someone turns to the Lord the veil is removed. Now the Lord is the Spirit, and where the Spirit of the Lord is, there is freedom. And we all, with unveiled face, beholding the glory of the Lord, are being changed into his likeness from one degree of glory to another; for this comes from the Lord who is the Spirit.

Paul develops this train of thought further in II Corinthians when he describes a threefold reflection of the glory. God's glory shines on Jesus Christ and God makes this glory shine in the hearts of believers as a cascade of spiritual light:

> And even if our gospel is veiled, it is veiled only to those who are perishing. In their case the god of this world has blinded

the minds of the unbelievers, to keep them from seeing the light of the gospel of the glory of Christ, who is the likeness of God. For what we preach is not ourselves, but Jesus Christ as Lord, with ourselves as your servants for Jesus' sake. For it is the God who said, 'Let light shine out of darkness,' who has shone in our hearts to give the light of the knowledge of the glory of God in the face of Christ.

Paul never encountered Jesus during Jesus' public life. Perhaps here he is making a passing reference to his own conversion experience as related in the Acts of the Apostles (9.3–10), where on the way to Damascus 'suddenly a light from heaven flashed around him', he heard Jesus' voice (there is no mention of 'seeing Jesus' in the pericope) and became blind for three days. Exegetes deny that in II Cor. 4.6 he is referring to the vision that he talks about in II Cor. 12.1ff. It appears to be an experience of faith.

For Paul, the glory which he mentions is on the borders of time and eternity: it is the risen Lord who is present in the hearts of believers through his spirit, but these believers are at the same time persecuted, dying; they 'see' and yet 'do not see'; 'we walk by faith, not by sight' (II Cor. 5.7). Only those who have a heart enlightened by God 'see' their glory. As an illustration, reference can be made to the pericope about the murder of Stephen (Acts 7.55–57):

> But he, full of the Holy Spirit, gazed into heaven and saw the glory of God, and Jesus standing at the right hand of God; and he said, 'Behold, I see the heavens opened, and the Son of man standing at the right hand of God.' But they cried out with a loud voice and stopped their ears and rushed together upon him.

Saul, the as yet unconverted Paul, had not seen anything of the glory. We are told quite laconically: 'And Saul was consenting to his death' (Acts 8.1).

In contrast to the Gnostics, Paul knows no dualism. There is no pre-existing God of light who is imprisoned in the darkness and frees himself from it again. One is glorified by conversion to the works of the Spirit in the Lord. It is the Lord who brings about this conversion. Glorification implies good actions (as John too will emphasize). We also find in Paul the contrast between the 'children of the light' and the 'children of darkness' which will be worked out in John. According to Acts, Paul declares that he has been sent to the Gentiles by Jesus 'to open their eyes, so that they convert from darkness to the light' (Acts 26.18).

In his First Letter to the Thessalonians, the oldest writing in the New Testament, Paul addresses the community as follows: 'But you are not in darkness, brothers and sisters, for the day to surprise you like a thief. For you are all children of the light and children of the day' (I Thess. 5.4–5). However, that does not apply to the 'Jews', who reject Christ and of whom he says mockingly: 'You who are sure you are a guide to the blind, a light to those who are in darkness' (Rom. 2.19).

The author of the letter to the Ephesians also emphasizes that the believers are children of the light (Eph. 5.8–11, 13–14):

> For once you were darkness, but now you are light in the Lord; walk as children of light (for the fruit of light is found in all that is good and right and true), and try to learn what is pleasing to the Lord. Take no part in the unfruitful works of darkness, but instead expose them . . . but when anything is exposed by the light it becomes visible, for anything that becomes visible is light. Therefore it is said,
> 'Awake, O sleeper, and arise from the dead,
> and Christ shall give you light.'

This last verse seems to be an early Christian baptismal hymn, which indicates that baptism is both resurrection from the dead (Rom. 6.4; Col. 2.12) and illumination (Heb. 6.4; 10.32).

Just as in the Old Testament the conscience is called light, so Paul sees it as an inner light that guides the believer. But in him there is a deeper, mystical dimension: believers allow themselves to be led by the indwelling spirit who is love and who teaches the doing of God by keeping one's gaze on Christ. Indeed, 'The natural person does not receive the gifts of the Spirit of God, for they are folly to him and he is not able to understand them because they can only be discerned in the light of the Spirit' (I Cor. 2.14), namely with 'the mind of Christ' (v.16). It is through this Spirit that the believer encounters Christ as the one who shows the way, a gift for which the Letter to the Ephesians utters the prayer (1.17–18):

> May the God of our Lord Jesus Christ, the Father of glory, give you a spirit of wisdom and of revelation in the knowledge of him, having the eyes of your hearts enlightened, that you may know what is the hope to which he has called you . . .

Paul, who is so concerned for the salvation of the non-Jews, the 'Gentiles', also knows the working of the spirit of Christ in their conscience. Indeed the light is also at work in history before Christ's coming and among those who have not yet encountered him through conscious faith. Moreover, in our multi-religious world the following passage from the Letter to the Romans gives us a perspective (2.14–16):

> When Gentiles who have not the law do by nature what the law requires, they are a law to themselves, even though they do not have the law. They show that what the law requires is written on their hearts, while their conscience also bears witness and their conflicting thoughts accuse or perhaps excuse them on that day when, according to my gospel, God judges the secrets of men by Christ Jesus.

For 'all those who are led by the Spirit of God are children of God' (Rom. 8.14). They are accepted by him and strengthened.

The Gospel of John

The Gospel of John, written just half a century after the letter of Paul to the Romans, sees Jesus above all as the Glorified One to whom the word 'glory', which is reserved for God, can be applied. The believers who read this Gospel know that Jesus is the Risen Christ who after his suffering and death is seen as the Glorified One in the midst of the community of faith:[8]

> And the Word was made flesh and dwelt among us, and we have seen his glory, the glory of the only-begotten son of the Father, full of grace and truth (John 1.14).

He gained his full glory through being faithful to death, after first having gone through total darkness, after the dying of the grain of wheat (John 7.39; 12.16, 24). The glorified Jesus is seen as the pivot of all creation. According to the prologue to the Gospel, Jesus has appeared among human beings from the mystery of God as from the primal source of all life (above all of Jesus' own life, cf. John 17.5), through which this light, so veiled in darkness, can become light.[9]

This coming of Jesus is a quite personal event for everyone, which essentially changes anyone who wants to be encountered by this light. The Gospel recognizes at many points that countless people reject the light: 'The light shines in darkness and the darkness does not overcome it' (John 1.5; also 1.11; 5.47; 6.60–65; 7.43–44; 8.59 etc.). Those who accept the light are themselves 'glorified'.

The conflict between light and darkness coincides with the duel between truth and lies. Jesus calls his Father 'someone who is truthful' (John 7.28; 8.26). Hence Jesus also appears as the absolutely righteous one, with a disconcerting sovereignty. He is aware that the true God becomes transparent in him, that the glory of his Father breaks through in him:

> If I glorify myself, my glory is nothing; it is my Father who

glorifies me, of whom you say that he is your God. But you have not known him; I know him. If I said, I do not know him, I should be a liar like you; but I do know him and I keep his word (John 8.54–55).

Jesus wants to liberate all human beings for his truth and transparency. This will be achieved by generally trusting in him as the one sent by the Father. Through 'seeing' him one encounters the depths of the being of the one who sends him. Through 'seeing' him one becomes a disciple.

Just before the pericope about the wedding feast in Cana, at which water is turned into wine, Jesus – after meeting the brothers Andrew and Simon Peter – meets their fellow townsman Philip. Philip urges his friend Nathanael to go in search of Jesus, 'Come and see' (John 1.46). Jesus recognizes that Nathanael is an honest man. Thereupon Nathanael says, 'How do you know me?' Jesus answers: 'Before Philip called you, when you were under the fig tree, I saw you' (John 1.48). Nathanael then 'sees' Jesus: 'Rabbi, you are the son of God.' The reply of Jesus which follows explicitly describes the whole weight and the double foundation of the 'seeing'. Nathanael 'sees' because he is honest, but above all because Jesus has 'seen' him. By this seeing he touches Nathanael's heart, with the promises that he will see even deeper into Jesus as the person in whom God's presence in this world is experienced: 'Because I said to you, I saw you under the fig tree, do you believe? You shall see greater things than these.' And he adds: 'Truly, truly I say to you, you will see heaven opened, and the angels of God ascending and descending upon the Son of Man' (John 1.50–51). Not only will Nathanael see God's glory perfected in Jesus, but so too will all the followers ('you') to whom the Gospel is addressed.

The very next pericope about Cana reads: 'This, the first of his signs, Jesus did at Cana in Galilee, and manifested his glory; and his disciples believed in him' (John 2.11). Here is an explicit beginning of something which is central to the Gospel (the significance of 'beginning'): the manifestation of God's glory in Jesus. And the sign of this is the miracle of abundant wine, just as later there is the sign of the raising of Lazarus: 'This sickness,' says Jesus, 'is not unto death; it is for the glory of God, so that the Son of God may be glorified by means of it' (John 11.4). Jesus repeats this to Martha: 'Did I not tell you that if you would believe, you would see the glory of God?' (John 11.40). In Cana the belief of the disciples is the consequence of the revelation of Jesus' glory, whereas in Bethany Martha's faith is the condition for this revelation. Jesus received this glory from the Father (John 1.14; 5.19; 8.38; 10.37–38; 14.10), but Jesus also reflects the glory back to the Father (John 11.4).

It is immediately evident that not everyone sees this glory (for example, this is not [yet] said of the 'brothers' of Jesus [John 1.12] or of Mary, who was also present in Cana). What then is this glory and who sees it? On this L.Geysels comments: 'It is that in Jesus which makes him a once-for-all gift for the believers, which from another world breaks into a world closed in on itself and radically renews it.'[10] In this sense, in John 6.34 Jesus says of himself, 'For the bread of God is that which comes down from heaven, and gives life to the world.' Here bread is the sign; in Cana it is the wine.

The disciples begin to see something of this, just as Martha really 'saw' God himself becoming visible: as he really is and not as many Jews thought of him. In all kinds of narratives, like the miracle with the loaves (John 6.1–16), that becoming transparent has to do with love: God will not let go of the world which has no perspective, the closed, 'hungry' and 'thirsty' world. However, 'seeing' Jesus calls for a change in the person who sees, and this is brought about by God. Then the person can freely begin to see: 'No one can come to me unless the Father who sent me draws him to me' (John 6.44). This verse ends with a refrain which mentions the abiding horizon: '. . . and I will raise him up on the last day'.

For the evangelist, that 'seeing' in Cana and in Bethany is a first phase. After Jesus' passion and death the second phase begins, namely the phase of the glory of the Risen Christ.

However, this is not 'seen' by all and it can also be experienced in the community of believers for whom the Gospel has been written. 'The glory which you have given me I have given to them,' says Jesus to his Father in the farewell discourse (John 17.22). The third phase is the eschatological phase, which is described in the last two chapters of the book of Revelation.

Jesus' appearance in Cana is far more than a 'miracle' to help people in need (it would be a pity if the feast were disrupted by a lack of wine). It is a 'sign' of the presence of another world with its own dimension. In the Old Testament, wine was also a symbol of the messianic age, of the breakthrough of paradise ('You have kept the best wine until last', John 2.10). And in the story Jesus himself also appears as the bridegroom of the messianic people, an image which he often uses and which is applied by the prophets to God.

However, the other dimension which has been mentioned has not been seen by many people. The author of the Gospel of John has experienced it in his community and seen how tensions, polarization and even splits have arisen over it.[11] To describe this drama explicitly in a typically Johannine style, among other things the Gospel resorts to the imagery of Isaiah, where Isaiah refers to the 'blind' whose eyes and hearts have not yet been opened. Reflection on the dramatic story of the healing of the man born blind is instructive here (John 9.1–38).[12]

This long pericope can be read as a catechesis, written from the context of persecuted Jewish Christians towards the end of the first century. Jesus encounters the man born blind as he is leaving the temple, the centre of Jewish religion. Before the blind man even has a chance to say anything, the disciples come to Jesus with a question which reveals their very archaic view of God: 'Rabbi, why was he born blind? Is it because of his own sin or that of his parents?' Thus according to them the bad behaviour of the man or his parents is to blame for the fact that he cannot see. But how could the man who has been blind from birth have committed sin unless God had already condemned him and he was fated to do so? And how free is he if he is imprisoned in the sinfulness of his parents? Jesus immediately rejects this image of God and sin (see also Luke 13.1–5).

Thus being born blind must also mean not yet having seen the light which is Jesus. However, for Jesus himself God is firmly involved: God makes the blind man the occasion for Jesus to reveal himself ('the works of God must be made manifest in him', John 9.3). Jesus heals this blind man on a sabbath (John 9.14), the day on which according to the strict interpretation of Jewish Law one may not work. However, for Jesus every day is a day on which he may work;[13] he stands above religion. And Jesus declares: 'We must work the works of him who sent me, while it is day; night comes, when no one can work. As long as I am in the world, I am the light of the world' (John 9.4–5). The 'we' does not refer only to Jesus but presumably also – in this text we are some generations after Jesus' death – to the faith community in which Jesus continues to be active. Even now he is the light of the world. The 'night' can be a reference to persecution, to opposition by the authorities, by the 'father of lies'. And here Jesus goes on to perform the (symbolic?) action of making mud from some sand on the ground and his spittle and putting it on the eyes of the blind man. Some scholars see here a reference to the creation story in Genesis, where the human being, with his eyes and his consciousness, is made out of earth, and also by the living Word from the mouth of God. Then Jesus commands, 'Go, wash in the pool Siloam': Siloam means 'sent'. In v.4 Jesus says of himself that he is the one 'who is sent', namely the one who brings the light from God. After the washing (is it a reference to baptism, as Augustine comments?), the blind man who now sees returns to the temple precincts. Perhaps he has not yet understood much. And in the meantime Jesus has gone away.

Next a second group is brought on to the scene: the neighbours. They know the blind man as a public beggar. They are so amazed that they first ask whether this man really is the blind man they know. The text gives the impression that, even before the blind man himself realizes it, they see that a deep change has begun in him. We may guess that the man not only acts as if he can see but also is a changed person. The physical healing is only one aspect of what has happened to him. And when the bystanders ask precisely what has happened to him, he can only tell them in detail what Jesus has done. He speaks only of 'a certain Jesus'. When the bystanders ask, 'Who is this man?', they are given the laconic answer, 'I do not know.'

Then we have a third category of people, the Pharisees: 'They brought the man who was blind to the Pharisees.' The bystanders are uneasy: the blind man was healed on a sabbath and that can have unpleasant consequences for everyone; so it is necessary to go quickly to the authorities to tell them what has happened. Now a new cross-examination by the Pharisees begins, and for the second time the man relates what has happened to him. The reaction of the Pharisees is divided (the Gospel already mentions a good Pharisee, Nicodemus, in John 3.1ff.). Meanwhile the man is getting a clearer view of what has happened, and when the Pharisees ask, 'What do you think, since he has opened your eyes?', he replies, 'That he is a prophet', in other words someone who comes from God.

Now the Gospel broadens the public to 'the Jews' (John 9.18), who want to summon the man's parents: is this your son, and was he really blind? They look for arguments so as not to have to 'see'. The parents answer both questions in the affirmative, but they have no explanation for his healing. They refer their questioners to their son: 'Why don't you ask him? He is old enough to speak for himself.' In fact they sense danger from the Pharisees and fear excommunication from the synagogue (something that the Jewish authorities did in fact practise with the Jewish Christians towards the end of the first century).

The Pharisees then begin a second interrogation of the man. This is a bit much: why go over the whole story yet again? Then he makes a dangerous remark: 'Do you too want to become his disciples?' The man has indeed meanwhile come to have a clearer view of his situation and has himself begun to be a 'disciple'. The Pharisees see through this, get rough and say, 'You are his disciple, but we are disciples of Moses. We know that God has spoken to Moses, but this man [Jesus], we do not know where he comes from.' Thereupon the man gets cross and retorts: 'Why, this is a marvel. You do not know where he comes from, and yet he opened my eyes? If this man did not come from God he would never have been able to do that.' Thereupon the furious Pharisees respond: 'And they cast him out.' In other words, he was excommunicated from the synagogue.

And now, right at the end of the pericope, Jesus appears again. He goes to look for the man himself, just as he had taken the initiative in healing him. 'And when he had found him', he puts the central question to him, 'Do you believe in the Son of Man?' However, the man does not yet see clearly and asks, 'Who is that, Lord? Then I shall believe in him.' Then Jesus becomes quite direct: 'You have met [literally seen] him; he is the one who is speaking with you.' Whereupon the man says, 'Lord, I believe', and 'he prostrated himself before him'. He recognizes God in his healer. There is no content to his confession of faith, but the man departs from the Law, from his 'religion', to a personal surrender which involves the whole of his existence, and he is ready to pay the price of his decision. All hesitation is over. He 'sees', not only with his eyes but also with his heart.

After the story, the evangelist makes Jesus put the Pharisees very firmly in their place (John 9.39–41):

'For judgment I came into this world, that those who do not see may see, and that those who see may become blind.' Some of the Pharisees near him heard this, and they said to him, 'Are we also blind?' Jesus said to them, 'If you were blind, you would have no guilt, but now that you say "We see", your guilt remains.'

There follows the parable of the Good Shepherd, which in the case of the Pharisees culminates in a new division. Some say that Jesus is possessed and raving. 'But others said: These are not the words of one who has a demon. Can a demon open the eyes of the blind?' (10.21). Here it is clearly demonstrated how Jesus came to bring about a division: those who accept the light and the others of whom John writes 'his own did not accept him' (John 1.11). Once again it must be repeated here that the whole of this text was written around the end of the first century, when the young faith community was experiencing to the full that it had become a sign of conflict in the great contest between light and darkness, between day and night.[14] And this was to remain the case right down the further history of the whole faith community.

Exegetes doubt whether Jesus himself ever said, 'I am the light of the world', because the 'glory' applies to him only after the resurrection. Moreover the question arises: isn't that emphasis on the light very one-sided for those who read the long dark history of human suffering, including the account of Jesus' passion? F.-J. Steinmetz investigates this.[15] He recognizes that we seek the light and that therefore sentences like those of the author of I John take this up: 'This is the message we have heard from him and proclaim to you, that God is light and in him is no darkness at all' (I John 1.5). But in that case, what are we to make of the story of the massacre of the children in Bethlehem? Of the beheading of John the Baptist? Of the crucifixion of Jesus himself? Of Auschwitz? Of anyone's suffering and death? In the Old Testament God is never identified with light. The more we human beings know, the more mysterious and unfathomable everything becomes. Isn't it better to put God, who is so strange, above light and darkness, as many mystics do? And isn't it striking that the Synoptics never make Jesus say that God – or he himself – is light?

However, in I John itself Steinmetz finds a commentary which explains the significance of the light. God is also given a different name in this letter: 'God is love, and he who abides in love abides in God, and God abides in him' (I John 4.16). Let's put another two verses alongside this:

> If we say [like the Gnostics] we have fellowship with him while we walk in darkness, we lie . . . ; but if we walk in the light, as he is in the light, we have fellowship with one another, and the blood of Jesus his Son cleanses us from all sin (I John 1.6–7).

And later:

> He who loves his brother abides in the light, and in it there is no cause for stumbling. But he who hates his brother is in the darkness and does not know where he is going, because the darkness has blinded his eyes (I John 2.10–11).

In John, light means love which pays the price (we need think only of the foot-washing), and darkness means sin against love. And the one who brings us out of darkness is the dead and risen Lord, he alone. The emphasis clearly lies neither on external light nor on the knowledge or knowing better of Gnosticism nor on a form of 'enlightenment', but on this other truth which is revealed only through living dealings with brothers and sisters. And here, because of their closed selves, human beings are darkness (John 12.35–36) and must constantly be illuminated and converted by Jesus.

Finally, it must be remarked here that the Gospel of John also avoids setting light and darkness against each other in an excessive way as the Gnostics do. These last have broken with the community (I John 2.18–19) and bring two parallel primal forces, light and darkness, into conflict with each other.[16] The Gospel and the letters avoid this dualism and dispute it. There the 'world' is not the evil adversary of light; the world is itself produced by the Light-Word. The world becomes darkness only in so far as it refuses the Light. Then human beings who are closed in on themselves, narcissistic; they are darkness and lies. In John 8.31–47 Jesus attacks the 'father' of 'lies' and his 'sons'. These do not seek the light and refuse to receive it. They regard their own, false 'glory', not that of God (John 5.44; 7.18; 12.43). For the Gospel of John, the 'world' is the sphere both of God's love and of the refusal of God's love. Josef Ratzinger points out here that the apparent dualism of John must not be understood ontologically, but historically. Departing from the Gnostic light-terminology, the Gospel takes up the Old Testament symbolism of light which here is associated with Jesus' person.[17] Moreover the Gospel does this with many primal symbols like bread, wine, water, way, fire and vine.

The Synoptic Gospels and Acts

As in Paul and John, so in the Synoptic Gospels and Acts the symbol of light is applied to Jesus and his followers, though less explicitly. The glory of God shines through in Jesus. In the hymn of Zechariah the Lord is announced as light, with reference to Isa. 9.1:

> When the day shall dawn upon us from on high
> to give light to those who sit in darkness and in the shadow of death,
> to guide our feet into the way of peace (Luke 1.78–79).

When Jesus is born, the shepherds see an angel of the Lord, 'and the glory of the Lord shone round about them' (Luke 2.9). The magi from the East 'have seen his star rising' (Matt. 2.2). And in the Jerusalem temple the pious Simeon 'on whom the Holy Spirit rested' (Luke 2.25) took the child Jesus in his arms and praised God: 'For my eyes have seen your salvation, which you have prepared in the presence of all people, a light for revelation to the Gentiles, and for glory to your people Israel' (Luke 2.30–32).[18]

At his first appearance in the synagogue in Nazareth, Jesus applies the prophecy of Isaiah to himself as the one who has been sent 'to preach the recovering of sight to the blind, to set at liberty those who are oppressed' (Luke 4.18). To John the Baptist in prison he gives as a sign that he has been sent 'the blind see' (Luke 7.22).

To put Jesus' 'departure' (Luke 9.31) through suffering and death in the perspective of his resurrection for the disciples, Luke narrates the transfiguration on the mountain, the place where God reveals himself, here presumably at night (Luke knows that Jesus liked to go up the mountain in the evening or at night to pray): 'And as he was praying the appearance of his countenance was altered, and his raiment became dazzling white' (Luke 9.29). Those who appeared before him with God were also clothed in this radiance, 'Moses and Elijah, who appeared in glory' (Luke 9.31). And then, as a sign from God which accompanied his people through the wilderness, 'a cloud (Matthew calls it a 'shining cloud' [Matt. 17.5]) came and overshadowed them; and they were afraid as they entered the cloud. And a voice came out of the cloud, saying, "This is my Son, my Chosen, listen to him"' (Luke 9.34–35). The evangelist writes this long after Jesus' death, for the believers, and thus wants to encourage them: now he is shining, risen; follow him!

We hear of this same experience of splendour when the women come to the empty tomb: 'Behold, two men stood before them in shining white apparel' (Luke 24.4). Matthew turns it into an apocalyptic vision ('Suddenly there was a great earthquake', Matt. 28.2), and he has only one angel appearing, who rolls the stone away from the grave and sits on it. 'His appearance was like lightning and his raiment white as snow' (Matt. 28.3).

Like Jesus and the angels, Jesus' followers must also be bearers of light. Thus Jesus says (Matt. 5.14–16):

> You are the light of the world. A city set on a hill cannot be hid. Nor do men light a lamp and put it under a bushel, but on a stand, and it gives light to all in the house. Let your light so shine before men that they may see your good works and give glory to your Father who is in heaven.

Then the believers, too, will finally prove, like the five wise virgins, to have sufficient oil in their lamps, even if the bridegroom (Jesus) arrives somewhat later than expected at the marriage feast of the definitive kingdom. They will go out to meet him with their lamps and enter it with him (Matt. 25.1–12). However, those who are not ready for this encounter are cast 'into extreme darkness' (Matt. 22.13). To them Jesus applies the prophecy of Isaiah (Isa. 6.9–10):

> You shall indeed hear but never understand,
> and you shall indeed see but never perceive.
> For this people's heart has grown dull,
> and their ears are heavy of hearing,
> and their eyes they have closed,
> lest they should perceive with their ears,
> and understand with their heart,
> and turn for me to heal them (Isa. 6.9–10).

Acts illustrates this, and tells how around the Mediterranean basin some people have their eyes opened and others remain blind, and this is the case with both Jews and Gentiles. It is striking how strongly it is indicated that the first Christians were almost literally fired with the Holy Spirit. In the house where eleven apostles were present with Matthias, who had newly been co-opted,

> . . . suddenly a sound came from heaven like the rush of a mighty wind, and it filled all the house where they were sitting. And there appeared to them tongues as of fire, distributed and resting on each one of them. And they were all filled with the Holy Spirit and began to speak in other tongues, as the Spirit gave them utterance (Acts 2.2–4).

Here the Christian reader of the first century will spontaneously have thought of God's fiery appearance on Sinai (Ex. 19.18). The passage also recalls John the Baptist, who denied that he was the Messiah: 'I baptize you with water. But one is coming who is mightier than I. He shall baptize you with holy spirit and with fire' (Luke 3.16). The disciples, initially so afraid, now begin to speak with other, fiery tongues and a bolder language.

In his first great speech Peter quotes the prophet Joel, where he says that God 'will pour out his spirit on all people' (Acts 2.17). And from Jerusalem this spirit-fire spreads throughout the Roman empire. It falls above all on the fierce young Pharisee Saul, who is on the way to Damascus, there to persecute the small

Christian community which is meeting in the synagogue. But on the way 'suddenly a heavenly light shone round about him' (Acts 9.3), so that he became blind for three days: 'although his eyes were open, he could not see anything' (Acts 9.8). His companions also see the light but do not hear the voice of the Lord ('Saul, Saul, why are you persecuting me?'). Then the disciple Ananias perceives through a vision that he must seek out Saul. Ananias lays hands on him: 'Brother Saul, the Lord Jesus who appeared to you on the road by which you came has sent me that you may regain your sight and be filled with the Holy Spirit' (Acts 9.17; also 21.6–16; 26.12–17). Thereupon he can see again; he gets up and has himself baptized, as a result of which he is now persecuted in turn – as it will prove, without success. Through Paul the Spirit breaks through in many communities, as a result of the breakthrough to the Gentiles.

Acts relates a typical anecdote during Paul's mission in the city of Philippi in Macedonia. A slave girl with the spirit of prophecy who had earned much money for her owners through her soothsaying follows on the heels of Paul and his companion Silas all day long. She pursues them everywhere, crying out, 'These men are the servants of the Most High God. They proclaim the way of salvation.' Paul silences her by 'driving a spirit out of her',[19] but her owners see their hope of income lost. They take Paul and Silas to the city authorities, with the result that both are put in prison. However, as a result of a sudden earthquake the doors of the prison are opened and the chains fall off. The jailer, who thinks that all have fled, is about to commit suicide: 'But Paul cried out, "Do yourself no harm, we are all here"' (Acts 16.28). The author relates: 'And he called for light and rushed in, and trembling with fear he fell down before Paul and Silas, and brought them out and said, "Men, what must I do to be saved?" And they said, "Believe in the Lord Jesus, and you will be saved, you and your household"' (Acts 16.29–31). He and all his family are converted. The light that the jailer asks for seems to have a double significance: light to be able to see in the darkness of the prison but also, more deeply, the light of faith.

The Book of Revelation

This is not the place to discuss the Book of Revelation or the Apocalypse, the last book of the Bible.[20] It is, however, important to emphasize the symbolism of light which is present there in many ways as a supplement which crowns the light symbolism that is to be found above all in Paul and John. Despite its considerable difficulty, the whole of the Book of Revelation is meant as comfort for persecuted Christians and as a warning against division and flagging ardour. The numerous images (white robes, golden candlesticks, stars, the innocent lamb, fire, sun, moon, a white cloud, a white throne, a white stone, jasper clear as crystal, twelve pearls, a clear river) indicate the triumph of light over darkness, of love over treachery, of life over death. The Apocalypse is *the* book of hope.

The last two chapters open up the perspective on the holy city of those who have risen, the 'new heaven and the new earth', which is depicted as a space radiant with God's glory:

> Behold the dwelling of God is with men. He will dwell with them, and they shall be his people, and God himself will be with them; he will wipe away every tear from their eyes, and death shall be no more, neither shall there be mourning nor crying nor pain any more, for the former things have passed away (Rev. 21.3–4).

Into this city flows 'the river of the water of life, bright as crystal, flowing from the throne of God and of the Lamb' (Rev. 22.1). And then follow the two marvellous verses which sum up the whole idea of 'glory' in the Old and New Testaments:

> They [the servants] shall see his face, and his name shall be on their foreheads. And night shall be no more; they need no light of lamp or sun, for the Lord God will be their light, and they shall reign for ever and ever (Rev. 22.4–5).

Face, name, forehead denote the 'person' with its unique property: those who are risen will experience the mysterious personhood of God each in their own personhod and thus develop to full clarity of spirit, heart and appearance. This is also the vision of I John:

> It does not yet appear what we shall be, but we know that when he appears we shall be like him, for we shall see him as he is. And every one who thus hopes in him purifies himself as he is pure (I John 3.2–3).

Now already there begins a definitive clarity in dealing between human beings, men and women, with one another and with the whole of reality.

And yet . . .

As J. Lambrecht has remarked, what Christians now in the meantime see is '. . . not God, far less Christ, God's image. In fact they can no longer see directly the glory of the earthly Jesus or the risen Christ. Believers see only the reflection of this that is present in the preaching of the gospel, in Christian life and in the visible working of the Spirit.'[21]

Indeed, the whole way through the light symbolism of scripture opens up a horizon on the mysterious Reality beyond all light and darkness. But although John makes Jesus say, 'Only he whom comes from God has seen the Father' (John 6.46), and 'he who has seen me has seen the Father' (John 14.9), it remains the case that Jesus 'dwells in light inaccessible. No man has ever seen him or can see him' (I Tim.6.16).

R. Guardini comments on this: 'Any attempt to penetrate directly to the Father encounters nothing but a universal divinity. One does not get to the real Father, the ultimate mystery, except through the Son.'[22]

Yet the holy Jesus also shows obliquely, namely through the way in which he acts and speaks, the light of the ultimate mystery.

Jesus' light does not bring us further than over the threshold. He does not compel anyone. On the contrary, complete trust is needed to enter a night which can become light – though always relative light. It remains a hesitant 'walking on the water' (Matt. 14.28). One does not get much deeper than into the shadows, where meaningful surrender offers stepping-stones of hope, where one is taken further, the further one allows oneself to be drawn through the clouds. Entering this sphere calls for a radical emptying. It is the silence of the afternoon of Good Friday, with sometimes the beginning of the dawn of Easter morning.

Anyone who with John bears witness that Jesus is 'the light of the world' must at the same time assert with the Synoptic Gospels that Jesus also shares an experience of night with Jeremiah, with Job, with the 'Preacher'. Only in this way is he completely human for all times, above all for what in a cultural sense is a post-Christian time, in which not only some mystics like John of the Cross, Thérèse of Lisieux or Simone Weil but also many ordinary believers see the suffering Jesus on Veronica's handkerchief rather than the triumphant pantocrator of the Byzantine icons.

A weary Christian at the end of the second millennium can then be fascinated by complaints like those of R. Schneider in his 'Winter in Vienna':

> Belief in the resurrection presupposes the longing to rise – or fear of nothingness. But neither that longing nor this fear can be taken for granted. They do not belong in a definition of being human – as far as such a definition is possible at all. Humanity can come into being and find a form without being disturbed by the question of immortality: it is here that the frontier of preaching lies . . . I know that he is risen. But my own life-force has sunk so deeply that it can no longer reach beyond the grave, can no longer desire and fear beyond death. I cannot think that any God could be so merciless that he would wake up a dead-tired sleeper under his feet, a sick person who has finally gone to sleep. No doctor, no welfare worker would do that, far less God . . .

And then Schneider asks the question:

> What can Christ's conquest over death mean for individuals and peoples who surrender to death, who do not want eternity?[23]

Then, from the author's despair, there rises the question, 'Who will refute this phenomenon, this gliding away from any horizon?' It is an echo of Nietzsche's question, 'Who gave us the sponge to wipe out the whole horizon?' It is the question of the person who comes up against the hollow wall of the void. There is nothing more to desire, nothing more to fear. The silence is ice-cold. One wakes for no one and is woken by no one.

Schneider's deep identity crisis recalls the moment in Gethsemane when Jesus 'began to be sorrowful and troubled' and Matthew makes him complain, 'My soul is very sorrowful, even unto death; remain here, and watch with me' (Matt. 26.37–38). He comes up against a radical loneliness and needs the support of Peter and the two sons of Zebedee. But even the three chosen disciples do not stay awake – only the anxious Jesus, who prostrates himself and prays, 'My Father, if it be possible, let this cup pass from me; nevertheless, not as I will but as you will' (Matt. 26.39). And after repeating this lament twice, he says, 'Arise, let us be going' (Matt. 26.46).

We are far from any experience of light. But Jesus is not broken by his experience of night, any more than were so many after him, from Stephen confronting the high priest to Thomas More in the Tower of London and Edith Stein in the Nazi extermination camp. Finally they were all supported by a shining horizon within, which allowed them to enter the night freely and in full trust. However, the whole of scripture indicates that those who despondently crouch against the wall of the void and see their identity sink deeply beneath them are not abandoned by the mysterious horizon. The bruised reed is not broken nor is the smoking flax quenched, although those who endure this are unaware of the fact. Believers know that 'God is greater than our heart and he knows everything' (I John 3.20) – even when a brother or sister has little prospect of sharing this trust and they have to bear this burden apparently impotently.

In the meantime Jesus' experience of night remains his mystery. However much he is in the grasp of the Spirit, he is quickly blocked by the opposition to his vision of the kingdom of God that has been orchestrated by the religious and political authorities. His brief and powerful public appearance takes him to a dark impasse that the evangelists honestly report. It seems clear that even he cannot escape the absolute emptiness and the silence of his Father. In the night which becomes sheer solitude, he remains faithful to the horizon of the kingdom of God which forms the heart of his life. He continues to believe in the value of that light which gives all meaning without for the moment seeing anything, as the powerless one who still continues to expect help 'from elsewhere'. And scripture teaches that after going through the annihilation of death, the horizon remains faithful to him by taking him into it.

Of course in this approach to the Jesus-event there no longer seems to be any room for any kind of pre-existence of an eternal Logos descending in human form.[24] The only thing that one can confess is that God's Spirit which Jesus accepted completely into himself never let go of him. And so he is saving event for those who have the same experience of emptiness, and that means all of us. Through the faithfulness of God's Spirit he is divinized without becoming identical with his Father. Central to the saving event is the expectation from God of God's coming, eschatological kingdom of which he is the present sign in concrete history.

Karl Rahner has summed this up sharply in one of his concentrated credal formulae:

> Christianity is a matter of keeping open the question of the absolute future which will give itself as such in self-communication, which has established itself eschatologically and irreversibly in Jesus Christ, and is called God.[25]

Jesus' whole life is focussed on the horizon of this absolute future which he calls his present Father. The core of his being is constantly fed by this horizon, to the end: 'Into your hands I commend my life.' Despite this bottomless trust that structured his whole personality, Jesus did not die with the firm insight, 'Tomorrow it will be over, then I shall be risen.' He too could not give a rational place to his night. The horizon took him through it. And to the end he named this horizon with a gentle word, his loving Father.

3

Light in the Community of Faith

Light continued to play a major role in the life of the churches: in the liturgy, prayer and art. Candles, lamps, stained-glass windows, bonfires, the use of gold and ivory, even the jubilation of choirs and fugues express experiences of light. We need think only of the Gothic cathedrals, of Van Eyck's 'Lamb of God', of the work of painters like Rembrandt and De La Tour, but also of composers like Vivaldi and Handel *(The Messiah)* – and above all Gregorian chant.

The mystics constantly resort to the symbolism of light to express their deepest experience of God. This long chapter can develop only a few aspects of this. The topic, which covers many phases of culture, is boundless. In addition to scripture it is vital to recognize the role of light in the traditions of the community of faith in order to display the wealth of light as the 'colour' of religious experiences. Here it must immediately be added that these experiences imply just as much shadow, night and darkness; in our time even to an increasing degree. The next chapter will go into that.

The first centuries[1]

The pre-Christian cult of the sun lasted until well into the 'Christian era'. The last words of the dying emperor Julian (died 363) are a typical illustration of this: 'Helios, you have forsaken me!'

The first Christians saw the cult of the sun and the starry heavens as a preparation for Christian symbolism.[1] They continued to draw on this reservoir. At the same time, however, Christianity dethroned the sun and the heavenly bodies. In Paul's letter to the Galatians we read:

> When we were children, we were slaves to the elemental spirits of the universe (4.3).

And later:

> Formerly, when you did not know God, you were in bondage to beings that by nature are no gods; but now that you have come to know God, or rather to be known by God, how can you turn back again to the weak and beggarly elemental spirits, whose slaves you want to be once more? You observe days, and months, and seasons, and years . . . (4.8–10).

Paul must have found that quite a few believers – from both Judaism[2] and paganism – tried to combine earlier views with Christian faith and went too far (he also seems to be concerned with this in Rom. 8.38–39). Thus the apologist Tatian (c. 120) writes:

> However, we are raised above fate, and in place of the 'powers' (the *daimones*) of the planets we know only the one ruler of the world who does not wander around.[3]

For him, the worship of Helios is superseded by baptism: Christ is 'the sun of righteousness'. Seen from a distance, this is an important step towards a liberating secularization.

And yet Christianity could take over the sun as a symbol. The doctrine of the divine light is developed throughout the whole of later theology. We also find aspects of the doctrine of illumination with Christ as '*Sol salutis*' (the sun of salvation) much later, for example in Scotus Eriugena, Eckhard, Hildegard of Bingen, Jakob Boehme and so on.

Of course the symbolism of light penetrated most deeply into the liturgy. In an agricultural society the church remained close to nature and the store of symbols available there. We need think only of the tendency towards the age-old fertility cult which is so characteristic of the first mariology. It is the moon (*luna*) which symbolizes Mary; both the Christmas moon and the Passover moon give light to the birth: the sun which is Christ.[4] Candlemas is the feast of the 'purification' of Mary. At a very early stage the symbolism of light developed spontaneously around the two great festivals of the church's year, Christmas and Easter, and that has continued to the present day.

Jesus died on the day of rest before the great sabbath and was raised on 'the day after this great sabbath', as the Synoptic Gospels report. For a while people continued to call the day 'the first day of the week' (Acts 20.7; I Cor. 16.2). But a distinctive feature of Christianity was that it gave the day a new name, 'the day of the Lord' (*kuriake*).[5] The 'Lord's supper' was celebrated on this day of the Lord (I Cor. 11.20).

It needs to be pointed out here that from the century before Christ the division of the weekdays according to the astrology of the Chaldaeans and the Egyptians had become general in the Mediterranean; in other words, each day bore the name of a heavenly body. According to this division the first day after the Jewish sabbath was called *dies solis* (the day of the sun). Jesus thus rose on the 'sun day'. For the pagans the Jewish sabbath was the day dedicated to Saturn (Saturday). For the pagans Sunday was the first day of the week.

In his letter to the Magnesians, Ignatius of Antioch (died c.110) writes that Christians 'no longer observe the sabbath but live according to "the day of the Lord", the day on which our life arose' (Mag. 9.1). Jesus' resurrection is a sunrise, just as his death was a sunset. In his letter to the Romans, Ignatius applies this to himself:

> It is beautiful to set like the sun, away from this world, so that I can have my sunrise in God (2.2).

It was at this time that Pliny reported to the emperor Trajan (98–117) that the Christians met on Sundays before sunset.

Certain pagans therefore thought that the Christians were a sect of sun-worshippers, as Tertullian reports:

> They regard the sun as the Christians' God because they have heard that we pray in the direction of the rising sun and that we are glad to see the day of the sun.

This was of course for quite a different reason from religious veneration of the sun. We should note in passing that for centuries it was a custom to orientate the choir of the church to the east so that the morning sun could shine in through a window.

In fact, as I have already mentioned, from the beginning the church was opposed to any form of astrological superstition. It was concerned exclusively with symbolism. However, in our Western languages the church has never been able to prevent the weekdays from retaining their old pre-Christian names. There was less objection to the use of the term Sunday for 'the Lord's day', since here the symbol of light was clearly decisive. Still, it was not Christianity but the Roman pagan sun cult which resulted in the first day of the week being shifted from Saturday to Sunday. What happens on Sunday is auspicious: both pagans and Christians valued 'Sunday's children', born on this day.

Moreover F.Böll rightly comments: 'The most lasting legacy which astrology has left us, even centuries after its collapse, is Sunday', while for millions – although they do not know it – the Lord's day has become a free day of rest. Russian Orthodox Christians still always call it 'the day of resurrection'.

Sunday and Easter Day are in fact closely interwoven. For Christians, the cyclically recurring celebrations of the mysteries are not the origin of this festival. Their festival involves the remembrance of a unique historical event 'under Pontius Pilate' which had lasting significance. But there was a desire to incorporate this remembrance into worship and culture as an annual feast.

According to John (18.29; 19.14) and the ancient tradition of Asia Minor, Jesus died on the fourteenth day of the spring month Nisan. At that time (in 30 or 33) this day fell on a Friday, the day of rest on which the Passover lamb was eaten. For Jews at that time Nisan was the first month of the year and began with the waxing of the moon. So on the fourteenth day there was the spring full moon. Moreover we can see that the Jewish feast of Passover was also involved in the alternation of the heavenly system.

Among the Greeks – where the reckoning of time was much more strongly bound up with nature – the day of Jesus' death fell on the day of Venus. He lay in the tomb on the day of Saturn and he rose on the day of Helios. For the Romans he rose in the middle of the month of Martius, also the first month of the year, and thus at the moment when the sun rises after the full moon, 'as bridegroom and brother'. All this was deeply rooted in the collective consciousness of the time, including that of the first Christians, and among other things explains the vigour of the dispute over the date of Easter'. The Christians of Asia Minor strictly followed the Jewish tradition: Easter always had to fall on 14 Nisan, and thus was not always on a Sunday. By contrast, the Christians of Rome, with their Greek and Latin tradition, also always had Easter falling around the same time, namely in the spring and at the full moon, but then always on a Sunday. It was the emperor Constantine who, after the Council of Nicaea in 325, imposed the Roman custom everywhere, all over the world; as Origen wrote, 'sun and moon are created simply to perform a dance for the salvation of the universe'.

In connection with this a whole Easter lyricism arose in which Christ was called 'the sun', which, after sinking into Hades – the underworld (or the antechamber) – dawns again. In antiquity Hades also stood for the extreme West where the sun sets (hence 'the gates of Hades', death, hell), whereas the light comes from the East. For the ancient world, which saw the earth as a flat disc around which the sun moved, all this was a great mystery. Many people thought that at night the sun went to light the dead. Moreover, the scriptural statements about 'the darkness' which came at Jesus' death (Matt. 27.45) and the sun which grew dark (cf. Luke 23.45) had a strong hold on the ancients.

An otherwise unknown author from the fifth century, called Pseudo-Augustine (*Sermon* 164.2; PL 39, 2067), illustrates the views that I have mentioned:

> Now the power of the seed breaks through the earth; its face is beautified with countless shoots. The whole of nature, which hitherto was dead, celebrates the resurrection with its Lord. The enchanting beauty of the trees in fresh green with their colourful decoration of blossoms, all this is a single expression of joy: everything hastens to the feast day. Hitherto the sky was grey and covered in clouds laden with darkness; but now it shines gently and softly on the earth. The vault of heaven and the surface of the earth come together in a common hymn of joy to Christ, God and man, who brought joy to heaven and earth and made them one. Sol, the source of light for all the stars, makes his face sparkle. Like a glorious king he decks himself with a starry diadem on this day of his wedding, and the joy of his heart, Luna, who, though scarcely born, immediately dies day by day, adorns herself for the Easter festival with a garment of light. Every creature, brothers, rejoices as it were in the holy worship of love for this day of our salvation.

This extract illustrates how the liturgy wove itself into contemporary culture. Thus the whole '*triduum sacrum*' took on a cosmic garb. The grace of the resurrection was communicated to believers as an 'illumination' by Christ the sun.

At the same time we should note the custom of baptizing catechumens on Easter Eve. The form of the liturgy indicates the great importance that was attached to the sun. Catechumens renounced the demonic sunset, with their backs to the west, by turning their faces to the east, to Christ.

Thus Jerome writes about the mystery of the light of baptism at Easter (*Commentary on Amos* 3.6, 14; PL 25, 1068):

> In these mysteries we first of all renounce him who is in the west and who through his sins is dead to us, and then, turning

to the east, we enter into a covenant with the sun of righteousness and confess that we shall serve him.

Here we hear an echo of the earliest church hymn, presumably a quotation from the baptismal liturgy:

Awake, O sleeper, and arise from the dead,
and Christ shall give you light (Eph. 5.14).

Baptism is participation in the sunlight of the resurrection. Moreover Christ is imagined as a young man who comes to meet the baptized with a torch. Through baptism Christians become 'a new creation' (II Cor. 5.17), for Christ is born in a new way in the heart of the believer. It must not be forgotten that during the first centuries the baptismal liturgy was concentrated on adults. Through catechesis they needed to grow to the conviction of the light of faith. These catechumens were called *illuminandi* (those who must be enlightened). Those who had been baptized were the *illuminati* (the enlightened). Baptism itself was an 'enlightening' (*photismos, illuminatio*). There is probably already a reference to this in the Letter to the Hebrews (Heb. 6.4; 10.26,32).

Baptism was in fact purification, liberation through the light of Christ. The immersion in the water symbolized rising to light from the darkness of death. For Augustine, the healing of the man born blind (John 9) points to baptism. In the early church, as we saw, baptism normally took place on Easter Eve and those to be baptized wore white robes. At many points the revised Easter liturgy has taken up this old practice and has also put much stronger emphasis on the symbolism of light. We might think of the gradual lighting of the many candles from the one Easter candle in the darkened church while the 'Light of Christ' is sung three times. The Easter candle is held in the water of baptism, since from the 'fiery water' come 'the children of light' (I Thess. 5.5; Eph. 5.8). Primal elements come together in this ritual while the community of believers sings a powerful *'Exsultet'*. And as an ancient epitaph says, the person baptized has become a 'child of the sun'.

The baptismal liturgy pointed to a new birth. Moreover the celebration of light connected with it was applied to Jesus' birth and incorporated into the festivals of Christmas (25 December) and Epiphany (6 January), which developed some centuries after the Easter liturgy. Easter Eve is connected with Christmas Eve. The Greek East concentrated on the feast of Epiphany, the Latin West on Christmas Day. But we do not have a precise date for Jesus' birth, as we do for Easter. Hence it was looked for in accordance with an artificial biblical-allegorical calculation and the symbolism of the sun, which was already used for Easter. Before there was a Christmas festival a cleric – probably African – in 243 suggested putting Christ's birth on 28 March, as it was thought that the creation took place in the spring – which began on 25 March – and that God had created man on 28 March, four days after spring night. Moreover here countless allegorical views were taken up – but in any case it is clear that the sun was closely involved.

The church in the Greek East did its best to call for a 'sunny' celebration of the birth of Christ as a reaction against the theosophy of Neoplatonism and the mystery celebrations of Isis and Mithras. In Alexandria, the mystery of the Aion born from a virgin was celebrated in the night before 6 January (presumably to be identified with Dionysius, and Dionysius in turn with the sun). The Gnostics celebrated the baptismal feast of Jesus (in the Jordan) on 6 January since then he was divinely born, according to their interpretation of Luke 3.22: 'You are my son, today I have begotten you.' In reaction to this denial of Jesus' humanity, the early church then put the physical birth of Jesus on this day, also in order to introduce a rival Christian feast on the same day as the pagan sun cult of 6 January.

In the Latin West the introduction of Christmas took another course. There too the emperors emphasized the cult of the sun with 25 December as its climax, the day on which the winter solstice was placed. We know that the feast of Christmas was already being celebrated at the end of the third century in Rome, in all probability in reaction to the ancient sun cult. The date of the Roman festival was gradually to displace the date of the Greek festival.

Jerome expresses his joy at the victory of the Christian feast over the pagan feast, and in a letter he enthusiastically writes that now the feast of Christmas is being celebrated in Bethlehem, in the very cave in which since the emperor Hadrian there had been a sanctuary of Adonis, the lover of Venus.[6] This also comes through in a Christmas sermon by Augustine: 'Let us keep this day holy, not like unbelievers because of the sun, but because of him who created the sun.' And even in the middle of the fifth century Pope Leo I reacted by saying that there are people who think 'that we venerate this feast not so much because of the birth of Christ but rather because of the rising of the new sun', and he complained that there were still Christians who on this festival 'turn to the sun with bowed head from the steps of the basilica of St Peter in honour of the shining disc', though this is only a reflection of the light of Christ.

It is evident from this whole summary of the process by which the great Christian festivals of light developed how long the earliest church had to struggle to shift the worship of dead heavenly bodies in the direction of a liturgy in which the person of the risen Christ was to be central. Just how difficult this fight was is well expressed in the second letter of Clement of Rome (c.160) to the Corinthians:

> We were blind in our understanding, worshipping stone and wood and gold and silver and copper, the works of men, and our whole life was nothing else than death. We were covered with darkness and our eyes were full of mist; but we have received our sight, and by his will we have cast off the cloud which covered us (1.6).[7]

Moreover, from the beginning spiritual illumination needed to be expressed in deeds of light, as is emphasized by the Letter of Barnabas:

Break your bread with the hungry, and if you see a naked man clothe him; bring the homeless into your house, and if you see a humble man, do not despise him, either you or your family. Then shall your light break forth as the dawn and your robes shall soon shine. And your righteousness shall go before you, and the glory of God shall surround you (3.3–4).[8]

From Augustine to Ruusbroec

It is impossible to summarize the further development of the symbolism of light in the liturgy, theology, art and the customs of the faith communities. I can only point to some of its aspects and the significance which it had for a limited number of great Christian figures. For lack of space I have to leave aside the light mysticism of the great Greek church fathers – above all Basil, Gregory of Nazianzus and Gregory of Nyssa.

The change in Jesus' countenance on the mountain (Tabor according to the tradition) inspired many. Taking this up, it is said of a number of Egyptian monks that they 'shone with the light of grace'. In the Life of St Sabas, Cyril of Scythopolis relates that Justinian (in 530) 'saw a shining divine grace in the form of light, like a crown on the head of the old man, and this radiated rays of the sun'.

Of course sects were also 'kindled by the holy fire'. For example, the Messalians exalted the mystical light to such a degree that they measured the degree of perfection of a soul by its capacity to see Jerusalem, the city of light, in a vision or the glorious raiment of the Lord. In the fourteenth century Barlaam, a monk of Calabria, accused the monks of Mount Athos of Messalianism, since according to him they claimed to see the uncreated Light. At the Council of Constantinople in 1341, Gregory Palamas, archbishop of Thessalonica, defended the monks and developed a whole mystical theology around the light of Tabor. The whole discussion with Barlaam centred on the question: is the light of glory created or not? For Palamas it was clear that the majority of the church fathers opted for the uncreated Light. But a transformation had taken place among the apostles: by God's grace they could see Jesus as he was, blinding in his divine light.[9]

Augustine of Hippo

We begin with Augustine of Hippo. Although his mother, St Monica, had given him a Christian education, he had not been baptized, nor had Christian belief made much of an impression on him. At the age of twenty, in his North African city of Carthage he came into contact with Manichaeism, which intrigued him; for almost ten years he became a candidate-disciple. It attracted him because he thought that it was rational and would free him from an obsession with the strict God of the Jews with his many commandments and prohibitions.[10] Augustine found it attractive not to have to take too much responsibility for his actions. But he was and fundamentally remained a seeker after the firm ground of truth.

His encounter with Bishop Ambrose of Milan was very important for his later life. Ambrose's preaching showed Augustine that Manichaeism gave a false picture of the Old Testament and Christian faith. This last did not seem to be a teaching for the less gifted:

> I felt that the Catholic doctrine was more unassuming and honest, in that it required to be believed things not demonstrated (whether it was that they could in themselves be demonstrated but not to certain persons, or could not at all be), whereas among the Manichaeans our credulity was mocked by a promise of certain knowledge, and then so many most fabulous and absurd things were imposed to be believed, because they could not be demonstrated.[11]

However, before becoming a Christian under the influence of Ambrose, the hesitant Augustine made one more detour through Neoplatonism. Now the gifted orator began to steep himself in philosophy. That was not difficult in Milan. In Christian circles there people were trying to reconcile Christianity and Neoplatonism. Ambrose, too knew Plotinus and quoted him in his sermons. Thus Augustine gradually discovered the transcendent divine reality deep within him. But the quest went further. He also wanted to encounter and experience the divine reality. Reading Paul was to put him on the way to this. A philosophical approach to the truth was not enough. And while Augustine in his garden paused in reading Paul's letters, in a neighbouring house he heard a child's voice repeatedly singing, 'Take, read, take, read.' Affected by it, he returned to his reading and in the letter to the Romans came upon the passage 'But put on the Lord Jesus Christ, and make no provision for the flesh, to gratify its desires' (Rom. 13.14). This time the text which he had already read made an impression on him – as he later writes in the *Confessions* (I 1, 2) – through the help of God, 'The Father of our awakening and our illumination'. The very sensual seeker had now found his identity and felt liberated. And in his *Confessions* he was later to write a splendid passage on this:

> And being then admonished to return to myself, I entered into my inward self, with you as my guide: and I was able to do so, for you became my helper. And I entered and beheld with the eye of my soul, (such as it was) above the same eye of my soul, above my mind, the Light Unchangeable. Not this ordinary light, which all flesh may look upon, nor as it were a greater of the same kind, as though the brightness of this should be manifold brighter, and with its greatness take up all space. Not such was this light, but other, far other from all these. Nor was it above my soul, as oil is above water, nor yet as heaven above earth: but above to my soul, because it made me; and I below it, because I was made by it. He that knows the Truth, knows what that Light is; and he that knows it, knows eternity. Love knows it. O Truth, you who are Eternity, and Love, you who are truth, and Eternity, you who are Love! You are my God; to you I sigh night and day. When I first knew you, you lifted

me up, that I might see there was what I might see, and that I was not yet such as to see. And you beat back the weakness of my sight, streaming forth your beams of light upon me most strongly, and I trembled with love and awe: and I perceived myself to be far off from you, in the region of unlikeness, as if I heard this your voice from on high: 'I am the food of grown men: grow, and you shall feed upon me; nor shall you convert me, like the food of your flesh, into yourself, but you shall be converted into me.' And I learned that you for iniquity chasten man, and you made my soul consume away like a spider's web. And I said, 'Is Truth therefore nothing because it is not diffused through space, finite or infinite?' And you cried to me from afar, 'Yes indeed, I Am that I Am.' And I heard, as the heart hears, nor did I have room to doubt, and I should sooner doubt that I live, than that Truth is not, which is clearly seen being understood by those things which are made.[12]

After many more heart-searchings Augustine made a definitive choice. He had himself baptized on the Easter Eve of 24–25 April 387, along with his friend Alypius and his fifteen-year-old son Adeodatus, and he further resolved to go through life as a voluntary celibate, in continence. In North Africa he gathered a small community around him. In these tranquil surroundings he began to write more than twenty books to refute Manichaeism. Thorough study of the scriptures was to help him here. Without any great feelings about it, in Hippo he was ordained priest. There he became a bishop with an apostolic monastic community around him. He had occasion to give around one hundred sermons in which he gave many commentaries, above all on the theme of love and light in the Gospel and Letters of John.

It is impossible to say more here about Augustine, who has continued to prove fascinating, except about the great attention which he paid in various writings to the light of the conscience. The Word illuminates his 'inward eye' and he constantly asks, 'Beloved light, what do you say to me?' (*Confessions* X, 17, 26).

Indeed, 'our whole work in this life, dear brothers, consists in healing the eyes of the heart so that they can see God'. That is how Augustine also sums up his own life in a sermon in Hippo.[13]

V. Paronetto justly writes:

> The whole of Augustine's life was a way to the endless light. For Augustine, dying meant seeing God. 'He has given you eyes to see the sun. Should he not also give you the possibility of seeing him, he who has created you?'[14]

Dionysius the Areopagite

Because of the influence which he exercised through the Middle Ages as far as John of the Cross, the mysterious Dionysius the Areopagite remains an important author in connection with the history of the quest for light. For a long time it was thought that he was Paul's Athenian convert (Acts 17.23), something that gave the writer authority. Much later it proved that his writings date from the beginning of the sixth century: hence his present name, Pseudo-Dionysius. To an important degree he stands at the origin of the line of 'darkness' in mystical theology: everything that can be said about God must also be denied; although God is, no one has penetrated into his real being.[15]

But Pseudo-Dionysius is an authentic theologian of light. In his *Heavenly Hierarchy* the light descends from 'The Father of all light' through Jesus Christ to the creation. Thus he sees the whole of reality as a gradual emanation of light from God via the angels to the human spirits and the universe. The soul is then a ray of that divine Primal Light which is the One and the Good. Among other things through the sacraments (above all baptism and eucharist), angels accompany the soul on its way to the perfect union with the divine light. However, the author leaves obscure precisely how this comes about. Moreover the whole event seems to be an entering into a dark reality which is beyond comprehension.

Thus the doctrine of Pseudo-Dionysius becomes a dialectic of light and darkness: the divine darkness is that unattainable light 'of which one says that God dwells in it' (*Letter* V). One knows by not knowing (*agnosis*).

He writes very sharply:

> If it happens that, seeing God, one understands what one sees, one has not seen God himself (*Letter* I).

The '*via negativa*' which this apophatic (speechless) theology indicated was later followed by many mystics, authentic and false, in order to indicate their inability to put into words a dark experience of illumination. The theme of the darkness which both veils and points to the light is central in the symbolism: step by step one puts aside all ways of knowing. A biblical and a Neoplatonic inspiration keep crossing . . . and the language becomes incomprehensible non-language.

Some fragments from the *Mystical Theology* of Pseudo-Dionysius which also use the language of the old mystery cult will serve as an illustration:

> Trinity, you who are above being and above the divine and above the good, you who guide Christians to the knowledge of the divine things, lead us to the supreme summit of the scriptures, truly unknowable and fully illuminating. Above them the simple, absolute and unchangeable mysteries of theology are hidden in the whole shining darkness of the indwelling silence; and in the total darkness, this darkness makes Him shine in an exceptional way who surpasses any shining light; beyond measure it fills the spirits which have no eyes with a shining and all-surpassing beauty. That is my prayer . . .
>
> We ardently long to penetrate that whole shining darkness and also to see and to know, through not-seeing and not-knowing, what exists above any seeing and any knowledge, precisely through this not-seeing and not-knowing . . .

Icons

Judaism has always rejected any images of God, basing itself on the second commandment of the Decalogue: 'You shall make no images' (Ex. 20.4).[16] But this commandment was not completely absolute (cf. Ex. 25.18): one could make golden angels for the ark – and this was not sinful.

The Jews were particularly strict at the time of the Maccabees, for fear of Greek and later Roman contamination. Moreover the Jewish view also influenced Islam later. However, in the Diaspora there was a greater or lesser degree of assimilation by the Jews dispersed there, as is evident from the third-century synagogue of Dura Europos in Mesopotamia. Among the Greeks, who drew on older Eastern traditions, images sometimes preserved a magical character, as they did among the Romans. Because of this many philosophers were opposed to them, though without success. Popular religion was stronger, as Plato himself conceded. Beyond doubt the Greek and Roman customs influenced the first Christians, as is evident from the whole Byzantine tradition of art.

Yet initially the early church remained very restrained, among other reasons because it included many poor people who could not allow themselves any luxury, and also because it was regularly persecuted and had to keep a low profile. Pagan images were gradually Christianized, as in the decorations in the catacombs, where the depictions of the dead made them look with open eyes towards the light of the kingdom of God. However, these pious images were not venerated.

Christian artists have always tried to give new expression to the paradox that the divine Light escapes any depiction and yet must be depicted, albeit as something that escapes us. St John of Damascus (c.650–c.750) expressed this paradox in a text directed against those who rejected images (PG 94, 1239):

For you have not seen his face (Deut. 4.15); what wisdom in the lawgiver! How can one make an image of the Invisible? How can one imagine the features of the one who is like no one? How can one depict that which knows neither quantity nor extent nor limits? How can one give a form to one who is without form? What then does one do with this mystery? If you have understood that the Incorporeal has become human for you, then it is clear that you may express his human image. For the Invisible became visible by accepting the body; you may form the image of the one who was seen.

Moreover it is not surprising that the early suspicion disappeared at the time of Constantine. The images of the emperor were transferred to Christ the Pantocrator, the ruler of the universe. Constantinople became the centre of Christian art, above all of icons.

A deep religious power was attributed to the icons as a result of the contact that they brought about with God. But there were also misunderstandings, above all as a result of the influence of Monophysitism, which confessed only Christ's divinity, and of paganism. These led to the primarily Eastern council named 'in Trullo' (690) – because it was held in the imperial palace – laying down limitations. The tensions, not least with Rome, did not stop the Byzantine emperor Leo III (717–741), in part inspired by the attitude of Islam and in opposition to the patriarch Germanus and the people, forbidding the use of images – after he had interpreted a devastating volcanic eruption as a divine sign in his favour. This was the beginning of iconoclasm. A popular revolt was forcibly put down and Leo III deposed the patriarch. Pope Gregory III and the holy monk John of Damascus reacted in vain.

Gradually iconoclasm was condemned (in the period between 780 and 813) and icons were again allowed until the dispute subsided once more (813–842). The fact that both Charlemagne and the popes had condemned the iconoclasts only made the gulf between the Eastern and Western churches wider. On the other hand the Eastern monks, who had continued to venerate icons in secret, increasingly gained influence (not least among the monasteries on Mount Athos). After the fall of Constantinople in

1453, above all Crete, Macedonia and Serbia, but also Venice, became centres of iconography.

Meanwhile great schools of art had developed in Russia between the thirteenth and the sixteenth centuries, above all in Moscow. The most important artist is Andrei Rubliev, a pupil of Theophanus the Greek, who emigrated from Constantinople. Rubliev was the master in the Monastery of the Trinity in Zagorsk and among other things painted the famous icon of the Holy Trinity.[17] Later, of course the art became more refined, but also more influenced by a certain superficial rationalism.[18]

Icons occupy a very special place in the churches of the Christian East, among other things because of the iconostasis or wall of images which separates the choir from the nave of the church. Icons are also venerated in private dwellings in the 'red corner' where an oil lamp or candle burns. They are deeply involved in births, marriages and deaths (for example an icon is put on the breast of the dead person). Theologically they emphasize, contrary to many heresies, the incarnation of God, the manifestation of the Light, and their attention to the face gives them a markedly personalistic stamp. They are understood as a kind of sacrament in which God himself (or Mary or another saint) shines through to the believers. Therefore in principle one must be a firm believer to be able to paint an icon authentically. The artist must himself be someone who has a clear personal experience of God's mystery.[19] Gold, white and red are the preferred colours in painting icons. Since icons arose in a Neoplatonic climate, in the visible and sinful world they give a view of the harmony of the spiritual world.

L. Ouspensky describes the deep religious significance of icons like this:[20]

> The icon is the image of a prototype which is not only ensouled but also divinized. It does not represent the transitory body which is destined to dissolution but the transfigured body, illuminated by grace, the body of the coming time (see I Cor. 15.35–46). It translates with material means, visible to our

mortal eyes, the beauty and the glory of God. We might note that at the Seventh Ecumenical Council the Fathers did not limit themselves to pointing to the difference between a portrait and an icon, between the image of an ensouled man and that of a divinized man. They say that the icon is to be venerated and is holy because it communicates the divinized state of its prototype and bears his name. It is for this reason that the grace proper to its prototype is present in it. In other words, it is the grace of the Holy Spirit which brings about the holiness both of the person depicted and of his icon, and it is through grace that the relationship of the believer with the holy is brought about through the icon of this last. The icon participates as it were in the holiness of its prototype, and through the icon we in turn participate in this holiness through our prayer.

We may really say that for Orthodox believers the icons have a sacramental significance:

Through the icon a certain spiritual reality is communicated in a sober and by no means exalted way. Just as grace illuminates the whole person so that its whole spiritual and bodily existence is grasped through prayer and remains in the divine light, so the icon in a visible way fixes the person who becomes a living icon, an authentic likeness of God. *The icon does not present the deity; it points to participation of human beings in the divine life.*[21]

A remarkable illustration of the link between holiness, light and living icons is offered by the life of St Seraphim of Sarov (1759–1833), who is much venerated in Russia. As a young man he went out into the 'wilderness' (*poestinia*, from *poestota*, emptiness), namely the monastery of Sarov in a great forest. Later he became a monk. Many witnesses tell the following story about him:

It happened in the winter of 1831 when he was living in his

monastery, deep in the forest. Starets Seraphim had a conversation with a layman, Motovilov, whom he had healed and who had chosen him as a spiritual guide. Seraphim, who for a long time had led an ascetic life in silence, seemed to be directly ensouled by the Spirit. He prayed constantly and thousands sought counsel from him. He read their hearts, prophesied and healed soul and body. Tormented and restless, Motovilov asked the old monk how one can discern the presence of the Holy Spirit. Seeing that simple words would not help, Seraphim suddenly showed himself to him completely transfigured and let him enter the light: 'We are both in the fullness of the Holy Spirit. Why do you not look at me?' 'I cannot, father, flashes of light shoot from your eyes. Your face is brighter than the sun.' 'Do not fear, you are as bright as I am. You are now also in the fullness of the Holy Spirit, otherwise you could not see me. Dare to look at me. God is with us.'

'And I looked,' related Motovilov, 'and an even greater fear seized me. Just imagine someone speaking with you, and his face is like the mid-day sun! You see the movement of his lips; the expression of his eyes changes; you hear the sound of his voice; you feel his hands pressing on your shoulders, but at the same time you do not see his hands, or his body, or your own, but only a shining light which spreads around, to a distance of several metres. And you see how this illuminates the snow lying on the meadow and falls gently on the great starets and on me.' Thereupon with a number of questions St Seraphim helped Motovilov to become aware of his new state. And he had to confess that he felt 'extraordinarily good', filled with 'an inexpressible stillness and peace'. With the peace came gentleness, joy, warmth and a very special perfume. Motovilov remarked: 'Formerly, when I went dancing, before the ball my mother would sprinkle me with perfume which she went to buy in the best shops . . . However, their fragrance was not to be compared with this aroma.' And Seraphim explained that the Spirit enlightens not only the soul but also the body, prevents it from feeling cold and even transforms the organ of smelling, that most archaic sense, bound up with the deep odour of the earth. 'That is how it should be,' says the saint; 'the divine grace dwells very deep in us, in our heart. The kingdom of heaven is in you, says the Lord. By the kingdom of heaven he meant the grace of the Holy Spirit. This is in us at this moment; it warms and enlightens us, delights our senses and fills our heart with joy.'[22]

In the writings that St Seraphim left behind, the following sentence was found: it sums up all that has gone before. 'All those who honestly hope for God will be lifted up to him and lightened with the clarity of the eternal life.'[23] And the Russians venerate the icons of St Seraphim.

Churches as houses of light

Meanwhile light had triumphantly penetrated the whole of the West with a number of late-Romanesque churches, but above all with Gothic, which introduced height and great windows into the buildings and allowed lighter material. André Malraux[24] speaks of 'golden churches' and of 'the marriage of the church and the sun'. E. Castelnuovo gives a very apt description of this atmosphere:

> Works of art play a major role in our attempts to imagine, to visualize, the Middle Ages; and among the images that we have formed of this period one comes most strongly to the fore, helped by monuments, chronicles and documents. More than all other eras, this era looms up before us, clad in a white garment of churches teeming with sculptures, mosaics, multi-coloured windows, glittering examples of the gold- and silver-smith's art, books illuminated with small miniatures, carved ivory, enormous bronze doors, enamel work, murals, panelling, borders, materials and fabrics in colours with constant reflections and strange designs, decorative panels inlaid with gold leaf.[25]

The imagination which fed this creativity was in every respect impressive. G. Duby indicates this in a chapter that he devotes to 'the most royal church of all' which is not a cathedral, namely the monastic church of Saint-Denis-en-France. He entitles it 'God is Light (1130–1190)'.[26]

For the sake of this light the Benedictine abbot Suger, inspired by Dionysius the Areopagite's theology of light, removed the organ loft which, like a dark wall, divided the nave of the church in two. He wrote:

> When the new rear part was connected to the front part, the church glittered at the centre, which had now become light, since all glass shines radiantly. So the noble building shone, permeated by the new light.

When the foundation stone was laid, King Louis VII had some precious stones placed there, while the monks sang 'Your walls are of precious stones.' Suger noted:

> Whenever, filled with the enchanting beauty of the house of God, I experience the fascination of the multicoloured precious stones and these lead me to translate all that is material into the immaterial and to reflect on the differences between the holy virtues, I really seem to be in a strange part of the universe. Here is a space which never existed previously, either in the dirt of earth or in the purity of heaven, and by the grace of God I can rise in an anagogical way from this heaven to the higher heaven.

Saint-Denis does not stand alone. Dozens of cathedrals and village churches breathe the same spirit of brightness. Duby gives this commentary on the Sainte-Chapelle in Paris, which was built later:

> The upper part of it was nothing but an ethereal snare, set to trap light and hold it prisoner. On all sides the light penetrated a space which had become completely homogeneous.[27]

Indeed, 'light, reaching for an incarnate God, insight and logic: those were the characteristics of the new aesthetics which in 1190 had put down deep roots throughout the north of the kingdom'.[28] Moreover it was in such lucid surroundings that Thomas Aquinas wrote his *Summa*. Some centuries later the same spiritual climate was among other things to influence his brother Dominican Giovanni da Fiesole, known as Fra Angelico (1387–1453) for the frescoes of San Marco in Venice.

One building which cannot be overlooked here is the Cathedral of Our Blessed Virgin in Chartres.[29] 'Here is paradise regained,' said Paul Claudel. F. van der Meer has remarked that its architecture is of a kind of epic simplicity.[30] And then he goes on:

> When you enter, you find darkness within. It is high and dark, although the walls are pure and white. And immediately light dawns on you: the people who put in this glass within a period of twenty-five years – with the princely gifts of the bishop and chapter, the king and the queen mother, the lords of Chartres and Dreux, and all the guilds of the city – did not want to build a church with overpowering light, but a church with a particular, intense atmosphere. By chance Chartres is also the church in which the experiment with colossal clerestory windows rising as it were like glass walls above the side aisles was first of all made . . . The church is clearly thought of as a lofty hall, hung and decorated with illuminated tapestries which more or less replace the walls. The glass is not an incidental addition; it is as essential as the plan or elevation of vaulting. It is certainly not intended to bring light into the church. On the contrary, the windows screen the light. They transfigure it, change the prosaic light into something which bathes the interior in an unearthly, bewildering glow, which moreover still wholly or partially brings out and illuminates the piers and sinews of the extremely slender architecture.
>
> Once again, what is the origin of this orgy of glass? . . . The answer is not technical. The technique was only a means. Nor

was it that the Westerners who had seen the golden Byzantine mosaics on the First Crusade wanted to replace the dreary frescoes of their barbarian Romanesque churches with something which would compete with these. Beyond doubt, however, they realized the possibilities of a new technique. But what lies behind it, behind this enigma, is a notion: as always in these centuries, one of the great notions of the liturgy.

The liturgy that I mean is the office of the dedication of a church, in those days one of the high points of all church life. That office is now wholly inspired by this one greatest notion, that the material church here on earth, with its liturgy of signs which veil and reveal – the sacraments – is a foreshadowing of the immaterial church, the eternal church, the city above, where the heavenly liturgy is constantly celebrated before the throne of God and the Lamb. That is it: the cathedral is an image of the heavenly city, Jerusalem.

In fact it is a figure in stone and glass of the Apocalypse, the last book of the New Testament. It indicates the 'idea', the meaning and the goal of the whole of Christianity.[31]

The masterpieces of the Flemish primitives fit into such cathedrals. They know the transparency of light.

In his commentary on Jan van Eyck's 'The Virgin in a Church' (Gemäldegalerie, Berlin), E. Panofsky remarks that the light is from the north:

> If he decided to shift the laws of nature, he had a reason for it. This reason is simply that the light that he paints is not meant to depict the natural light, but the supernatural, supersubstantial light that illuminates the city of God: the divine light, under the appearance of ordinary daylight. In Jan van Eyck, this light, although independent of the laws of astronomy, is not independent of the laws of symbolism . . . By challenging the laws of astronomy the apparently natural light reveals its truly supernatural character.[32]

In fact on the embroidered hem of the splendid red robe of the

Virgin there is a text – a deliberate choice by Van Eyck, also on the Ghent retable – which is sung in Flanders, northern France and the Lower Rhine on the feast of the Assumption of Mary:

Haec est speciosior sole, super omnium stellarum dispositionem. Luci comparata invenitur prior. Candor est enim lucis aeternae, speculum sine macula Dei majestatis.[33]

And Panovsky adds:

What more telling image could one find of this light, set above the order of the universe, not followed by night and extending to the ends of the world, than a sun which shines in the north and in so doing proclaims that it never sets?

The mystics

Francis of Assisi

The time of the great cathedrals is also the time of the great mystics. Through their personal spiritual power they most strongly translated the focus on God in these centuries. Here it was a matter of their own experience of the divine light. Here too an abundance of witnesses makes choice difficult. We begin with one who, after Jesus Christ and Mary, is the most venerated and the clearest saint, Francis of Assisi (1181/1182–1226).

Despite all pious legends, he appears as a very simple minstrel of total harmony. We can rightly apply to him what the historian A. Vauchez says about the mediaeval saint: 'the saint is a being of light'.

Shortly before Francis, half-blind, sick and somewhat depressed, at the age of around forty-five sensed the approach of death, he wrote the 'Hymn of Brother Sun and of the Creation', which is better known as 'Hymn of the Sun'.[34] Here is an extract. However, Francis also praises Brother Wind, Sister Water, human beings, and Sister Death:

All praise be yours, my Lord, through all that you have made,
And first my Lord Brother Sun,
who brings the day and light you give to us through him.
How beautiful is he, how radiant in all his splendour!
Of you, Most High, he bears the likeness.
All praise be yours, my Lord, through Sister Moon and Stars;
In the heavens you have made them,
bright and precious and fair.
. . . All praise be yours, my Lord, through Brother Fire,
through whom you brighten up the night.
How beautiful is he, how gay, full of power and strength . . .

When Francis was dying, the brothers brought Clare and her sisters to him again. And after Clare's death a brother wrote about her:

> After prayer her angelic face was even brighter and more beautiful, so much did it shine with joy. The gracious and generous Lord so filled his lowly bride with his rays that she really spread the divine light around her.

Although here we have the customary language of the time, the atmosphere which dominated in San Damiano and throughout Assisi among the followers of Francis and Clare, something inexpressible is translated in it. It is striking that even now anyone who visits Assisi is affected by it.

The Divine Comedy

Of course many people will hesitate to put Dante, Francis's fellow-countryman, among the mystics. But in my view the depth of his insights into the mysticism of light seems to leave a modest place for him here, although he was not a saint in the accepted meaning of the word.

We rediscover the luminous harmony of the Gothic cathedral in the '*dolce armonia*' of *The Divine Comedy*, which Dante Alighieri

(1265–1321) himself called *La Commedia*. It is a perplexing hymn to the light that is God, which fills, purifies or repels. Only Dante's genius can put the abundance of imagery and allusions to predecessors and contemporaries in one earthly and heavenly perspective. On the one hand Dante is infinitely far from the relativizing thought of our post-modern world, from any rationalism and also from theology after Vatican II; however, on the other hand he is so sensitive to the kaleidoscopic human spirit that many present-day figures can be found mirrored in the hundreds of figures which he presents in his comedy.

Dante lived in the middle of a time of discoveries: everything was opening up in all directions and, having travelled much throughout Europe, he took part in them, in depth and in range, with an unparalleled Florentine exuberance. He sees the darkness of countless political rogues. He was a sworn enemy of Popes Boniface VIII and Clement V – he puts most of the popes whom he describes in hell, his description of which recalls the depictions of Hieronymus Bosch. Nothing happens there because there is no love. He sees the true church in heaven, where above all the simple and modest lay people and founders of orders live, all those who truly love. For him, everything flows together into a last synthesis of an universal spirit, filled with symbolism, but always very personal, and not anonymous as in the intellectual monuments which Thomas Aquinas composes: politics, history, science, astronomy, mysticism, classical antiquity, Old and New Testaments, contemporary Christianity. All this is summed up in his strophes.

The Divine Comedy is a poem about an imaginary journey which begins in hell on the evening of Maundy Thursday and after a journey through purgatory ends in heaven on the morning of the Thursday after Easter. Dante is accompanied on his journey by Virgil, on the prompting of St Lucy, whom Dante venerated greatly, and his beloved Beatrice, sent to accompany him to the gates of heaven. There Beatrice herself becomes his guide. The poem is both an ascent to the heavenly light and a love-song for Beatrice, who waits for him in the light. It is 'love which moves all things', as the very last verse says, *'l'amor che muove il sole e l'altre stelle'* (*Paradise* 33, 145). Moreover all three parts end with the word *'stelle'* (stars). We shall follow Dante on his journey, illustrated by some quotations.[35]

On entering the first circle of hell he writes:

> So dark it was and deep and misty, that peer as I would into the depths, I could distinguish nothing there (*Hell* 4,10).

Virgil accompanies him deeper and deeper, where everything becomes blacker and fearful figures everywhere threaten to come to the two of them in the deepest ice-hole, with Lucifer, 'the wicked worm who pierces the world' (34, 108).

They then creep upwards through the centre of the earth, where they can again see stars. Here there is mention of light, white and blue colours (sapphires). Again, as in hell, there is a clear hierarchy. Dante makes those who converted at the last moment say:

> At that moment a light from heaven admonished us, so that, repentant and forgiving, we departed from life at peace with God, who stirs in our hearts the longing to behold him (*Purgatory* 5, 54).

On the way Virgil constantly encourages Dante with the prospect of his meeting Beatrice:

> It is Beatrice I mean: you will see her above on the summit of this mountain, smiling and blissful (*Purgatory* 6, 46).

Virgil stops, as a good pagan, to offer a hymn to the sun:

> O kindly light, trusting in whom I take this new path, conduct us as we need to be conducted in this spot. You warm the world and enlighten it. When other reason does not prompt a different course, your rays should ever guide us (*Purgatory* 13, 16–21).

When they reach the end of Purgatory, Virgil has to leave Dante and finally entrust him to Beatrice.[36]

> Within a cloud of flowers which uprose from the angel's hands, and descended again both within and without, there appeared to me a lady crowned with olive over a white veil, and wearing beneath a green mantle a robe of the colour of living flame (*Purgatory* 30, 28–33).

Beatrice accuses him of being unfaithful to her and to God's light all too often after her death. Dante repents and has a fit of remorse on seeing her heavenly beauty.[37] Thereupon Dante is washed clean, Beatrice can take off her veil, and the choir sings:

> that he may see the second beauty that you conceal.

Thereupon Dante exclaims:

> O radiance of eternal living light . . . where the heaven with its harmonies shows your perfect image, when you unveiled yourself in the open air (*Purgatory* 31, 137–45).

With Beatrice he then goes through the reborn earthly paradise on the summit of the Mount of Purgatory so that together they can enter the nine heavenly spheres and from there ascend the highest heaven, the empyreum, where he sees the blessed in the form of an enormous rose, illuminated by the light of God. The whole of the third part, Paradise, is a song of praise to the divine Light. This light becomes transparent in those who are risen:

> With the divinest light of the lesser ring I heard a modest voice reply, like that of the angel addressing Mary: 'So long as the festival of paradise shall last, our love will radiate around us such a vesture. Its brightness will correspond to our fervour, the fervour to our power of sight, and that is in proportion to the grace it has in addition to its natural gift. When the glorious saintly flesh has been resumed, our person will be

more acceptable because of its completeness' (*Paradise*, 14, 34–48).

And in that light he sees 'the sun of my eyes', Beatrice:

> For within her eyes there appeared a smile so glowing that I thought I had fathomed with my own the depths of my grace and my blessedness (15, 34–36).

Dante looks round:

> I saw faces persuasive to love, decked with another light and their own smiles, and gestures graced with every form of seemliness (*Paradise* 31, 49–51).

However, Beatrice, on whom 'the rays of eternal light play', is taken up into the rose which Dante now, in his earthly life, cannot yet reach. He is accompanied further by Bernard:

> Here the power of my lofty fantasy failed (33, 142).

For him and for the blessed, God's deepest light remains unattainable, just as, conversely, was the floor of hell:

> O how defective is language, how feeble to respect my conceit; and this, compared with what I saw, is so slight that 'little' is too weak a word (33, 121–126).

Half a century earlier than Dante a woman, just as powerful a poet, had sung her own experience.

Hadewijch

We have no direct biographical information about Hadewijch. Presumably she lived and wrote in the middle of the thirteenth century (c.1210–c.1260) in Antwerp or Brussels. It is certain that she belonged in the broad current of the Beguine movement, that she inspired a group of like-minded women, was very refined and cultivated – her language is splendid – and had a decisive influence on John Ruusbroec (1239–1381).[38]

She wrote a number of *Visions*, *Letters* and *Poems in Stanzas*. In them she tried to avoid both the 'rationalism' of Peter Abelard (and the scholastics with their Aristotelian spirit) and the influence of Dionysius the Areopagite, for whom God dwells unattainable in the darkness. At the same time she avoids deriving religious experience predominantly from the feelings (something of which Bernard of Clairvaux was accused). At first sight she seems to follow Bernard, among other things by her emphasis on true love, inspired by the poetry of the French troubadours, and on the God who can be experienced intensely in mysticism. However, her writings show that she did not despise 'reason', although she wanted to keep this in its place (see for example *Letter* 18): for her, God is indeed greater and he removes human beings to such a great abyss that there is room for his space.[39]

However, Hadewijch does not want to disappear into this abyss completely; in her mystical life she wants to remain a proud, free woman. She talks of 'free love' (*Poems in Stanzas* 31). Her own unique and always passionate personality does not disappear under the force of God's love.

We must limit ourselves here to just one aspect of her spiritual life, namely clarity. Her encounter with an enjoyment of the unattainable God in the wilderness is at the same time a great clarification, since everything is clear and direct: 'In this way the soul sees and does not see' (*Letter* 28) and she is at the same time 'illuminated' and 'blinded' (*Letter* 11). There is brilliant 'lightning' and dark 'thunder' (*Letter* 30).

In *Vision* 6 Hadewijch writes:

> [At the age of nineteen] above that lofty seat in this lofty place I saw a crown that surpassed all diadems. In its great breadth it embraced all things beneath it, and beyond the crown was nothing . . .

And there she corrects herself:

> And I saw him whom I sought. His countenance revealed itself with such clarity that I recognized in it all the countenances and all the forms that ever existed and ever shall exist ...

It was a total vision of a personal Light in which immanence and transcendence flow into each other. And in *Vision* 12 she writes:[40]

> Once at Epiphany, during Mass, I was taken up out of myself in the spirit; there I saw a city, large, and wide, and high, and adorned with perfections. And in the midst of it there sat Someone upon a round disc, which continually opened and closed itself again upon hidden mysteries. And he who sat there above the disc was sitting in constant stillness; but in the disc his Being circled about in unspeakable swiftness without stopping. And the abyss in which the disc ran as it circled about was of such unheard-of depth and so dark that no horror can be compared to it. And the disc, seen from above, was set with all kinds of precious stones and in the colour of pure gold; but on the darkest side, where it ran so fearfully, it was like fearful flames, which devoured heaven and earth and in which all things perished and were swallowed up. And he who sat upon the disc was One whose countenance none could perceive without belonging to the terrible flames of this disc and being thrown into the deep abyss which lay underneath. And that countenance drew all the dead to it living; and everything that was withered blossomed because of it; and all the poor who saw it received great riches; and all the sick became strong; and all who were in multiplicity and division became one in that countenance. And he who sat in this high place was clothed with a robe whiter than white, on the breast of which was written: 'The Most Loved of all Beloveds'. That was his name. Then I fell down before that countenance in order to adore the truth of that terrifying Being whom I there saw revealed.

The language is apocalyptic and sets out to express the

inexpressible in metaphors of light which are barely understandable. She uses the same language in *Vision* 1 to express her encounter with the Holy Trinity, which she compares with three pillars (Spirit, Father and Son respectively). An angel asks her to turn from him:

> And I turned from him, and I saw standing before me a cross like crystal, clearer and whiter than crystal. And through it a great space was visible. And placed in front of this cross I saw a seat like a disc, which was more radiant to see than the sun in its most radiant power; and beneath the disc stood three pillars. The first pillar was like burning fire. The second was like a precious stone that is called topaz; it has the nature of gold and the brightness of the air, as well as the colours of all gems. The third was like a precious stone that is called amethyst and has a purple colour like the rose and the violet. And in the middle under the disc, a whirlpool revolved in such a frightful manner and was so terrible to see that heaven and earth might have been astonished and made fearful by it.[41]

Hadewijch herself recognizes that she is perhaps not writing very clearly, as in *Letter* 22:

> I am distressed that I dare not say or write to persons what is worth the trouble, or write any words about the depths of my soul.

The *Letters* – from her more mature period – use a more comprehensible language. At the beginning of *Letter* 1 she speaks of 'the clear love':

> Since God has manifested by his virtues that radiant love which was uncomprehended, whereby he illuminated all the virtues in the radiance of his love, may he illuminate you and enlighten you by the pure radiance with which he shines resplendent for himself and for all his friends and those he most dearly loves.

> The greatest radiance anyone can have on earth is truth in works of justice performed in imitation of the Son, and to practise the truth with regard to all that exists, for the glory of the noble love that God is. Oh, what great radiance it is that we let God act with his radiance! For in it Love works – for himself and for all creatures, each one according to its rights – whatever his goodness may promise to give it, in justice and radiance.

And later in this letter she asks:

> Illuminate your mind and adorn yourself with virtues and just works; enlarge your spirit by lofty desires towards God's totality.

Indeed, for her as for Ruusbroec, the light must shine on the others (*Letter* 12):

> With the great fieriness of the unified burning life they will be enkindled; and with the flames of burning charity they will be illuminated.

But she herself cannot do other than let the deep Light clothe her wholly. 'In the riches of the clarity of the Holy Spirit, the blissful soul celebrates wonderful feasts' (*Letter* 28). For, she says, 'I have seen the land of clarity' (id.), and 'The flame burns every moment in the marrow of my soul' (*Letter* 24). Again we see the old images of sun and moon, in which God as the sun illuminates the soul by becoming one with her (*Letter* 19):

> The souls engulfed in God who are thus lost in him are illuminated on one side by the light of Love, as the moon receives its light from the sun. The simple knowledge then received by them in this new light, from which they come and in which they dwell – this simple light then catches their darker half, so that the two halves of the soul become one; and then there is full light. If you had demanded this light to

choose your Beloved, you would be free. For these souls are united and clothed with the same light with which God clothes himself.

And yet, faithful to the old tradition, she will repeat with Augustine: 'All that man comes to in his thought of God, and all that he can understand of him or imagine under any outward form, is not God' *(Letter* 12).

Hadewijch, too, comes up against the dark cloud. Her *Poems in Stanzas* sound like 'songs of lament over the absent Beloved', who yet remains present. Hadewijch wants the encounter with the Other as Other and refuses to shut herself up in enjoyment in her own loving longing. Some stanzas indicate this:

> For I saw a shining cloud rise,
> Over all the dark sky; and its form seemed so beautiful,
> I fancied I would soon with full happiness
> Play freely in the sunlight:
> But my joy was only a fancy!
> If I should die of it, who would blame me? (*Poem* 17, 7).

> Alas, noble Love, in what season, when,
> Will you restore serene days to me
> And a change from my darkness?
> How glad I'd be to see the sun!
> You alone know
> How I mean this:
> Whether I wish anything but your pleasure (*Poem* 19, 7).

John Ruusbroec

After Hadewijch, Ruusbroec. Perhaps he had fewer literary gifts, but he was the greatest teacher of mysticism in the Low Countries, with influence all over Europe.[42] As chaplain of Sint-Goedele in Brussels and later as prior of the Augustinian monastery of Groenendaal in the Zoniënwoud, which gave him much imagery, he was one of the last to express the subtle balance betwen theology and spirituality which characterizes the heyday of the Middle Ages. Here his serenity and his 'discernment of the spirits' in a period of church decline, plague and war, and wild religious movements, are striking. Again I shall point out the motif of light by means of some extracts from his numerous writings, which need to be interpreted predominantly as trinitarian mysticism.

The title of a smaller work, *The Sparkling Stone*,[43] already indicates his perspective. It is a dialogue with a monk. Ruusbroec himself refers to Rev. 2.17 ('I shall give him a white stone'). And he comments as follows:

> By this sparkling stone we mean our Lord Jesus Christ, for according to his divinity he is a beam of the eternal light (Wisdom 7.26), a ray of God's glory, and a spotless mirror (Heb. 1.3) in which all things have their life. Whoever overcomes and transcends all things is given this sparkling stone, through which he receives light, truth, and life. The stone is also like a fiery flame, for the fiery love of the eternal Word has filled the whole world with love and wishes all loving spirits to be consumed in the fire of love.

That light comes to dwell in us 'by combining reason with our faith in God'. But this presupposes a basic renunciation:

> There we will abide – unified, empty and imageless – raised up through love to the open bareness of our mind, for when we transcend all things in love and die to all rational observations in a dark state of unknowing, we become transformed through the working of the eternal Word, who is an image of the Father. In the empty being of our spirit we receive an incomprehensible resplendence which envelops and pervades us in the same way that the air is pervaded by the light of the sun. This resplendence is nothing other than an act of gazing and seeing which has no ground. What we are is what we see, and

> what we see is what we are, for our mind, our life, and our very being are raised up in a state of oneness and united with the truth which is God himself.

Later he explicitly mentions this 'being transformed' by God's clarity through which the reasoning understanding must be silent.

> Nevertheless our power of reason remains standing with its eyes open in darkness, that is, in a groundless state of unknowing. In this darkness the fathomless resplendence remains covered and hidden from us, for its overwhelming groundlessness blinds our reason. It does, however, envelop us in simplicity and transform us through its inmost self.

However, Ruusbroec is a personalist. Entering the light is not an abolition of consciousness:

> If we could be blessed without our knowledge, then a rock, which possesses no knowledge, could likewise be blessed. If I were lord of all the earth, but did not know it, what good would that be?

Nor can human beings shut themselves off in the light. He distinguishes four forms of consciousness in 'the enlightenment'. Here it is striking that one of them involves 'going out of oneself to all human beings with the trust of brotherly love'. In the meantime he recognizes the difference between 'the enlightenment of the saints' in the beatific vision and 'the highest enlightenment which we can attain in this life'.

> God's shadow enlightens our interior desert on earth, but on the high mountains of the Promised Land there is no shadow. Still, it is one and the same sun and one and the same resplendence which enlighten both our earthly desert and also those high mountains . . .

Meanwhile 'with blinded eyes we will then be drawn by the sun into its own resplendence, where we will attain unity with God'. But,

> Our own state in the Christian faith is still in the coolness of dawn, for the day has dawned for us. We therefore 'walk in the light' and sit in God's shadow, for God's grace is an intermediary between him and ourselves.

Ruusbroec's masterpiece, *The Spiritual Espousals*, is a commentary on Matt. 25.6: 'Behold the bridegroom comes, go out to meet him!' This is of course an inner seeing, the encounter with God who enlightens human beings like a sun.[44] Some extracts again point to the important theme of light. The 'spark' of the soul will, like Zacchaeus, see God, his light that comes to us in us:

> Thus there arises a higher light of God's grace which, like a ray of sunlight, is cast upon the soul without its being merited or desired. In this light God gives himself to us out of his gratuitous goodness and beneficence, a gift which no creature can merit in advance.

He sees this grace as being 'like a lamp full of precious oil . . . Through the fire of charity it provides a flame and bright light.' Sometimes a sudden, ecstatic illumination comes:

> Sometimes God gives some people short flashes of spiritual insight, just like flashes of lightning in the sky. These are short flashes of singular resplendence which shine forth from out of a simple bareness. In an instant the spirit is raised above itself, but at once the light is past and the person comes to himself again. God causes this himself and it is something very exalted, for those who experience it often become enlightened persons.

As with Hadewijch, for Ruusbroec words and images are inadequate to describe such experiences:

By means of the enlightened reason the spirit raises itself up in interior observation, contemplating and observing its inmost depths where the touch abides. At this point, reason and all created light are unable to go further, for the divine resplendence which hovers there and which constitutes this touch blinds all created powers of vision by its presence, which is unfathomable. All powers of understanding which are enlightened by merely created light are here like the eyes of a bat when confronted with the sun's brightness . . . The enlightened reason is constantly led to ask ever anew where the touch comes from and to make new soundings in order that it may follow this vein of honey to its source. But it knows as much about this on the first day of its attempt as it will ever know. Consequently the powers of reason and observation confess, 'We do not know what it is', for the divine resplendence which hovers there repulses and blinds all powers of understanding by its very presence . . .

In a last, brief part about a life which sees God, Ruusbroec wrestles with the images of light and darkness in order to have some sense of what they are about. In the total emptying the absolute light breaks through, constantly renewing and welling up from the core of the Trinity, which is itself a 'bottomless pit of simplicity'. The mysterious reality is described by impotent words:

> In the abyss of this darkness in which the loving spirit has died to itself, God's revelation and eternal life have their origin, for in this darkness an incomprehensible light is born and shines forth; this is the Son of God, in whom a person becomes able to see and to contemplate eternal life. This divine light is shed upon a person in the simple being of his spirit, where the spirit receives the resplendence which is God himself above and beyond all gifts and creaturely activity in the empty idleness of the spirit, where the spirit has lost itself in blissful love and receives God's resplendence without intermediary. The spirit ceaselessly becomes the very resplendence which it

receives. See, this hidden resplendence, in which a person contemplates all that he desires in accordance with his spirit's mode of emptiness, is so great a resplendence that the loving contemplative neither sees nor feels in the ground of his being, in which he is at rest, anything other than an incomprehensible light. In the simple bareness which envelops all things, he feels and finds himself to be nothing other than the same light with which he sees. This is the first point, describing how a person is made capable of seeing in the divine light. Blessed are the eyes that see in this way, for they possess eternal life.

Julian of Norwich

The English eremitical mystic Julian of Norwich (1342–1416) also calls for our attention. She was presumably influenced by John Ruusbroec and the Rhineland mystics Tauler and Eckhart. She was only rediscovered in the middle of the nineteenth century.[45] Thomas Merton puts her on the same footing as John of the Cross and calls her the greatest English theologian alongside Newman

In her *Revelations of Divine Love* she offers what R. Maisonneuve calls a 'pedagogy of sight'. Terms like 'see', 'look' and 'behold' constantly occur. For her, human beings are blind people for whom the world has not yet become transparent. They must grow out of their prison towards the consciousness that they live under the loving and active gaze of God. This is brought about by looking at the life of Jesus, his suffering, the origin of abiding joy. She herself experienced anxieties and night; her time too was characterized by plague, famine, war, the Western schism. But she remained deeply convinced that God's spirit brings people into the mystery of the Father where all shall be well. God is always deeply present in the ground of human beings. She constantly emphasized her own experience, as a woman, for her theory (she knows that men would not always take her seriously because she was only 'a woman, unlettered, feeble and frail').[46]

At the end of her *Revelations*, in Chapters 83 and 84, she talks about the three central attributes of God, namely life, love and light:

> Our faith is a light, coming to us naturally from him who is our everlasting Day, our Father, and our God. By this light Christ, our mother, and the Holy Spirit, our good Lord, lead us through these passing years. The light is measured to our individual needs as we face our night. Because of the light we live; because of the night we suffer and grieve. Through this grief we can earn reward and thanks from God. With the help of mercy and grace, we know and trust our light quite deliberately, and with it we go forward intelligently and firmly. When we are done with grief our eyes will be suddenly enlightened, and in the shining brightness of the light we shall see perfectly. For our light is none other than God our Maker and the Holy Spirit, in our Saviour, Christ Jesus. So did I see and understand that faith is our light in darkness, and our light is God, the everlasting Day . . . This light is love . . .

Nicholas of Cusa, The Vision of God

Nicholas of Cusa (1401–1464) occupies a quite special place in the transition between the Middle Ages and the Renaissance.[47] A European diplomat and cardinal, and later Bishop of Brixen, he was a truly universal spirit who was attracted by both astronomy and jurisprudence as well as by mysticism. At the same time he worked for the unity of the church, which was then so divided internally, and, in the footsteps of Ramon Lull, for reconciliation between the religions.

His *De Docta Ignorantia* expresses the core of his philosophical thought: neither knowledge through the senses nor abstract discourse is enough for true knowledge. Only intuition makes it possible to know the ground of everything, God. Any knowledge of God must at the same time confirm and deny any statement about him. We can encounter God in one sense through his presence in creation, but as the one who is completely transcendent he always escapes our knowledge. For Nicholas of Cusa, Christ remains the saviour who opens the door both to earth and to heaven because he combines the two dynamically in himself.

The Cusanus Society in Trier published a critical edition of his extensive work and has devoted many colloquia to this attractive and in many respects still topical figure. Here we must limit ourselves to his *De Visione Dei* (The Vision of God), a work which he addressed to the Benedictines of Tegernsee in 1453. The spirituality of this abbey was governed by the *Devotio Moderna* and by the mystical theology of Dionysius the Areopagite.

As a dialectician, Nicolas of Cusa wants to teach the monks that love and insight need to go together. The dialectic of light and darkness constantly appears. Here as an illustration are some short extracts from the brief work.[48] Nicholas of Cusa wants constantly to reconcile a total immanence of God in the cosmos with God's absolute transcendence. He explains his purpose in the introduction:

> I shall endeavour to lead you into the divine darkness in the simplest and most understandable way, so that you can discover and note it yourselves. As soon as you are there and experience the presence of the inaccessible light, each of you, to the degree that God grants him, will spontaneously try to get closer and closer to him and here, as a kind of firstfruits, to taste in advance the full sweetness of the heavenly banquet of eternal bliss, to which we are called in the Word of Life by the Gospel of the Christ who is blessed for ever.

He then develops the 'seeing face to face':

> Your gaze, Lord, is your face. So the one who thus looks upon you with loving gaze will find your face looking lovingly at him. And the more lovingly he tries to look upon you, the more lovingly he shall be looked upon by you. Whoever looks upon you with wrath will be looked upon in the same way. Whoever looks on you with joy will know himself to be looked

on joyfully, depending on the face with which he looks upon you. Just as the bodily eye that sees everything through a red glass judges that everything that it sees is red, or green if it looks through a green glass, so shall the spiritual eye which is blinkered by limitations and passivity judge you, the object of spiritual vision, according to the nature of this limitation and passivity (53f.).

He says this about the beauty of the face of the Lord:

> The one who is on the way towards seeing your face is still far removed as long as he still has some concept of it. A concept of a face falls short of your face, Lord. Any beauty that one can think of falls short of the beauty of your face . . . In all faces one sees the face of faces: veiled and mysterious. One does not see it unveiled until, above all faces, one enters a remote hidden stillness where there is neither knowledge nor concept. Beneath this mist, cloud, darkness or ignorance which the one who seeks your face enters, your face can only be found veiled, but this very darkness unveils the presence of the face beyond all veils.

The invisible can be seen in the visible:

> So you, my invisible God, are seen through each and every gaze. Through everyone who sees, in every visible thing and in every act of seeing, you are seen, who are invisible and completely detached from all that, and infinitely high above it. So, Lord, I must leap over the wall of invisible vision beyond which you are to be found. Now this wall is at the same time all things and nothing. For you who encounter us as if you are at the same time all and nothing of that all, dwell within this very high wall which no reason can climb over by its own power.

Nicholas of Cusa is, however, very well aware that his talk of God constantly remains stammering:

> Through the words that I use I make the taste more rather than less pleasant. But your goodness is so great, my God, that you yourself make even the blind speak about the light and proclaim the praise of him of whom they know nothing and cannot know anything but what is revealed to them.

Fortunately it is Jesus, the Word incarnate, who opens the door to the invisible:

> The Word of God illuminates the intellect as the sunlight illuminates the world. In you, my Jesus, I see the life of the senses illuminated by the light of the intellect, the light of the intellect as illuminating and illuminated light, and divine life as only illuminating. For in that invisible light I see the source of light, namely the Word of God, which is the Truth that illuminates every intellect.

We note how Nicholas of Cusa constantly seeks in a subtle way to maintain the balance between the indwelling of God in his creation and his total transcending of it, through which the personal can still be addressed. Later, Giordano Bruno would disturb this equilibrium by doing away with the transcendent pole in the field of tension with his pantheistic explanation. However, the Enlightenment was even less successful in maintaining the dialectic and would reduce God to a theoretically necessary principle of order.

But on our short journey we must pause again, at the point before the West partially came under the spell of this one-dimensional reduction, to consider some great visionaries of the Light in the darkness.

John of the Cross

The Carmelite John of the Cross is not only the great master of Spanish mysticism (1542–1591) and a contemporary of Teresa of Avila, but at the same time he is one of the most remarkable literary figures in the Spanish language.[49]

John of the Cross constantly combined his mystical experience, expressed in poetry, with theological commentaries. Like Dionysius the Areopagite, he does not see the classical stages of prayer, namely purification, enlightenment and union, as a succession of phases; they overlap and are woven into one another.

There is an enormous amount of literature about his teaching. He had a deep influence on such different figures as Henri Bergson, Edith Stein, Dag Hammarskjöld, Daniel Berrigan, Salvador Dali and Maurice Béjart. Here of necessity I shall limit myself to a few extracts from his poetic work which as a whole take up the theme of this book. For John the symbols of flame and wound are of great significance: by this he means the change in his own person under the influence of the divine love. In his poetry he is strongly influenced by the language of the Old Testament Song of Songs. Above all his own 'Song of Songs', some verses from which he asked to be read to him on his death bed, is inspired by this. In it we read:

> Where have you vanished,
> Beloved, and have left me full of woe?
> And like the hart have sped,
> wounding ere you did go
> your love who followed,
> crying high and lo . . .
> O end my torments here,
> since none but you can remedy my plight.
> And to these eyes appear,
> for you are all their light
> and but for you I value not their sight.
> O crystal spring so fair,
> might now within your silvery depths appear,
> even as I linger here
> these features ever dear
> which on my soul I carry graven clear.

He wrote his most typical poem, 'The Dark Night', as a prisoner in the monastic prison of Toledo. Here are just a few lines:

> Kindled in love with yearnings,
> in the dark night when none saw me
> when I could see nothing.
> Without light or guide,
> save that which burned in my heart.

In the commentary John emphasizes the great difference between the light of nature and that of the consciousness and the spiritual light of God that the soul experiences through the way of suffering and complete darkness.

John's last great work, 'The Living Flame of Love', is also a poem which begins like this:

> O living flame of love
> that tenderly wounded my soul
> in its deepest centre.
> Since you are no longer oppressive,
> defeat me now if it be your will,
> break the web of this sweet encounter.

In his commentary on this poem, John writes:

> The grace which God has given the soul earlier is a light. With this light he has enlightened the depths of the eye of the spirit by breaking it open for the divine light. So he has made it ready for himself. Now this abyss of grace has opened up another abyss: the divine transformation of the soul in Christ ... so that we may say that God's light and the light of the soul are simply one light. The natural light of the soul has then become one with the supernatural light of God. In the other life this comes about by means of the light of glory; in this life by means of very enlightened faith.

Teresa of Avila

Whereas John constantly talks about 'God' and strikingly rarely about Christ, there is much more about Christ in the mysticism of the woman Teresa.[50] She constantly calls him 'His Majesty'. Her writings – she too wrote a 'Song of Songs' – are more about inwardness and 'tenderness' than about 'light', though she too speaks of 'the shadow of the deity' and of the 'shining sun under the cloud'. In her main work, the *Castillo Interior* (The Interior Castle), written in Toledo when she was imprisoned as a rebel nun, but not in the first person, in order to avoid persecution by the Inquisition, the motif of light plays a role, but it is more limited than in John.

In Chapter 1 of the first Mansion she wants 'to see the soul as a citadel, wholly made of just one diamond or of a very clear crystal'. She uses the images of citadel and diamond alternately. She wants to guide the reader from imprisonment in the dark outside to the very clear innermost mansion, into which only God leads. There the soul changes 'from an ugly worm to a white butterfly'.

However, she too recognizes the painfulness of a comfortless purging process to which His Majesty awakens the soul: 'It is as if a falling star shoots by, there is a flash of lightning or a clap of thunder, but she sees no light and hears no sound . . . This glittering is like broken light. Like a sun under a very fine veil. Like a diamond, if you can polish it. His garment looks like Dutch linen.' She, too, speaks of a wound 'as by a fiery arrow'. Everything then culminates in a spiritual marriage of the soul with God . . . 'just as in a place with two windows through which the full light falls, the initially separate sources of light fuse into a single light' (cf. I Cor. 6.17): 'Then the king is in his palace.'

But light does not only come directly from God. We receive it from each other. In one of her *Letters of Conscience* from Seville (November 1575) she expresses disquiet about 'her father', Gracian, who was sick:

> Suddenly he appeared to me in such a way that it could not be my imagination. A light extended deep within me. I saw how he went his way with a happy and shining face. Of course the light that I saw had to make his face shine like that of all in heaven. I asked myself whether it sometimes shines through the splendour and the light which emanate from our Lord.

Teresa had a fiery soul and a relatively weak psychological make-up; neither humour nor sound understanding got in the way of it. Far less tormented than John of the Cross, she had a happy nature. Although a Carmelite nun, she had an extremely busy life. Throughout, that life was directed towards one goal which she repeated, sitting upright, on her deathbed.

> My Lord and my Bridegroom, now the time has come for which I have longed. It is time to see each other...

And Marcelle Auclair ends:

> The Countess of Alba put a garment of cloth of gold over the body of one who during her lifetime had chosen a habit of the coarsest material.

Between the certainty of yesterday and the doubt of tomorrow: Blaise Pascal

From the seventeenth century on, the shift in the European intellectual climate accelerates. Not only did the confusions of Reformation and Counter-Reformation further attack the old coherence of the world-view, but doubt in thought increased, while an empirical-scientific approach to it contributed to the discovery of more and more new territory. To an increasing degree the collective consciousness disintegrated.

Blaise Pascal saw the certainties of yesterday removed for good, but he punctured the newly offered triumphs of substitute certainties. He saw both the greatness and the brokenness of human beings. He seems to us to be more modern than his contemporaries. Jean Brun locates him like this: 'Therefore he is neither the philosopher of the reassuring firm ground under our feet nor the philosopher of intoxicating dizziness, but the philosopher of the abyss.'[51] Pascal felt very strongly that the alternative is the fire of God or the chill of nothingness. And he chooses, not blindly (a mistaken interpretation of the famous 'wager'), but in the light of experience.

As a thinker, Blaise Pascal (1623–1662)[52] came under the influence of Michel de Montaigne (1533–1592) and René Descartes (1596–1650), both of whom emphasized the individual subject with its self-consciousness. Pascal was to define it as a 'thinking reed' (347). However, at the same time he was a scientist who among other things invented a calculator, a distant forerunner of the computer.

As a Christian, Pascal was for a while a fervent Jansenist, sharply aware of the presence of evil in the world. The new picture of the world which science increasingly opened up intensified his feeling of solitude: are human beings just a speck of matter in immense space and endless time (194; 205; 693)? As a scientist he rejected any religious dogmatism; nevertheless he wanted there to be a connection between his life as a scholar and as a believer.

The question of God will not let him go: did God exist or not (230)? He complains about 'seeing too much to deny and too little to be sure' (229). Not seeing always makes him dizzy before the possibly bottomless abyss of existence: 'Our whole groundwork cracks, and the earth opens to abysses' (72). And there is the emptiness of death: 'The last act is tragic, however happy all the rest of the play is; at the last a little earth is thrown upon our head, and that is the end for ever' (210). He never developed a system for finding an answer. But the question 'What is it that I am?' (323) and 'Am I a bottomless abyss?' (425) continued to torment him. And in his fourth letter to Mademoiselle de Roannez we read: 'All things are the veils which cover God. He usually hides himself and discloses himself rarely.' Pascal sees darkness everywhere.

He looked almost despairingly for an authentic experience of God. The reasoning mind does not give this. It must have a deeper foundation: 'It is the heart which experiences God, and not the reason. This, then, is faith: God felt by the heart, not by the reason' (278). However, for the perceptive Pascal, understanding by the heart is not a question of feeling. Pascal calls the 'I think' the heart, and this thought lies deeper than rational understanding. It is a quest for the fullness of existence. He refers explicitly to Jer.31.34: 'I will put my spirit and my fear in your heart', and he adds: 'To prophesy is to speak of God, not from outward proofs, but from an inward and immediate feeling' (731).

And then – when Pascal was thirty-one – an experience struck him in a flash, on the evening of 23 November 1654. He was alone in his room. Then he experienced something that was to become so fundamental to him that he immediately wrote it down with a trembling hand on a piece of paper and later copied it on to parchment. This famous Memorial barely fills a page.[53] It begins:

> The year of grace 1654
> Monday 23 November, festival of St Clement, pope and martyr, and others of the martyrology, vigil of St Chrysogonus and others, from about half past eleven in the evening until half an hour after midnight,
> FIRE
> God of Abraham, God of Isaac, God of Jacob, not of philosophers and scholars.
> Certainty, certainty, heartfelt joy, peace.
> God of Jesus Christ.

Pascal repeatedly returns to this experience in his *Pensées* (556; 544). Clearly he does not mean to belittle philosophers and scholars, but here he experienced quite a different dimension of experience from the reflective or the experimental.

Meanwhile he continued to engage in further scientific investigations, including mathematics. We know how involved he was in the Jansenist disputes, and in his *Provinciales* he could dispute vigorously with the Jesuits. Pascal was not a saint at that time, as Guardini remarks.[54] But later he confessed his error and was reconciled with the church. In his last months, when he was seriously ill, he united himself with the suffering and death of Jesus[55] and tried constantly to help poor people, among other things by inventing a successful plan for cheap transport in Paris.[56]

Nietzsche, who admired and abhorred Pascal, called him a great Christian. In his *Posthumous Works* he wrote, 'When I speak of Plato, Pascal, Spinoza and Goethe, I know that their blood streams in my veins . . .', and in *Ecce Homo*: 'Not only do I read Pascal, but I revere him as the most instructive victim of Christianity . . .' Both saw the abyss, but Pascal saw the light and had deep veneration for the suffering Jesus.

The quest continues: the nineteenth and twentieth centuries

After the Enlightenment and the French Revolution, which in many countries was followed by a different relationship between church and state and between faith and science, the quest for God between darkness and light became if possible even more individual and varied. We find novelists like Sigrid Undset and the first Luise Rinser, musicians like Messiaen, painters like Rouault and Chagall, journalists like Emmanuel Mounier, poets like Charles Péguy and film-makers like Tarkowski. From the many possible figures I have chosen four very different representatives of the nineteenth and twentieth centuries: John Henry Newman, Thérèse of Lisieux, Pierre Teilhard de Chardin and Dag Hammarskjöld.

John Henry Cardinal Newman

John Henry Newman (1801–1890) was certainly as sensitive to the quest for the 'inner light' as Augustine himself; after a long phase of seeking, from being a priest in the Church of England he came to be a cardinal in the Roman Catholic Church.[57] He was still an

Anglican at the age of thirty-two when, somewhat weary after hard study, he became very ill on a journey to the Mediterranean, in Castro Giovanni on Sicily. Raving, he whispered, 'I have not sinned against the light'. However, he recovered very quickly and wanted to return as soon as possible to England. It was quite clear to him that a task was waiting for him there. Because there was no passenger ship, he secured passage on an orange boat heading for Marseilles. But the boat lay becalmed, with loose sails, in the Straits of Bonifacio. Newman looked at the warm summer night and then composed his prayer, which is now among the most popular hymns in the Anglican church:

> Lead, kindly Light, amid the encircling gloom,
> lead thou me on;
> The night is dark, and I am far from home,
> Lead thou me on.
> Keep thou my feet; I do not ask to see
> The distant scene; one step enough for me.
>
> I was not ever thus, nor prayed that thou
> Shouldst lead me on;
> I loved to choose and see my path; but now
> Lead thou me on.
> I loved the garish day, and, spite of fears,
> Pride ruled my will: remember not past years.
>
> So long thy power hath blest me, sure it still
> Will lead me on;
> O'er moor and fen, o'er crag and torrent, till
> The night is gone,
> And with the morn those Angel faces smile,
> Which I have loved long since, and lost awhile.[58]

Back in Oxford (on 10 July 1833) he became the head and heart of the Oxford Movement, by which he wanted to renew his church. But his quest did not cease, and in 1845 he entered the Roman

Catholic Church after making an impressive confession of faith in a sermon[59] in the Church of St Mary the Virgin. The experience of light during his journey from Sicily had become normative for his life:

> I shall wait for the light of thy guidance, and when I receive it I shall act in accordance with it, in simplicity and without fear. I believe I shall not be impatient if thou always bringest me darkness and defeat.[60]

For Newman, the experience of light was intensely bound up with his reflection on the conscience. It had very deep roots in his childhood years.

A simple story that he read much later offered such a precise account of his own experience as a child that he copied it out. It is about a boy of four who sees a tortoise creeping past. The child has a stick in his hand and is about to hit the animal. Then something so powerful unexpectedly happens in him that he runs to his mother and says to her, 'Mama, what was that? It told me that I mustn't do it.' Moved, the mother takes the child into her arms and replies: 'Some people call that the conscience. But I call it the voice of God. If you listen to it carefully, you will always understand better. But if you do not listen, then this voice will slowly go away.'[61]

Time and again Newman keeps returning to this. It becomes the firm ground for his argument that a personal Reality is at work above human beings. This voice compels him to leave his Anglican surroundings, which are so familiar and in such exalted society, and to opt for the Roman Catholic Church, which was to cause him so many problems. Some brief extracts can illustrate this basic conviction:

> Conscience does not repose on itself but vaguely reaches forward to something beyond self, and dimly discerns a sanction higher than self for its decisions, as is evidenced in that keen sense of obligation and responsibility which informs

them ... (It is) a voice, or the echo of a voice, imperative and constraining, like no other dictate in the whole of our experience ...

If (a person) has been betrayed into any kind of immorality, he has a lively sense of responsibility and guilt, though the act be no offence against society, – of distress and apprehension, even though it may be of present service to him, – of compunction and regret, though in itself it may be most pleasurable, – of confusion of face, though it may have no witnesses.[62]

What I am emphasizing here is that this voice commands, that it approves, that it disapproves, threatens, that it points to a future, that it bears witness to the invisible. The conscience is more than the human self. Man himself has no power over it, or does so only with the greatest difficulty; he has not made it and he cannot destroy it ... The sunshine presupposes that there is a sun in the sky, although sometimes we do not see it. When there is a knock on our door at night, the presupposition is that someone is standing outside in the darkness and asking to be let in. So too it is with this word in our innermost parts.[63]

And in his novel *Callista*, Newman makes the philosopher Polemo bear this witness. He comes to visit Callista in prison and makes her reply to the question of God like this:

'Well,' she said, 'I feel that God within my heart. I feel myself in His presence. He says to me, "Do this: don't do that." You may tell me that this dictate is a mere law of my nature, as to joy or to grieve. I cannot understand this. No, it is the echo of a person speaking to me. Nothing shall persuade me that it does not ultimately proceed from a person external to me. It carries with it its proof of its divine origin. My nature feels towards it as towards a person. When I obey it, I feel a satisfaction; when I disobey, a soreness – just like that which I feel in pleasing or offending some revered friend. So you see,

Polemo, I believe in what is more than a mere "something". I believe in what is more real to me than sun, moon, stars, and the fair earth, and the voice of friends. You will say: Who is He? Has He ever told you anything about Himself? Alas! No! – the more's the pity! But I will not give up what I have, because I have not more. An echo implies a voice; a voice a speaker. That speaker I love and I fear.'[64]

Newman found his light in the conscience and there he found God. He is convinced by his experience. But he recognizes that his personal experience need not necessarily be universal; it can be governed by temperament and milieu.[65] Newman also concedes that the step from the experience described to the existence of God implies surrender in faith. And he must equally recognize that in the second half of the nineteenth century, he sees very little of the step towards faith in the world around him.

In his *Apologia pro Vita Sua* he develops his view of what he interprets as a darkening of God:[66]

Starting then with the being of a God (which, as I have said, is as certain to me as the certainty of my own existence, though when I try to put the grounds of that certainty into logical shape I find a difficulty in doing so in mood and figure to my satisfaction), I look out of myself into the world of men, and there I see a sight which fills me with unspeakable distress. The world seems simply to give the lie to that great truth, of which my whole being is so full; and the effect upon me is, in consequence, as a matter of necessity, as confusing as if it denied that I am in existence myself. If I looked into a mirror, and did not see my face, I should have the sort of feeling which actually comes upon me, when I look into the living busy world, and see no reflection of its Creator. This is, to me, one of the great difficulties of this absolute primary truth, to which I referred just now. Were it not for this voice, speaking so clearly in my conscience and my heart, I should be an atheist, or a pantheist, or a polytheist when I looked into the world.

And then, like so many before him, Newman comes up against the incomprehensibility of evil:

> I can only answer, that either there is no Creator, or this living society of men is in a true sense discarded from His presence ... if there be a God, since there is a God, the human race is implicated in some terrible aboriginal calamity.

In the end Newman did not know what to make of what he judged darkness.[67]

Thérèse of Lisieux

Apparently uninfluenced by the criticism of Christianity and brought up in the very closed Catholic milieu[68] of the French provincial town of Alençon, in 1888, at the age of fifteen, Thérèse Martin entered the strict Carmelite convent of Lisieux.[69] She died of tuberculosis on 30 September 1897. In 1925 she was declared a saint.

Anyone who now reads her writings cannot avoid the impression that the atmosphere in this Carmel was very artificial, if not stuffy and childish. The power of Teresa of Avila or John of the Cross seems a long way away. A solid modern theological foundation of post-Jansenist spirituality, which characterized the prevailing piety, was completely lacking. The amazing thing is that this gentle and strong girl, under an apparently very serene exterior, wrestled for the last eighteen months of her life with an all-encompassing void, which began at Easter 1896. In June 1897 she, who had called God's face her sun, wrote:

> Then suddenly the fog which surrounds me becomes more dense; it penetrates my soul and envelops it in such a way that it is impossible to discover within it the sweet image of my Fatherland; everything has disappeared! When I want to rest my heart, fatigued by the darkness which surrounds it, by the memory of the luminous country after which I aspire, my

torment redoubles; it seems to me that the darkness, borrowing the voice of sinners, says mockingly to me: 'You are dreaming about the light, about a fatherland embalmed in the sweetest perfumes; you are dreaming about the eternal possession of the Creator of all these marvels; you believe that one day you will walk out of this fog which surrounds you! Advance, advance; rejoice in death which will give you not what you hope for but a night still more profound, the night of nothingness.'[70]

The only thing that still remained for her until her death was love and trust in the night in which she could no longer 'see' anything.[71]

Pierre Teilhard de Chardin

From a very different background and with a fundamental optimism, despite the many dramas in his life, the palaeontologist and Jesuit Pierre Teilhard de Chardin (1881–1955) sees one great movement to the light throughout evolution:

> Every being in the world stands somewhere on the slope that rises up from the shadows to the light.[72]

Gripped by the phenomenon of evolution in living matter, he tried to reconcile the unfolding of this energy which can be observed everywhere with a development from 'inside' human beings: 'Man, on whom and in whom the universe enfolds itself.'[73]

For him this is beyond any doubt a collective process in which an acceleration of the progressive socialization of humankind plays a great role, above all because of an evolution which is conscious of itself, among other things through the ever greater influence that all individual brains together exercise in it, and an increase in personal freedom:

> The ultimate centre of each one of us is not to be found at the

term of an isolated, divergent trajectory; rather, it coincides with (though it is not lost in) the point of confluence of a human multitude freely gathered in tension, in reflection and in one common mind, upon itself.[74]

He sees the whole of this movement ultimately directed to a universal focus of psychical inwardness, the 'Omega' point. But even Teilhard does not say that this process will necessarily succeed. The evolution towards consciousness is at the same time an evolution towards freedom and ethics – and thus towards possible mistakes.[75] But he hopes that the keystone of the whole of evolution will be the point of encounter between the universe which has reached the limit of centring and another Centre which is even-deeper – a self-subsistent Centre and absolutely highest Principle of immutability and personalization: the only true Omega.[76] Even for Teilhard the believer, this scientific philosophical approach still remains the outside.

Many texts indicate a deeper personal experience which is brought out above all in the last years of his life, in *The Heart of Matter*[77] and 'The Mass on the World', culminating in 'The Christic', written in New York a month before his death. The title of the introduction to *The Heart of Matter* is 'The Burning Bush', pointing to Moses' encounter with God on Sinai. He sees his whole quest as a process of illumination:

> Progressive extension, in every being and every event, of a mysterious inner clarity which transfigures them. But even more a gradual change of radiance and degrees of light, combined with the complex interplay of three universal components, the cosmic, the human and the Christic ['the Christic' is a term peculiar to Teilhard] – explicitly present in me (at least the first and the second) from the first moments of my existence, but which required sixty years of passionate effort for me to discover that they were none other than successive approaches of one and the same basic reality . . . Purple lights from matter, imperceptibly involving to the gold of the Spirit,

finally to change into a 'universal personal' reality - and all this permeated, ensouled, anointed with a breath of Unification – and of Femininity.[78] . . . So through contact with the earth I have experienced the transparency of the divine at the heart of a burning universe. The divine radiating from the depths of a fiery matter.[79]

He recognizes that constantly a certain 'love of the Invisible' (which he understands as a supreme Someone) has been at work in him. And it was the humanity of Jesus (his heart where the fire of matter and the divine energy coincide) which held together the 'pagan' and Christian sides of his deepest being and to which he immediately gives a universal significance in and above time.[80] Here love takes on a central significance: in its many forms as God's voice it has always attracted him. At the end of *The Heart of Matter* he prays:

> Lord, because with every instinct of my life and through the opportunities which I have been given, I have never ceased to seek you and to place you at the heart of universal matter, in the dizzy blinding of a universal transparency and a universal conflagration I shall have the delight of closing my eyes.[81]

In 'The Christic' Teilhard goes deeper into one point: the whole of reality is to be consummated as shining love. All religions point the way here, but in Christianity this movement culminates in the focussing of evolution on a resurrection of the cosmos and humankind in love. And in a note written three days before his death, he refers to I Cor. 15.26–27, which he writes in Greek: *en pasi panta theos* (God all in all).

A prayer from 'The Mass on the World' ends this short encounter with Teilhard:

> So, my God, I prostrate myself before your presence in the universe which has now become living flame; beneath the lineaments of all that I shall encounter this day, all that happens to me, all that I achieve, it is you I desire, you I await.

Dag Hammarskjöld

From a similarly global background to that of Teilhard, Dag Hammarskjöld (1905–1961) sees 'the way inwards' as a journey to the light. The son of the governor of Uppland in Sweden, a member of a well-to-do family, a very gifted alumnus of the University of Uppsala, which was dominated by an agnostic climate,[82] in 1953 Hammarskjöld became Secretary-General of the United Nations. In the midst of the pressures of an extremely complicated political task, reading the great mystics each evening was a serene point of rest for this solitary man, as is shown by the many quotations in his book *Markings*.[83] A quotation from Meister Eckhart (in German) indicates his fundamental concern always to remain honest with himself:

> The soul that would experience this birth [just before, he has written 'Of the Eternal Birth'] must detach herself from all outward things: within herself completely at one with herself . . . You must have an exalted mind and a *burning* heart in which, nevertheless, reign silence and stillness (124).

This concern also comes through in an early note from 'The Middle Years', 1941–1942:

> The more faithfully you listen to the voice within you, the better you will hear what is sounding outside. And only he who listens can speak. Is this the starting point of the road towards the union of your two dreams – to be allowed, in clarity of mind to mirror life, and in purity of heart to mould it? (35).

One does not arrive at true belief without this fundamental honesty with oneself:

> The road to self-knowledge does not pass through faith. But only through the self-knowledge we gain by pursuing the fleeting light in the depth of our being do we reach the point where we can grasp what faith is. How many have been driven into

outer darkness by empty talk about faith as something to be rationally comprehended, something true? (37).

As a Swede, sensitive to nature, he experiences a transparency of the supernatural:

> A line, a shade, a colour – their fiery expressiveness.
> The language of flowers, mountains, shores, human bodies: the interplay of light and shade in a look, the aching beauty of a neck-line, the grail of the white crocus on the alpine meadow in the morning sunshine – words in a transcendental language of the senses (54).

From 1953 on he regularly quotes the Psalms and his sensitivity to the light becomes stronger, but so does his experience of the night.

> Like light. In light, lit through by light, transformed into light.
> Like the lens which disappears in the light it focusses.
> Like wind. Like light.
> Just this – on these expanses, on these heights (112f.).

That is how he comments on 'the light shines in darkness, and the darkness has not overcome it'. And in a commentary on Psalm 37 (in November 1956):

> Every hour
> Eye to eye
> With this love
> Which sees all
> But overlooks
> In patience,
> Which is justice,
> But does not condemn
> If our glances
> Mirror its own
> In humility (121).

And he takes up the image of the lens again in a note dated 28 July 1957:

> You are not the oil, you are not the air – merely the point of combustion, the flash-point where the light is born.
> You are merely the lens in the beam. You can only receive, give and possess the light as a lens does.
> If you seek yourself, 'your rights', you prevent the oil and air from meeting in the flame, you rob the lens of its transparency.
> Sanctity – either to be the Light, or to be self-effaced in the Light, so that it may be born, self-effaced so that it may be focused or spread wider (154).

But from his guard post in New York until his death in a plane crash in Katanga, he uninterruptedly experienced the darkness – in humility, even in himself. A long note dated 24 February 1957 goes into this and recognizes the 'point where it becomes possible for us to recognize and understand Original Sin, that dark countercentre of evil in our nature – that is to say, though it is not our nature'. And then he explains:

> It is when we stand in the righteous all-seeing light of love that we can dare to look at, admit and consciously suffer under this something in us which wills disaster, misfortune, defeat to everything outside the sphere of our narrowest self-interest. So a living relation to God is the necessary precondition for the self-knowledge which enables us to follow a straight path, and so be victorious over ourselves, forgiven by ourselves (128).

Finally he only finds meaning, though this is complete meaning, in the 'light of union', in 'God's union with the soul' but in the service of others. And after a quotation from the Our Father, he adds:

> You wake from dreams of doom and – for a moment – you know: beyond all the noise and the gestures, the only real

thing, love's calm unwavering flame in the half-light of an early dawn (140).

Although many who knew him less well regarded him in their commentaries after his death as a detached aesthete who was never in fact a believing Christian, Sven Stolpe rejects this interpretation, certainly for the period after 1953. And one of Hammarskjöld's best friends, the theatre director and poet Karl Ragnar Gierow, said in a commemorative address that he had never met a more 'shining' person. An old colleague in Uppsala told me how deep Hammarskjöld's faith was and how much support he found for it in a Catholic woman friend.

Although the motif of light resounded strongly in all the testimonies cited, the shadow of darkness was never absent. This shadow presses in increasingly.

4

Through the Night

The threatening void

On 16 July 1944 Dietrich Bonhoeffer wrote from his cell in Tegel prison, Berlin, in a letter to his friend Eberhard Bethge:

> Anxious souls will ask what room there is left for God now; and as they know of no answer to the question, they condemn the whole development that has brought them to such straits. I wrote to you before about the various emergency exits that have been contrived; and we ought to add to them the *salto mortale* (death leap) back into the Middle Ages. But the principle of the Middle Ages is heteronomy in the form of clericalism; a return to that can be a counsel of despair, and it would be at the cost of intellectual honesty. It's a dream that reminds one of the song 'If only I knew the long way back to Children's Land.' There is no such way – at any rate not if it means deliberately abandoning our mental integrity; the only way is that of Matt. 18.3,[1] i.e. through repentance, through *ultimate* honesty. And we cannot be honest unless we recognize that we have to live in the world *etsi deus non daretur*. And this is just what we do recognize – before God! God himself compels us to recognize it. So our coming of age leads us to a true recognition of our situation before God. God would have us know that we must live as those who manage our lives without him. The God who is with us is the God who forsakes us (Mark 15.34). The God who lets us live in the world without the working hypothesis of God is the God before whom we

stand continually. Before God and with God we live without God. God lets himself be pushed out of the world on to the cross. He is weak and powerless in the world, and that is precisely the way, the only way, in which he is with us and helps us.[2]

This long quotation from the Lutheran minister and pastor – perhaps his most important text – contains a warning. The previous chapters about light might seem perhaps to be a naive therapy. One must indeed dare to descend into the void, into the chill darkness, in order, wearily wandering, to become open to the true Light.

In *Thus Spoke Zarathustra*, Nietzsche makes Zarathustra ask: 'Where is man, if not above abysses? Seeing itself – isn't that seeing abysses?' And in the long term, Nietzsche sees nothing but 'nothingness', empty consciousness, empty thought, with a Dionysian vitalism as the only way out, and the only perspective – which he later also abandons – the perpetual recurrence of identical reincarnations. Even the man who constantly tried to give hope by interpreting the whole of evolution positively also felt doubts now and then about the great night of much suffering.

In the introduction to *The Spiritual Energy of Suffering*, Pierre Teilhard de Chardin wrote:

> To a clear-sighted observer looking at the earth from a great height, our planet would first seem blue all over because of the oxygen which surrounds it, then green from the vegetation which covers it, then very bright – increasingly bright – through the thought that becomes more intense on its surface; but also darker – ever darker – through the suffering which increases in quantity and fierceness, in time with the rhythm in which consciousness grows in the course of the ages. Yes, the more human human beings become, the more the problem of evil intensifies and gets worse in their bodies, in their sinews, in their spirit: understanding evil, enduring evil.[3]

No one can avoid the disconcerting discovery that every culture is built upon rubble, the result of the violence of the natural elements or human violence. There is no one who is not hurt, who does not carry around a shadow, who does not have some deep dark cellar somewhere. Serene wholeness is a dream; individuals and their relationships are characterized by conflict and discord. Auschwitz, the symbol of countless massacres of human beings by human beings, is not what first makes us ask the question 'Where is God?'. But where are human beings? Over-protected and over-informed Westerners in particular soon feel themselves to be on the edge of a black hole: in the end perhaps nothing makes any sense. Then everything becomes covered with a grey helplessness. Some – more than before – leap into the abyss. The void makes us dizzy, like inexperienced mountaineers, and the lack of any prospect can exert a strange attraction: at that point any sense of responsibility slips away. Fortunately, for most people the passion for life remains stronger than cynicism or nihilism. Under the surface they are supported by a fundamental trust.[4] However, many of them muffle just as deep a fear by escaping into the activity of the moment or the magic of drugs.

I shall not be offering here a parallel anthology of descriptions which bring us down into regions of atrocious wickedness, of boundless meaninglessness or a darkening of faith with no hope. Almost every day, we all look at tears, lies and perversity. Above all those who long for the light are tormented or disturbed here. There is in fact a hellish side to human beings and humankind. The Bible itself relates in detail and in abundance a centuries-long history of murder, torture, faithlessness, corruption and the killing of children and saints. In our centuries millions of baptized Catholics, Protestants and Orthodox 'Christians' have killed millions of their fellow-believers in two world wars. Almost the whole Jewish population disappeared in extermination camps. And tens of millions have been liquidated under the governments of Stalin, Mao, Pol Pot and others.

Big numbers depersonalize, but for every victim there is the terrible lonely confrontation with meaningless evil. This is far worse than for the man Job, for whom in the end everything came good again on this earth, since the God who allowed his testing remained faithful to him even in this life.

Before Albert Camus's *The Plague* and Shusaku Endo's *Silence*, Dostoievsky described this when Ivan Karamazov put his brother Alyosha to the test:

> People sometimes speak of man's 'bestial' cruelty, but this is very unfair and insulting to the beasts: a beast can never be so cruel as a man, so ingeniously, so artistically cruel. A tiger merely gnaws and tears to pieces, that's all he knows. It would never occur to him to nail men's ears to a fence and leave them like that overnight, even if he were able to do it. These Turks, incidentally, seemed to derive a voluptuous pleasure from torturing children, cutting a child out of its mother's womb with a dagger and tossing babies up in the air and catching them on a bayonet before the eyes of their mothers. It was doing it before the eyes of their mothers that made it so enjoyable. But one incident I found particularly interesting. Imagine a baby in the arms of a trembling mother, surrounded by Turks who had just entered her house. They are having great fun; they fondle the baby, they laugh to make it laugh and they are successful: the baby laughs. At that moment the Turk points a pistol four inches from the baby's face. The boy laughs happily, stretches out his little hands to grab the pistol, when suddenly the artist pulls the trigger in the baby's face and blows his brains out . . . . Artistic, isn't it? Incidentally, I'm told the Turks are very fond of sweets.'
>
> 'Why are you telling me all this, Ivan?' asked Alyosha.
>
> 'I can't help thinking that if the devil doesn't exist and, therefore, man has created him, he has created him in his own image and likeness.'

And Ivan continues to test Alyosha's faith with his hard facts.

Only those know the true significance of the 'glory of God', of his kindly light, who dare to wade through the sea of the deepest suffering that is born of evil. Paul saw the 'fullness' (*pleroma*) only through the 'emptying'. Because of an excess of information this last has perhaps never been so challenging as it is now.

The mystery of evil

There is evil everywhere, as wickedness or suffering, and no one understands this. Karl Lehmann – now President of the German Conference of Bishops – once rightly wrote:

> Nowadays we choke on this idea of a 'higher harmony' as the explanation of evil and suffering in the world . . . We find such an explanation of evil rationalistic and harmonistic. Human suffering is theologically so misused that today we have to pay for it a thousandfold: suffering comes from God's hands; the root of sickness is sin; there is complete health only in the kingdom of God; suffering is God's exalted method of training refractory human beings . . . What has become problematical is not the attempt to arrive at a personal and existential explanation of suffering – people have always striven for this, each in their own way, with greater or lesser success. What is problematical is the subsequent theological systematization; it always gives the incontrovertible impression of having no respect for pain and fundamentally cherishing only an abstract compassion.[5]

Paul Ricoeur knows that he cannot unravel the 'meaning' of evil. He refuses to reduce evil to an ethical misuse of human freedom.[6] He recognizes that in the end he has no answer: 'I see only one possible direction for meditation', in fact an attempt to deprive the apparently absolute 'power' (and impasse) of evil of its force. He counters the experience of evil with the experience of reconciliation: reconciliation is expected despite evil, and this 'despite' can then become a modest 'because of'. The Light is stronger through forgiveness. Evil as such is not 'something' or 'someone'; it is pure negation. One can only defend oneself against this negation by an 'and yet' of hope, namely that ultimately evil will not triumph.

Here any philosophy in the style of Hegel which attempts to give meaning to evil through a dialectic with a positive direction certainly falls short. Moreover any theodicy which makes God 'insensitive' to evil and which underestimates the tragedy of evil avoids the real challenge. Evil cannot be interpreted by a rational approach; only symbolic language can grasp it in any way:

> All symbols make us think, but the symbols of evil show in an exemplary way that there is always more in the myths, in the symbols, than in the whole of our philosophy, and that a philosophical interpretation of the symbols will never produce absolute knowledge. The symbols of evil from which we read the failure of our existence at the same time represent the failure of all thought-systems which might seek to swallow up the symbols in absolute knowledge.

According to Ricoeur, evil is at the opposite pole, not to the Good but to the Holy, also in the sense of the inviolate. Human beings must first confess that they are 'unfit' and then, laboriously, be reborn to a second, authentic innocence ('reflection is both an archaeology and an eschatology of consciousness'). This can only – Ricoeur is a believer – come about through the working of grace (Rom. 5.20): from outside the individual is set on the way to a 'redemption' which is more than 'liberation'. Instead of disconnecting God from evil by mystery, evil must be overcome by the mystery of the love of God, which in the Old and New Testaments always proves to be stronger than what is said about his 'wrath'. Here the figure of the father of the prodigal son provides the key. Moreover Ricoeur's last word is a surrender to hope: 'to produce the potential of hope, to express the future of the resurrection' (cf. Deut. 30.19–20; Rom. 5.15–20). Only this hope can give light (*'spero ut intelligam'*): 'evil and hope are more in solidarity than we might ever think'. Only this hope gives freedom, since it defeats the idols of evil. And here Ricoeur is also giving the last answer that Alyosha gave to Ivan: surrender to the only One who can wipe away evil, 'the only One who is without sin'.

In every celebration of the eucharist in every church the words 'for the forgiveness of sins' are repeated. Ricoeur and Dostoievsky both point to Jesus as an answer to the mystery of evil.

Jesus and evil

We can rightly read the whole of the New Testament as a duel between the light and the powers of darkness, and we can see Jesus above all as one who conquers these powers by going through the darkest night: he rescues men and women from their many fears, and thus brings definitive salvation. Certainly for Jesus the emphasis does not lie on evil (or the Evil One), but on the growing kingdom of God, on beatitudes, on the ultimate breakthrough of liberating light. But perversely to reduce Jesus completely to a dear, gentle man would be to fail to recognize the constant struggle against evil in his life: in words and actions, here he was harsh, indeed brutal (see for example his diatribe against the Pharisees). For him evil is everywhere, and certainly in the human heart.

The whole brief course of Jesus' public life apparently ended in a defeat. Evil succeeded in eliminating him quickly: Gethsemane, Golgotha, the tomb. Paul proclaimed 'the Crucified and Risen One', but inevitably first 'the Crucified One', the scandal of a fiasco. Only after Pentecost did an atmosphere of triumph prevail among the Christians: we have won through him! Good is victorious over evil – or is it 'the Evil One'? One question which inevitably keeps coming up is: what/who is evil/the Evil One for Jesus?[7] This question still remains very real, even now, after secularization. The 1990 European Values Study, which is representative of more than half a billion Europeans and North Americans, tells us among other things that in Europe 21% believe in the devil (North America 62%) and 19% in hell (North

America 63%), with considerable differences between countries. Thus in Ireland 53% believe in the devil, in Italy 35%, in Great Britain and Poland 30%, in Finland 27% and in the Netherlands and Belgium 17%. Tens of millions believe in the devil and hell. 51% in Europe believe in sin as opposed to 83% in North America. Nor is it surprising that satanic sects arise here and there.

What about Jesus and the devil?

Jesus was a Jew. The Old Testament sees the devil[8] as the opponent, the 'adversary'; from this, above all in Judaism, a kind of 'satan' developed. Satan is the one who disrupts relations between God and Israel. Although in the New Testament he is called 'the prince of this world' and leads an army of 'demons', he does not appear as God's adversary in his own right (Tobit 6.8; Matt. 8.3). Of course popular religion has constructed all kinds of legends around this dark figure. In the New Testament Jesus makes the kingdom of God the heart of his message. However active the devil is, he continues to lead a shadowy existence. Jesus and the evangelists grew up in the context of their time; they automatically adopted the symbolism of the devil as a personification of evil. Jesus 'saw' evil at work and used the usual terminology for it.[9] Was the devil a person for him? This seems difficult to discover from scripture: where does Jesus' terminology appear and where is his deepest conviction on the matter expressed? Exegetes are even divided over the words 'Deliver us from the Evil One/evil' in the Lord's Prayer. But it is certain that Jesus incessantly combatted the effects of evil.[10]

This is not the place for a comparative study of the significance of the devil in the New Testament. In the Synoptic Gospels we can distinguish between (*a*) exorcisms, the symbol of the beginning of the kingdom of God,[11] and (*b*) the general battle waged by Jesus against the 'prince of this world', who among other things is active through anyone who lies or falsifies (the 'Pharisees', the high priests, the so-called 'righteous'). Matthew

23 is exceptionally sharp. The Gospel of John and also the letters attributed to John above all go into this second aspect, though with a very dualistic terminology, which is sometimes reminiscent of Qumran.[12] Here the opposition between light and darkness is also much more explicit. The devil appears as the evil one from the time of creation in paradise, as 'a murderer and a liar from the beginning' (John 8.44). Although he will continue to be active until the end of history (I Cor. 15.24–28), a 'stronger one', Jesus (Luke 11.12), is conquering him.[13] The devil tries to divert Jesus from this task, from the beginning of his public ministry (the 'temptations' in the wilderness, Luke 4.10–13) to the phase of the passion 'when Satan entered into Judas' (Luke 23.3) and 'darkness reigns' (Luke 22.53). But right from the beginning the spoilsport has lost (Gen. 3.15; John 12.31: 'now shall the ruler of this world be cast out'). Similarly, after Jesus' resurrection the devil continues to threaten the faith community as the power of the antichrist (I John 4.2–3; II John 7),[14] who presents himself as a 'liar' disguised as an 'angel of light' (II Cor. 11.14), making many 'children of the devil' (I John 3.10) and giving the impression that Jesus himself is 'possessed by the devil' (John 8.48).[15] The Apocalypse describes not only the dramatic battle between light and darkness, life and death, which is carried out by the faith community and in the faith community itself, but also the final victory (Rev. 12.9–13).

In any case Jesus never speaks of a 'divinity' of evil as an equal to God himself, which is such a characteristic view for earlier and later Gnosticism, nor does he show that evil can be overcome by knowledge. Only faith and love are decisive.

Apart from baptism (also an 'exorcism'), in the first centuries there was little talk of the devil and hell: everything was focussed on the salvation that Jesus brings. People were optimistic: paradise was certainly coming. Origen and Gregory of Nyssa indeed spoke about the devil, but they thought that God could save even the devil in the final restoration of all things (the *apokatastasis*). This doctrine was later condemned (by an edict of the emperor Justinian in 543). In the meantime, under the influence for example of Augustine (*The City of God*) and Gregory the Great (also for pedagogical reasons), attention was more strongly focussed on the Last Judgment and hell. In the Middle Ages this trend was even further accentuated with much imagination (numerous visions of hell, not least in order to persuade the believers through fear to repent lest they found themselves in the 'claws of the devil').[16] As with the choirs of angels, so too a reverse 'order' of devils arose, with Lucifer (Luke 10.18), the untrustworthy bearer of the false light, right at the bottom – according to Dante not in fire but in ice. Presumably purgatory, a kind of counterpart of reincarnation, arose in the twelfth century.[17]

Luther rejected the doctrine of purgatory and put more emphasis on the tension between God and the devil than on that between heaven and hell. Hell faded right into the background in the later Lutheran tradition. The Enlightenment criticized the whole of traditional Christian eschatology; as a result there was a revival of early views among Catholics and Protestants (as in the case of Newman, who saw hell and the existence of God indissolubly connected).[18]

Present-day theology has difficulties with angels and devils. Christian Duquoc recognizes that the devil has almost completely disappeared from theology; people hesitate to allow him a real existence and find it difficult to imagine the absolute 'crystalline' freedom of the fallen angels before the fall. A fallen angel could no longer be converted because, since he is incorporeal, any decision is total, without any possibility of forgiveness or repentance. Here God finds no guilt: the one who is absolutely free always chooses in total freedom. This was also the opinion of Thomas Aquinas.

Meanwhile modern science has robbed the devil of his former functions: the contingency of nature explains much evil and suffering. Moreover God is innocent here. But what about the abuse of human freedom, its passions, its diabolical side? An introduction of the devil here can amount to an exoneration of human beings: it is the devil that destroys history and my life. But is that the case? Doesn't this make history an abstraction? Its meaning and meaninglessness are not imposed, but written by those who respond positively or negatively to the invitation to the kingdom of God. According to Jesus, eternity as such has only a positive significance. Moreover Duquoc (with Edward Schillebeeckx) says that anyone who definitively refuses this invitation does not fall into hell with the devils but literally into 'nothingness', a nothingness in which the imagined devil is also to be found.[19] Isn't the devil then that facet of the human spirit which wants to exclude God, to reduce God to nothing and in glorifying itself appropriate all light and every way to the light?

The strange longing for innocence

The possibility that angels, devils or eternal hell[20] do not exist does not affect the fact that Jesus really says that human beings are guilty ('If you, evil as you are, know how to give good things to your children . . .', Luke 11.13; also his quotation from Isaiah in Matt. 12.14). 'What is guilt?', and, more profoundly, 'What is innocence?' Péguy wrote his *Mystery of the Holy Innocents*, prompted by 'innocent children'. In *Crime and Punishment* Dostoievsky has the girl Sonia appearing as a prototype of innocence, just as Alyosha appears between his guilty brothers and Prince Myshkin as a naively-intelligent and unworldly saint (in *The Idiot*). All the great religions and world-views have their relatively innocent martyrs (Gandhi, Martin Luther King, Sadat, Romero, Rabin, the seven Trappists murdered in Algeria). For all Christians and for many others Jesus is the innocent *par excellence*.[21] Centuries of Western and Eastern Christian culture have venerated Mary as the absolutely innocent woman (the Immaculate Conception, without any original sin), as has the Qur'an in Surah 19.

Often, and wrongly, innocence is confused with being intact, with physical virginity or naivety. Of course rape, prostitution and paedophilia provoke opposition, but so too does the starvation and murder of the defenceless. A deep reflex projects innocence on to certain animals: tiny birds, the white lamb, seals killed 'innocently' for their skins. It is even projected on 'innocent' nature, which precisely because of this calls for reverence. The person who collects flowers can also trap human beings. Very deep down, here we touch on a kind of archetypal dream of a primal paradisal state in which nothing can threaten the clarity, where no one causes harm, where no word is ambiguous, false or murky, where everyone can rightly be vulnerable and trusting. Gertrud von Le Fort describes this atmosphere in a poem about a roe, suddenly encountered in an open space in a wood:[22]

The Roe

There stood the golden roe,
and listened to me,
her eyes pretty and shy
and terribly gentle,
as though in the dear animal
there dawned the submerged soul of creation.

In his play *The Love-Girl and the Innocent*, which is again set in a Stalinist labour camp, Solzhenitsyn describes the relationship between Njemov, head of the production division, and Ljuba, the camp prostitute. Out of self-respect Njemov refuses to force productivity and thus exploit his position. He is aptly called 'the innocent'. Njemov and Ljuba (whose name in Russian means *agape*) are not saints, but very deep down both have preserved a simplicity, in counterpoint to the hell of their surroundings. The Communist authorities banned this play, and the world première took place in America. Njemov, who sees who Ljuba really is, says to her, 'You should wear a white silk jacket, with lilies of the valley . . . here, on your breast . . .' And during a short, loving conversation Ljuba replies, 'Only for you can I change myself and become pure and clean again, as before.'

Most people have a naive longing for the state of innocence, rooted in a strange longing to be a child again, what Bachelard calls the 'true archetype of simple happiness'. The great mystery religions were attempts to achieve a catharsis. The Old Testament also knew many rituals of purity, on the basis of a mixture of physical pollution (for example contact with blood), the transgression of cultural rules, sinfulness, and anxiety about the mystery of life and death. Here sociology, ethics and religion overlap.[23]

Jesus also talked about regaining the clarity of a child (Matt. 18.3). But those who remain stuck in this first naivety will never grow up. And Jesus also emphasizes that: no return there is possible; one has to grow into another innocence. This is something that requires a change, a personal conversion, being 'born again'. According to the Gospel of John, Jesus talked about this in his nocturnal conversation with Nicodemus (John 3.1–21). Nicodemus was stuck; he came – typically – 'to Jesus by night'. This conversation has nothing to do with a glorious return to a dreamed-of primal state of complete freedom and security, characteristic of many Gnostic tendencies in which those who are egocentric and usually androgynous redeem themselves for themselves and thus, completely healed, become 'children of the light'.

If we are to understand the significance of Jesus' view of innocence we must return to the Old Testament. Here in Leviticus 10.8–11 there is an emphasis on the sharp distinction between clean and unclean, coupled with the distinction between sacred and profane. Whatever corresponds to the divine ordering of society is clean.[24] 'Becoming unclean' denotes some transgression of this order,[25] which becomes strongly ritualized. There is a strong accent on the coherence of the Jewish people as distinct from all other peoples. Of course this ritualization can result in an imprisonment of the individual in the group, in the name of the required reverence for the sacral, for God. In that case the authentically sacral degenerates into magic and (human) sacrifices are offered in the name of God to restore order. No room is left for a personal conscience – and its innocence.[26] Time and again the Old Testament makes the prophets stand up against the ossified 'system'. However, unavoidably these prophets, too, were partially imprisoned in that system, however much they too were persecuted for their courageous complaints.

Jesus himself endured this persecution and complained about it (Matt. 23.1–39, about those who murder the prophets). He had seen through the ambiguity of the division into 'clean' and 'unclean'[27] and the Pharisaic misuse of it. He emphasized the innate law of the conscience:

> But what comes out of the mouth proceeds from the heart, and this defiles a person. For out of the heart come evil thoughts, murder, adultery, fornication, theft, false witness, slander. These are what defile a person; but to eat with unwashed hands does not defile a person (Matt. 15.18–20).

Jesus is the prototype of an innocence which is not naive. Innocence – it is significant that this word appears rarely, if at all, in most encyclopaedias, even theological ones – has different dimensions. Innocence has to do with real authenticity, with existential truthfulness,[28] in which people unfold the core of their being without falsification. It is listening to the voice within: 'become who you are', as Nicholas of Cusa put it:

> When I rest in the silence of contemplation, you, Lord, reply within my heart, saying: 'Know yourself; than I shall belong to you.'[29]

Of course the dimension of authenticity is closely bound up with ethics: we must seek and make our own authenticity, and thus make choices from our contextual freedom. Here, as far as possible, any ambiguity must be avoided. In the Sermon on the Mount, Jesus says, 'Let your yes be yes and your no no. Anything else is of the evil one' (Matt. 5.37). However, scripture also says that an absolute 'yes' can be said completely only by Jesus himself: 'He was not Yes and No; but in him it was always Yes' (II Cor. 1.19). Scripture shows that both Paul and Peter, and John and his brother James, made mistakes in their quest and had to confess this with regret.

Inevitably, even the most noble people make mistakes in their quests. To become oneself involves negotiating many crossroads which are veiled in the mist of determinisms, ignorance and powerlessness. Everyone, however free, in many respects remains a prisoner. Within a personal history the way to the land of light crosses unavoidable frontiers, with more or less responsibility. In this twilight zone, beforehand it is far from clear whether one is entering greater light or greater darkness (we need think only of the complex questions in bioethics or business ethics). Moreover it can rightly be said that no one is completely innocent.[30] Everyone carries the shadows of their own mistaken attempts and experiments with them. Any memory, individual or social, is ambiguous.[31] Even Mary did not understand her son Jesus for a long time. We saw that Augustine had a child, Deodatus, by a woman whom, given his status, he could not legally marry, and his (saintly) mother Monica 'misled' him, in the expectation that he would find a good partner, to liaise with a kind of call-girl. Later he was to write, 'Was I ever innocent?' And Dostoievsky, from his Slavonic feeling of universal responsibility, can say, 'We are all guilty of everything and to everyone.' The nobility of one or another moment in which clear love becomes transparent can reveal not only one's own guilt but also the longing for innocence . . . and the evil will to destroy innocence, as was the case with the two brothers of Alyosha Karamazov.

A good deal has been written about guilt. Historians of religion write, not completely wrongly, that Augustine gave the whole of the West a guilt complex. Be this as it may, J. Delumeau has given an impressive description of the influence of the sense of guilt and sin on Western collective thought.[32] It is certain that the Christian West coloured ethics with a religious feeling of guilt, in contrast, for example, to the Eastern socio-psychological sense of shame to be found among the Japanese. This feeling of guilt is even fatalistically interpreted by determinism, transferring error and guilt to God in the doctrine of irrevocable predestination. Jansenism, and a certain kind of Calvinism and Lutheranism (we might think of the films of Ingmar Bergman), have burdened whole generations with a pessimistic image of God, the breeding ground both for agnosticism and for New Age movements.[33] In reaction, from Jean-Jacques Rousseau to the May revolt in 1968, with great naivety there has been an emphasis on the 'natural innocence of human beings'. God was to blame for the guilty conscience; he was the great alienator of human beings. Nietzsche condemned and denied such a God and therefore put human beings above good and evil.

However, rough, everyday reality teaches us that the Gospel saying about 'pearls' before 'swine'[34] continues to be applicable to interpersonal and universal history. No matter how one interprets original sin,[35] centuries of experience from the symbolic Cain onwards reveal the reality of the evil of which the biblical serpent has become the primal image. And whether one personifies that evil as the 'devil' or regards it as an indeterminate, faceless 'power', in the world and in every human being there remains a dark side, which, while it does not do away with freedom, at least hinders it (Rom. 7.15–24).

Human beings are also victims, not only of their own evil, but also of Evil. Those who think themselves wholly innocent are as immature as those who allow themselves to be imprisoned in guilt-feelings. Anton Vergote rightly says of the 'narcissistic paradox of perfection':

If because of an exaggerated feeling of guilt one attributes an absolute value to the commandment to be perfect, outside any context, it degenerates into an obsessive hunt for this one thing: gaining perfection by means of the inner fight against desires and pleasures. With a splendid picture before one's eyes in which one is reflected and which one wants to match, one can only be furious at the moments of impurity and deception.[36]

On the way, everyone must laboriously kill the idealized child which does not accept the inevitable conflicts and tensions between becoming a self and being there for others, whether out of fear or for other unconscious motives. All must accept that they are in a boat in stormy water, or are sitting on a capricious mount which completely escapes any firm control. Somewhere the chaos of instinct, imagination and play is part of human nature, just as much as the constant concern for creative order and clarity in thought and action. Only in this way can one maintain human equilibrium without sinking into the quicksand of narcissism.

However, it would be pretentious not to apply to oneself the Gospel parallel about the good grain and the tares growing together, humbly allowing both to grow up side by side (Matt. 13.24–30). Every candle casts its shadow. Jesus too knew temptations in the wilderness, and he too could be hot-tempered. All Puritanism was alien to him. He knew 'what was in man' (John 2.25): the wise and foolish longings, the good and evil desires. This recognition is the simplicity of realism. Not to succumb fatalistically here is a sign of the abiding hunger for salvation, for entering into a room without idols and without night. However, in a finite world, no one can fully succeed here. Still, the hunger for that perspective keeps people human; this comes through in T. S. Eliot's *Four Quartets*:

> And all shall be well and
> All manner of thing shall be well
> When the tongues of flame are in-folded
> Into the crowned knot of fire
> And the fire and the rose are one.[37]

But the fusion of light and tenderness does not belong to the brief existence on this side of reality, except for brief, privileged moments.

Leaving the nursery of the 'first naivety' – which is an ethical task – requires the choice of what Paul Ricoeur calls a 'second naivety'. The freedom which makes us responsible for the evil that we share in causing at the same time makes us responsible for growth towards a second innocence, which also has interpersonal, social and cosmic implications.

Here the light of forgiveness opens the way. Above all those who are ethically most sensitive suffer most deeply under the shadow which remains with them because of earlier objective or subjective error and guilt. However much effort they make when possible to compensate for the suffering that has been caused or the injustice that has been done, the memory of it remains a scar, among other things because it is not always possible to make good, especially where the fault through word or writing affects anonymous people. For those who continue to feed their inner dialogue with the 'Father', what first weighed heavy can turn into liberation. God is then recognized as the merciful light which does not condemn but 'embraces': both the 'prodigal son' and the son who thought himself to be without fault, but valued justice higher than love and thus lost his innocence. The 'prodigal son' again wears 'the finest clothes' and a ring (of a new covenant); the one who was guilty from the beginning now attains his innocence and comes home. The Father has to urge the 'innocent' oldest son, who excluded himself, to confess the shadow which fell upon him by his choice to exclude himself from his brother (Luke 15.11–32). By forgiving the other the Father also forgives our shadow, for he 'is greater than our heart and he knows all things' (I John 3.20). The innocence produced is in fact the first innocence: it is not ours to achieved or keep; it is given. We cannot free ourselves from the burden of the shadow. Everyone has to be liberated, not only by the mercy of the other but by that light which brings complete liberation from the darkness.

What applies to interpersonal relations equally applies on the social level. Whole groups carry around shadows, falsifications of the collective memory, recollections of evil and vengeance, of an unassimilated past.[38] Really an all-embracing and lasting process of forgiveness is indispensable for clarifying relations between the generations, the sexes, races, social classes, religions and churches and ridding the future of an explosive burden. However, history teaches us how difficult such a process is and how fragile it remains. Yet movements like Pax Christi, education, the media and especially the European Union and the Council of Europe can call for a social 'conversion', taking account of the scriptural saying that when the house is purged of one devil, seven devils can quickly take its place (Luke 11.26). And however old-fashioned the word may sound, without voluntary 'sacrifices' (R. Girard) it does not look as if this purging of mentalities will come about. Only the readiness of the defenceless to defend themselves can break the spiral of subtle or brutal violence and replace it with constructive solidarity.

However, there is not just the night of the evil persons. The deepest night is that of the good person, including the committed honest believer. Hans Andreus, the seeker, put this cry into words, addressed to 'God knows who':

only unimaginable nameless, you who
are clothed and veiled in so many names
where no one knows or wants to know,

let me sometimes see that you are there,
not in a flash of insight, like lightning,
but as a lightness breathing in me.

Veiled or absent light

There are blind people who have never seen anything: not a smile, not a colour. There are also blind people who know how much beauty they saw and will never see again except in their memory and their imagination. But those who feel deep within themselves the strong longing for the light and its transparency in people who are close, in society and nature, can suffer greatly from the experience of the many veils that cover that light, from the lasting absence of that light.

Any spiritual light is experienced in veiled form. The Old Testament teaches us that to see God unveiled is death. God transcends human beings, in both time and eternity. Yet the experience of light, which one sometimes has in meeting a transparent person, veils more than it unveils. The innermost being of the other person, however near, remains unattainable and therefore attractive. The other person remains irreducibly other, a 'strange love'. For those who know that the being of the other is rooted in the being of God, the most intimate and unfathomable, the light of the other will always be experienced as surrounded with a soft veil; because whatever of God they have attained must necessarily remain the veiling of an unveiling. That is the case within the dimension of existence before death. And in a way which can now be grasped only as an analogy – that remains in what believers intimate as a risen existence for which they hope. There too the loving encounter with the other, though definitively shining and becoming brighter, veils because the God present in it remains veiled, despite the transparency. God can be encountered only through the veil of the other.

Perhaps that is the deeper meaning of one of the last verses of the Bible: 'They shall see his face and bear his name on their foreheads' (Rev. 22.4). Face, name, forehead point to the unique core of one's person. They are to know the divine core of the person in the core of one another's persons. But no one becomes the personal core of God; nor is anyone identified with the personal core of the other. This limitation is essential for existence itself. And so for every existence that is not God, the shining must remain veiled as a sign of a constantly imperfect participation in the divine reality. Those who recognize the divine reality 'dialogically' in themselves can only situate the encounter with God through the prism of an interpersonal encounter.

Perhaps this is the deepest significance of one of the first verses of the Bible: 'And God created the human as his image; in the image of God created he him; male and female created he them' (Gen. 1.27). C. Verhoeven rightly says:

> 'Human beings are capable only of a veiled perception. They could not bear a direct experience of the unveiled reality.'[39]

But this theological view does not remove the pain of God's absence or the perplexity about it.

At one point in his *Frankfurter Hefte*[40] Walter Dirks describes one of his last conversations with Romano Guardini. In it the old man told him that at the Last Judgment he would not only answer questions, but also ask them. He steadfastly hoped that the angel of the judgment would not refuse to give him the answer which no theology, no dogma, no magisterium nor even scripture itself had been able to give: 'Why, God, these fearful detours before you give salvation? Why all that darkness, all those complications in our lives? Why the guilt and why all that suffering of innocents?'

The Jew Martin Buber describes a similar experience in a conversation with an old professor with whom he was lodging and who had asked him to read out something from the proofs of his book.

'When I had finished,' Buber relates, 'at first hesitantly, but then, caught up in his own concerns, all the more passionately, he asked: "How can you keep saying 'God' time after time? How can you expect that your readers will understand this word in the sense in which you want it to be used? ... What word of the human language is so misused, so polluted, so damaged as this? All the innocent blood that has ever been shed has robbed it of its splendour. All the injustice which it must serve to cover has removed its character. When I hear mention of the most high 'God', sometimes it sounds to me like blasphemy." His clear, childlike eyes flamed ...'[41]

No one can deny that many people, including professed Christians, share a darkness about God at this end of the second millennium. A comparison of the writings of two Carmelite sisters, Teresa of Avila and Thérèse of Lisieux, demonstrates this. For many people God is not just absent – 'God is no longer there,' says Bishop Karl Lehmann – but also dead.[42] Marx, Nietzsche, Freud seem to have abolished him. Bernard Welte quotes a verse that the dying philosopher W. Weischedel asked to be written down:

> In the dark base of the cup
> the light of nothingness appears.
> The dark shine of Godhead
> thus becomes the light of nothingness.[43]

Jung saw God as no more than a projection: human beings have to understand their own self-realization through self-consciousness as the incarnation of God. Nietzsche's interpretation can be taken in a very different way, but just as godlessly. Thus T. van den Hoogen writes:

> In a Nietzschean perspectivism De Lubac describes human existence as a 'dance in the middle of an empty heaven': being approaches becoming so closely, he says,[44] that there is no longer any question of ontology. One could say that the stream of all being (*physis*) is so dominant that there is no longer any room for the 'source'. That raises the theological question whether in that case one can still continue to talk of 'God's heaven', as the faith tradition does. Doesn't that image inevitably call for thought about being in which there can still be talk of the difference between the stream and the source, beings and Being?[45]

The question raised is: where do I find a firm standpoint, with all my longings and desires? Where is there a dynamic support? Is everything always in flux? Or is there a true source which at the same time makes room for getting back over this void? Certainly we walk over an abyss of the void. Scripture does not deny this. The book of Ecclesiastes, which was Karl Rahner's favourite in his last years, is a reflection on the vanity of everything: 'Vanity of vanities, all is vanity' (1.2). And:

> Again I saw all the oppressions that are practised under the sun.
> And behold, the tears of the oppressed,
> and they had no one to comfort them!
> On the side of their oppressors there was power,
> and there was no one to comfort them.

And I thought the dead who are already dead more fortunate than the living who are still alive;
but better than both is he who has not yet been,
and has not seen the evil deeds that are done under the sun (4.1–3).

But Ecclesiastes does give an answer. This deep lament is addressed to God. God hears, and people can continue to trust him, although he is absent. The tortured Jeremiah bore the same witness to God: 'Am I not a God who is far off? No one can hide himself without my seeing him' (Jer. 23.23–24). And Martin Buber continued the conversation with his colleague like this:

> ... Certainly they draw caricatures and write 'God' under them. They murder one another and say 'in God's name'. But when madness and deception fall upon all of them, when they stand before God in deepest darkness and no longer say 'He, he' but sigh 'You, you', cry 'You', just that one word, and when they add 'God', is it not the real God that they all invoke, the One, the Living One, the God of the children of men? Is it not he who *hears* them? ... We cannot wash the word 'God' clean and we cannot make it whole. But stained and abused though it is, we can pick it up from the ground and elevate it above an hour of great oppression.[46]

Meanwhile we continue to walk over an abyss of nothingness. The book of Genesis tells us that we come from nothing, formed from chaos, directed to one another before God whose voice is heard, but whose face is not seen. Henri de Lubac quotes a profound saying by Robert Grossteste (died 1253), a famous bishop of Lincoln: 'In any created being, not-being comes before its being.'[47]

One can only fall 'upwards', so one is held firm – by trustful longing. God rescues us from the nothingness. Here human longing coincides with God's hope, with the mysterious way in which God calls us to light.

The last answer here must be given by the free person, in the night: however much I quiver before the abyss, I dare to walk over water, I trust the invisible hand which holds me fast. Here one does not get by with the result of a theoretical argument. Here is the step of the completely emptied person who modestly nods to Jesus' often repeated question, 'Do you trust me?' The Lord asks the essential question which God himself raises. And just as often the Lord repeats, 'Do not fear, I am with you.' But he also remarks, 'Blessed are those who do not see and yet believe.'

Inevitably everyone feels a question here, in particular the honest believer who is most existentially affected: isn't this answer in fact an impasse? If God is affirmed as both light and darkness, as both knowable and unknowable, where do we start? The First Vatican Council of 1870 stated in the canons on faith:

> Whoever says that the one and true God, our Creator and Lord, cannot certainly be known through what is made with the natural light of reason, let him be anathema.[48]

However, centuries beforehand, Hilary of Poitiers (c.315–367) had written: 'Nothing is more worthy of God's glory than to put him outside the limits of human intelligence.' Is there no expedient which surmounts the pressure of final and impossible sheerly rational proofs? For Francis, Teresa of Avila, Teilhard de Chardin and so on, this way is also the divine man Jesus – not a concept, but someone: he is the light among us that points most transparently towards the light. Nowhere did he 'prove' God. By his way of living and dying he led his group of followers to experience that the history of each of them individually and of humankind in general does not end up in nothingness. It is striking how, after the Spirit was given, Paul and the first church could not keep silent about the 'glory' of God which constantly breaks through in the human adventure, 'through the Lord Jesus'. For Christians, the way to the light therefore irrevocably runs through the unique and continued event of Jesus. In this mysterious person the darkness of evil, suffering and death also find their place, not theoretically, but concretely. The resurrection is the sign of that concrete nature. This was Alyosha's answer to the objections of his unbelieving brother Ivan.

People should not go on rationalizing, but take the words of the Lord seriously. Moreover Hans Küng rightly says that christology is the place for believing theology. Eberhard Jüngel also writes:

> Christian theology arose as the explicitation and self-criticism of faith in Jesus of Nazareth. To believe in Jesus means to understand him as that person through whom and in whom God has become definitively accessible . . .[49]

However, doesn't that light of Jesus seem infinitely far away from many present-day believers, not to mention all those who have never heard of him or have heard of him only in a distorted way? It is Jesus himself who points to the brothers and sisters who are fellow-pilgrims as the place where he and his God can always be found, namely the kingdom of God, above all where they beg fir light through their poverty and yet also give light.

The deeper significance of Matthew 25 lies here: 'Truly, I say to you, as you did it to one of the least of these my brethren, you did it to me' (Matt. 25.40). This takes up A. Gesché's question:

> Rather than being thought, said and looked at, doesn't God first of all in a sense need to be 'done and acted on', because it is there that people encounter him?[50]

God is found where people take quite seriously their responsibility for the neighbour 'for whom one gives one's life' (John 10.15; 15.13). There the dimension of the other light breaks through. This runs directly counter to the tendency to seize the meaning of existence in order possibly to grasp the divine through Eastern or Western techniques of contemplation or methods for expanding consciousness. The interpersonal 'liturgy' of foot-washing by which Jesus becomes a slave to his disciples is in fact more central than a solemn celebration of the eucharist. Moreover, the eucharist retains its meaning because of its emphasis on what the foot-washing symbolizes.

I John states that very clearly: 'He who says that he is in the light and hates his brother is in the darkness still. He who loves his brother abides in the light, and in it there is no cause for stumbling' (I John 2.9–10). And: 'No man has ever seen God; if we love one another, God abides in us and his love is perfected in us' (I John 4.12).

It is evident from Matthew 25 that the encounter with the Light through the services of others does not necessarily imply that one is a conscious believer, a baptized Christian or belongs to a church. The mediaeval theologians already talked quite openly of the *Ecclesia ab Abel*[51] (the church from Abel). The community of believers already begins with the first 'righteous pagans'. Here Jacob's exclamation at Bethel, 'Truly the Lord is in this place and I knew it not' (Gen. 28.16), applies to everyone.

Nor can it be surprising here that for Jesus the two commandments, love of one's neighbour and love of God, are one (Matt. 23.37–40). Here love of God remains the 'first commandment'. Christianity is not a Gnosticism; it is a recognition that God's light is active, concrete love by human beings. Where this is experienced authentically, there is God. However, this perspective also forbids – as with Feuerbach and others – a divinization of the other or a reduction of God to one's fellow human being.[52] The omnipresent brutality of human beings, who are in many respects so corrupt, prevents any reduction of the other to an idol. For the believer, the relation with the other is always the finding place and the absence of God. The other reveals and veils God. For many of our contemporaries, and initially for the apostles and even Mary, his mother, the light in Jesus himself remained hidden.

But what if the divine dimension in Jesus, of whom it is said that he is the place where God is to be found *par excellence*, also remains hidden in the other? What if in this sense one can apply to oneself the scriptural saying 'It was now dark, and Jesus had not yet come to them' (John 6.17)? What if the divine dimension is 'asleep' in them, the sea is raging and they are afraid in their small boat and made even more afraid by the fear of the others? Jesus, who says 'No one comes to the Father but by me' (John 14.6), also says 'No one can come to me unless the Father who sent me draws him' (John 6.44). Isn't that a vicious circle? Scripture itself shows how many people very slowly discovered the other, divine dimension in Jesus: first the apostles themselves, from Peter to Thomas, but also Nicodemus, Pilate's wife (Matt. 27.19), the centurion (Luke 23.47). Nowhere is it said that the last two become followers, but they had 'seen' something in Jesus.

In John there is a short statement which can take us further here: 'He who does what is true comes to the light' (John 3.21). In the first instance this 'doing the truth' means the revelation which Jesus has brought, taking it into oneself and allowing it to permeate one's whole being. But in the light of the universal will for salvation which Jesus himself attributed to God, one can go further: all those 'righteous' who honestly follow their conscience, do the truth and somehow experience the light although Jesus (or his divine dimension) remains unknown to them, even if for them God remains the unknown who perhaps does not exist. However, the believer cannot but suspect that they have seen something of the divine reality, without needing to subscribing to Karl Rahner's view of 'anonymous' Christians – something that Muslims, Hindus or agnostics would find insulting.[53]

May we raise the question whether for Jesus, too, God's light remained hidden, at least at times? His trepidation on the Mount of Olives, his ambiguous complaint on the cross, were a stumbling block for the first church. According to the Qur'an, it was not Jesus who died, but a double. Yet scripture is explicit: he went the way to the end, alone. Nowhere is it said that he doubted, but that he was afraid of the night of his failure and death. He went on alone, but he had to have his cross carried for him. With Pilate it was Jesus and not Pilate who triumphed.

Who can fathom what was going on in his mind in the last hours of his mortal life? One thing is certain: in trust he went through his own night. He was convinced that the light would not let him go and that this light was nothing other than kindly. Even then God remained 'Abba', 'my dear Father'. And he knew that this voluntary departure through treachery and death would open up a way for many.

However they twist and turn, no one can completely shed the burden of not yet seeing, the never-ending lure of doubt. Even the old sage about whom Buber spoke in his *Tales of the Hasidim* ultimately gave the learned rationalist as a decisive answer the simple: 'But perhaps it *is* true.' The twilight is a burden which believers have to bear together (Gal. 6.2, 'Bear one another's burdens'). One can see something of the Light through others, with varying success: by a gesture or a word, a verse from scripture which suddenly illuminates a whole situation, a hymn or a glance. Those who experience the light in themselves can thus become a mirror for the inner light which is reflected from the other. A Jewish saying goes, 'The believer is the mirror for the believer' (cf. II Cor. 3.18). For the first Christians, the evening celebration of the eucharist must certainly have played a special role here as a mutual confirmation of faith, as an interpersonal experience of the Gospel saying, 'Where two or three are gathered together in my name, I am in their midst' (Matt. 18.20). Then they experienced the beginning of their resurrection through their common bond with the risen Christ. Augustine expressed this in concentrated form in a sermon to the catechumens in Hippo (*Sermon* 272):

> If you are the body of Christ and his members, then it is your own body on the Lord's table. It is your own symbol that you receive. So know what you see and receive what you are.

In our sometimes less stimulating celebration of the eucharist, in which the rite so often emphasizes the experience and witnessing of the faith, the mutuality which Augustine mentions is ignored far too much. Then all that is left in the pressurized life of a pluralistic society, which also stamps some family life, is the silent witness of a neighbour, a sister or brother. So I shall end this chapter with quite a long quotation from perhaps the greatest Catholic theologian of the twentieth century, Karl Rahner. In 'Experiences of a Catholic Theologian', published shortly before his death, he wrote:

> It could well be that the radical incomprehensibility of what is in fact meant by 'eternal life' is greatly underestimated, and that what we call looking upon God face to face in this eternal life is reduced to one of the attractive activities with which this eternal life is filled. How unspeakably unprecedented it is that the absoluteness of the Godhead itself should enter unveiled into our limited creativity! One can really make no real sense of this.
>
> It is clear to me that here a task is laid upon theologians of our time which, however precarious, cannot let them rest, namely the task of finding a better idea of this eternal life, one in which there is no longer any room for the misapprehension that I have just mentioned. But what will this look like in the name of heaven?
>
> When the angels of death have removed from our spirit all that unimportant rubbish that we call our history (though of course the real heart of what we have done with our freedom will remain), when all the stars of the ideals with which, in our overestimation of ourselves, we have decked the firmament of our existence, have faded and gone out – when death has brought a disconcertingly silent void and we have accepted this silently, in faith and hope, as our real being – when the life which we have led hitherto, however long, seems to us just one short explosion of our freedom instead of a protracted process – like a film in slow motion – an explosion in which what was a question is transformed into an answer, possibility into reality, time into eternity, and the freedom offered us into perfect freedom – and when, in the mighty fear of an ineffable

jubilation, it proves that this disconcertingly silent void which we feel to be death is in fact filled with the primal mystery that we call God, filled with the pure light and with his love which takes all and gives all – and when moreover from this unnameable mystery the face of Jesus, the one who gives blessing, looks on us, and thus all our true expectation of the incomprehensibility of the unnameable God is surpassed concretely in a divine way – then I would want to describe – no, not describe but indicate in a stammering way – roughly what you can provisionally expect: by already experiencing the decay which is death as the dawning of what is to come.[54]

5

Light, A Way to the Unnameable?

The media regularly report the appearance of a soft and comforting light in near-death experiences.[1] There still does not seem to be sufficiently serious scientific investigation into this. In any case, the people who entered this boundary area were living and not dead. They did not find themselves on the mysterious other side. So Karl Marx's statement has not been refuted: 'Religion is only the illusory sun which orbits round human beings as long as they do not orbit round themselves.'[2]

What emerges from the previous chapters is that numerous people say that they have had experiences of light. Of course we need to make a distinction between what is produced by a lively imagination, what is preserved from the memory of a dream and what is revealed in a vision.[3] Each time there is a different way of 'seeing'. Each time images appear, and in the re-telling also a language which is influenced by the person's own secular and possibly religious culture. Moreover, everyone knows that 'visions' or related phenomena can be produced artificially, perhaps through strict fasting or through drugs. They can be the result of a flight from reality by artificially filling a relative consciousness from the cellars of the unconscious.

However, this does not alter the fact that ordinary balanced people with a lucid consciousness[4] can be 'overtaken' by a very special experience which is described in terms of light. Sometimes others around them 'see' a radiance from this illumination which seems to them to be different from the natural glow of healthy young people or lively adult personalities. For those who experience these experiences, subjectively they seem like entering an 'other' reality; within time and space one rises above both. An experience which seems to last quite some time in fact proves to have taken a very short span of time. The space implied seems to be extended endlessly. What is more important is that people experience being taken up in to an immense shining reality without the dissolution of their own selves. Moreover the whole event is characterized by harmony, by peace and by feelings of goodness and love which seem to extend cosmically. Afterwards, although they remain themselves, they feel different: reborn, full of trust and dedication to an all-embracing higher reality.

Mircea Eliade wrote an important article about this immanent experience of light.[5] Like Jung, he finds empirical material in dreams of light which particular people related. His starting point, which I shall quote here, is a dream had by an American merchant, aged thirty-two, in the middle of the nineteenth century. He describes it like this:

> I found myself behind the counter in my shop on a bright sunny afternoon; in the twinkling of an eye everything became darker than in the darkest night, darker than in a mine shaft. The man with whom I was standing talking went down the street. I followed him, and although it was so dark I saw hundreds, indeed thousands of people, filling the street and wondering what was going on. At that moment I saw in the sky, to the south-west, a light as bright as a star, about as big as the palm of my hand. The light in fact seemed to be getting bigger and came closer; it began to lighten the darkness. As soon as it had reached the size of a man's head, it divided into twelve smaller lights, with a larger light in the centre, and it grew very quickly – at the same moment I knew that it was the coming of Christ. At the very moment I had the thought, the whole south-west of the sky was filled with a shining horde, and at the centre were Christ and the twelve apostles. Now it was brighter than the brightest day imaginable, and while the shining mass rose towards the centre, the friend with whom I

was talking exclaimed, 'It's my redeemer.' At that moment he left his body and ascended into heaven, and I thought that I was not good enough to go with him. Then I woke up.

At first the man was so much under the impact of the dream that he didn't dare tell anyone about it.

'A few weeks later,' he said, 'I told it to my wife and afterwards some others. Three years later, someone, known for his deeply religious life, said to my wife, "Your husband is born again and he doesn't know it. Spiritually he's a little child, with his eyes still closed, but he'll learn to see it himself."' Indeed, three weeks later, when our merchant was walking with his wife along Second Avenue in New York, he suddenly exclaimed, 'O, I have eternal life.' At that moment he felt that Christ had risen in him and that he himself would remain aware of that for ever. Later he had another experience of light on a boat in the middle of a large group of people, but he confessed that this waking experience of light never led him to forget the first, that of his dream.

To a psychologist of religion it seems that in this matter-of-fact, indeed very un-religious, person suddenly suppressed unconscious religious feelings broke through. It is surprising – something that one notes in most of these strange spiritual experiences of light – that those who experience them undergo a kind of essential mutation, like a new religious self-birth.

In the rest of his study, as a historian of religion Mircea Eliade goes through a number of parallel phenomena in the different religions, above all in the three great monotheistic religions.

However, the great question remains: are we here stuck in our imagination, in the sphere of our own consciousness, or do we really in some way touch on the Unnameable communicating itself? There is a great risk of remaining imprisoned in more or less aesthetic feelings, in self-expression, in projections, in narcissistic longings, in suppressed eroticism. And yet the need for experience and its importance have to be recognized. No less a figure than Karl Rahner repeatedly wrote prophetic words about this. For instance:

> The devout Christian of the future will either be a 'mystic', one who has experienced something, or he will cease to be anything at all. For devout Christian living as practised in the future will no longer be sustained and helped by the unanimous, manifest and public convictions and religious customs of all, summoning each one from the outset to a personal experience and a personal decision.[6]

And when at the end of his life he was asked, 'Where do you now see the most important theological questions?', he replied:

> It is really the oldest theological questions that are the most topical. How is authentic experience of God possible? How can I really experience that God has given his absolute and irrevocable communication of himself in Jesus Christ?[7]

Experience

What does it mean to 'experience'? J.-B. Lotz defines experience as 'the direct, involved grasping of a given reality'.[8] In his view, without being sheer intuition, experience belongs to this category: one in fact acquires a direct insight. However, any immediacy inevitably implies a number of intermediaries, provided by language and upbringing. A pure experience is an abstraction. Furthermore an experience is 'understood' only by a minimal reflection, thus by a degree of detachment from it. Then follows the question: what is absolutely objective truth here? Of course this cannot be detached from the subjective ground of experience. Only by reflection on the multiplicity of parallel experiences is 'objective' truth – which is always relative – attained, truth which at least seems trustworthy to the subject who experiences it.[9]

The experience of meaning is always a very special event. It emerges from a personal prehistory of a more or less explicit quest for truth, which relates to both the deciphering of the reality experienced and the truth of the correct reaction to it. Here insight into values and into a hierarchy of values comes into the foreground: the ordering of this whole which has grown slowly can lead to an experience of 'insight' which is more than a rational synthesis, because the whole of experience is involved in it.

Of course, here too the social-cultural context, which is strongly determined by history, also plays a part, since no experience stands apart from this context. That at the same time explains how for all great cultural areas, experiences relating to basic values can lead to very different hierarchies of values.[10] This does not alter the fact that for example the value of the 'conscience' seems to be an almost universal fact,[11] at least in the great cultures. Values prevent actions from becoming meaningless. For example, those who deny the value of longing or of hope cannot cope with either the orientation of their actions or the direction of their deepest aim in life. Conversely, central values can become transparent in action and thought through imagination and memory. A number of values, however important, is not enough to make life meaningful: what is equality without freedom and what is freedom if this is not focussed on a person or project? Without freedom love is worthless and any view of life becomes a prison.

Newman always gave experience a central place in his thought. He made a distinction between a rational approach to the mystery of existence ('notional') and an approach based on experience ('real'), since 'in effectivenesss intellectual ideas cannot compete with the experience of concrete facts'.[12]

Experiences can illuminate deeper dimensions; they can 'reveal'. These are dimensions of transcendence: they rise above the ordinary, they seem to escape the experimental and bring us into 'another domain in ourselves'.

Elizabeth Goudge has described this in a conversation between the two lovers in her book *Green Dolphin Country*:

'What does your country look like, Margaret?,' asked William.

'I can't describe it precisely,' she replied, 'but if I live in a particular way I tell myself that I'm now in my own country. That is when I live as simply as possible and the air is fresh and the wind cold, and there are no lies. When I'm there I get the idea that there's another door which opens on yet another land where my soul has always lived, and that one day I shall discover how to open the door.'

This is not to say that people *per se* experience 'another', absolutely transcendent Reality in that other domain. Philosophers and theologians try to clarify this sphere in which their own experience of transcendence and possible experience of the Transcendent can flow together. 'Revelation' is always ambiguous.

After an analysis of the advantages and disadvantages of different models of 'revelation', which are either too anthropomorphic or too abstract, Avery Dulles[13] opts for the model of 'symbolic mediation', and in so doing follows Samuel Taylor Coleridge: 'It is only through symbols that we can obtain intellectual knowledge of the divine' (131). In part supported by Paul Tillich, Karl Rahner, Paul Ricoeur, Langdon Gilkey, Louis Dupré and others, Dulles then develops his view. According to this approach a revelation never takes place through a purely inward experience or through a direct encounter with God. Symbolism is always necessary. Signs serve more to evoke and open up a fullness of meaning than to explicitate it. Such an experience of symbols always implies an authentic personal involvement of the person dealing with the symbolic event which happens in a language that can barely be translated. For many writers a symbolic statement, always in a particular context, is a metaphor (e.g. 'God is light') or is expressed in a myth (one might think of Plato's cave-dwellers). Thus parables about the kingdom of God or rites can also be metaphors. Scripture offers an enormous reservoir of symbols which through their somewhat ambivalent meaning are sources of reinterpretation.

Dulles sees revelation and symbolism as being very closely linked. He gives four arguments for this. First, symbolism does not imply a speculative but a participatory knowledge: the person is involved, since symbols are never objects and call for a personal interpretation from the moment that one enters the landscape of symbolic language. In fact one has to begin on a personal voyage of discovery. Secondly, symbolic language changes the person who is affected by it. Psychotherapy gives many examples of this. Thirdly, symbolism very strongly influences commitment and behaviour,, among other things by involving the imagination in feelings, with all the energy that flows from them (we need think only of the significance of national flags, or of the role of the sun in the many modern sects which give it a central place in their mythology). And finally, symbolic language leads into areas which normally are difficult for logical or analytical thought to reach, namely the whole sphere of the mystery about which poets and mystics talk. As Paul Tillich says, it opens up 'levels of reality which otherwise would remain closed to us . . . and it opens up divisions and facets of our soul which correspond to particular dimensions and aspects of reality'. And Thomas Carlyle remarks: 'In the symbol there is a concealing and at the same time a revealing.' Paul Ricoeur writes that the symbol 'makes us reflect'. It opens up a whole range of possible insights.

These four arguments can in fact be applied directly to the biblical symbolism of revelation, including the symbol of light. We need only think of an earlier quotation from I Timothy about God 'who dwells in light inaccessible' (6.16), or of the language of Pseudo-Dionysius or Nicholas of Cusa. In other words, really only symbolic language is suitable for speaking about the divine reality, and even Jesus himself can only bear witness to the Father in this way. The whole of Christian liturgy, including the most beautiful prayers and hymns, is symbolic language. Moreover Karl Rahner rightly speaks of 'mediated immediacy'.

Of course particular symbols are sociologically and culturally determined. Others (like water, fire, light, night) reach anyone who is in some sense open to them through their universal human depths, and they are the way *par excellence* for the interfaith dialogue in our multicultural world. One of the most special tasks of the churches is to preserve the reservoir of symbolic language and to help to interpret it, respecting the mutual complementarity of the symbols offered. It is not surprising that in a postmodern age which is distancing itself critically from the all too rationalistic phase in Western thought – supported by the philosophers of the Enlightenment and by a positivisitic and thus reductionist approach to reality[14] – a sense of symbolism is developing. This applies not only to Christianity but to any quest for the interpretation of an existence which is always mysterious.[15] Without the openness of symbolic language, even the most important 'dogmas' become empty formulae which hinder more than make space for that which essentially cannot be grasped.

Here in fact it has to be noted that Christian writers draw a distinction – though not always clearly – between religious experience and the experience of faith. We shall be returning to this. Here it may suffice to point to a comment by J.-B. Lotz:

> *Religious experience* is always mediated through the world and thus can make the world the Absolute. If it does not break through it, it remains stuck in an atheistic or pantheistic religious experience. But talk of the *experience of faith* can also divert into abstractions and miss any experiential basis. The two experiences need each other, the first in order not to fade away hopelessly without an 'answer' from the absolute 'You'; the second in order not to float meaninglessly because it has no basis in living experience – here at the same time it is necessary to avoid reducing the experience of faith to religious experience.[16]

From his Christian humanist background, Karl Rahner thinks in the same direction: 'one must break through to God with (and from) the earth'.[17] He explains:

> Hence in seeing, too, and not only in hearing, there is a kind

of sensory experience of transcendence, that serves as the foundation and mediation in referring the sense-endowed spiritual subject to God.

This is the Rahner who wrote: 'Without an experience of God, however little reflected upon and thematized, on the whole an experience of the self is impossible.' Rahnerian holism . . .

Religious experience and the experience of faith

From a historical perspective the religious is an all-embracing phenomenon, and for the non-believing observer, too, the religious, even after secularization, remains a topical category in existence and experience.[18] But religious experience in general – and the religious experience of light in particular – does not escape the ambivalence which characterizes most experiences. For example it is typical that Johann Baptist Metz writes this about the present-day European climate: 'Earlier people said, "Jesus yes, the church no." Now they say, "God no, religion yes." And here for many people "religion" is "the religion that I construct myself".'

Unique, individual experience is becoming not only the norm of ethical action, but at the same time the key to the understanding of reality. Moreover in a sense it cannot be otherwise: I have 'my' conscience and the perspective of 'my' consciousness. This approach derives, among other things, from the fact that the market of philosophy (with ethics) and religion, which offers very different methods and systems of interpretation, some of them with a 'scientific' basis, has become so complex that in order to escape a total relativism many people retreat to the island of their own experience: what I experience there is beneficial, and is true, at least for me now. We need think only of the title of the highly individualistic book by A. Frossard, which became a bestseller: *God Exists – I've Met Him*. Slowly, every special experience is being interpreted as mystical, and the Spirit is found in every form of ecstasy: before a tree in the evening sun, before a playful squirrel, before a powerful erotic impulse. Something of this comes through in Eichendorff's poem:

> A song sleeps in all things
> which dream there on and on;
> and the world will begin to sing,
> if only you can find the magic word.

In this way every person finds his or her god somewhere and tolerates the polytheism of the others. Support for this immanent polytheism can be found in depth psychology. Philosophical or ecclesiastical reflections are then swept away as theoretical limitations which are irrelevant. However, thinking people remain on their guard: what is the significance of all this subjective experience? Is it human to suppress the critical consciousness?

The first question then is, 'What is specifically "religious" in the experiences mentioned?' Rudolf Otto tried to introduce clarity here.[19] Of course religious experience is an individual event. But this event has objective characteristics: in it one comes upon something marvellous which deeply affects the subject. People trust this marvellous element and believe in it, even when they interpret it as an aspect of their own, albeit always unfathomable, existence. In that case what is the difference between the religious and the purely emotional? When does a loud or a silent inner 'enlightenment' become religious?

It is possible to use the definition of religion which Schleiermacher gave: 'Essentially it is neither a thought, nor an action, but intuitive contemplation and feeling.' But in that case are all deeper feelings religious? Or do we have to reserve the specifically religious for the feeling that arises when one experiences in oneself the span of the horizon of existence as 'in' and 'before' the individual consciousness, as Schleiermacher explains in his *Dialektik* (1853)? For him the horizon of existence is God, for we experience ourselves as wholly dependent on God in a living, conscious relationship. This links up closely with the Augustinian *'intimior intimo meo'* (more intimate than my deepest depth). Of course this approach can be applied to all the great historical religions; at any rate, it is not primarily about knowledge but about an intuitive experience. Nothing can be proved, but a basic personal experience can be recognized which Otto calls the experience of the 'Holy' and which in a great variety of social and psychological contexts proves fundamentally to be the same, as William James described it in his famous work *The Varieties of Religious Experience* (1902).[20] This primal experience inevitably already implies an interpretation. Without language, symbols, upbringing and thus the influence of a particular historical religion, it is impossible to interpret this primal experience. Otto recognizes that intuition and thought can never be separated. Therefore, he argues, intuition is at the same time a kind of knowledge, a conscious experience of tension, involvement and solidarity, whether this is labelled 'religious' or not.

On this approach one thus inevitably ends up in an impasse: doesn't such a subjective experience open wide the door to all forms of subjectivism (including those that are most alienating) by which each individual constructs his or her images of God, rituals and 'dogmatic' supports? Experience and the history of religion abundantly illustrate this legitimate concern. Depending on the spirit of the age, almost anything can be declared 'holy'.[21] Moreover in the religious sphere no one can act harmoniously in a purely individual way. Everyone needs some support and correction from society. Here Christians can participate on the basis of a long tradition of 'discerning the spirits' They are always aware of the working of the Holy Spirit in the conscience and in consciousness, and of the very individual and diversified character of this activity (among other things through the many 'charismas'). From the first century onwards, however, there were warnings against the baneful deviations which arose through an excessive emphasis on the subjective. Gnosticism has been a temptation from the beginning to the present day.

In his great work on the Holy Spirit, Yves Congar devotes considerable attention to this and develops a number of criteria for preventing 'charismatic movements' from sinking in the quicksand.[22] For Christians a 'church' remains necessary as a 'space for the spirit'.[23] But – and history also teaches this – the sphere of the church can also become a prison. Not only the divisions into so many churches but also the great suffering caused by them teach Christians that in the end even believers always partly stand alone with their very personal religious experience and their very personal 'inspiration'. Yet no one can get any further without some direction from the long collective experience of church theology and spirituality, with all its changes.

Here we must return to the central question: does an experience of light lead to the Light, implicitly or explicitly to the God of Jesus Christ? Or is it no more than a symbolic expression, a projection of one's own self-consciousness which is thus determined as an experience of oneself, seeing one's own free void? And is it thus – on reflection – a kind of reflection of light which first disturbs and then discourages because ultimately nothing is seen and nothing is encountered? A poem by Rainer Maria Rilke can illustrate this:

> Does God play with mirrors?
>
> Does God play with mirrors?
> Does racing appearance blind us?
> Is this splendour yours,
> or his playful mockery?
>
> Your clear feeling gleams –
> I storm your doors like wind –
> but when I touch its glow,
> it seems to me cool.[24]

Is it a flash of lightning in 'the god in the depth of one's thoughts', or is the divine reality truly touched in an experience of light to which it is not reduced? Of course the believer can usually settle for the absolute 'negative way': the experience of the Absence as a radical limit-experience reduces the human being to silence in the face of something that cannot be experienced, that perhaps is or is not, as a kind of 'Christian agnostic'.[25] No word, no symbol, can comprehend the unattainable Other which perhaps is still present. One patiently accepts its absolute silence. However, the believer can also recognize that there is a good reason why the motif of light keeps recurring in scripture. Of course light remains a symbol, but it clothes an inward 'seeing' of a reality which both penetrates and transcends believers: it becomes clear to them that an unfathomable mystery is touching them. Such a special experience, though it is not exceptional, will find a clarifying echo in the words of scripture, in the liturgy, in the encounter with others, above all in the discovery of the strange figure of Jesus. There the believer recognizes a transparency, a dimension which is quite different from anything within this world and which is experienced here and now, in the world, as the many witnesses have described it. On reflection the believer knows that this can be called something like a 'revelation' from God, which in one way or another must take form within the world. If God truly wants to share himself, it must be possible for human beings to experience him in some way as God. Moreover Hans Urs van Balthasar sees the central question of fundamental theology here: without the sight of a 'form', a self-revelation of God directed towards human beings is impossible. In this sense it is an 'aesthetic' problem: here the reality of faith must relate to the senses.[26]

What Augustine calls 'the eyes' of faith must really 'see' something, but this seeing cannot be reduced to an observing: it is a total experience in which all dimensions of the person are affected. Terminologically, this 'light of faith' comprehends the tension between trusting faith (*pistis*) and knowledge (*gnosis*). We might think of the experience of Mary Magdalene when she exclaimed 'Rabbouni!' (John 20.16). 'It's you!'[27]

Against this background it is not surprising that a debate has developed among believers about the value of experience in faith. Doesn't any belief in experience threaten the experience of faith?

The experience of faith always comes from God, who communicates himself freely and thus transcends any experience of self, and can in fact be reached only by a leap of faith which is given, and transcends any experience of one's own. One should therefore be suspicious *a priori* of any faith which is based, for example, on a subjective experience of light. For Anton Vergote, emphasis on belief in experience indicates a crisis in Christianity: one believes what one can experience. 'By contrast, in the experience of faith, "faith" qualifies experience.' He recognizes that a certain *experience* of faith is possible, but that faith can be threatened by belief in experience of faith, a belief which is defined and limited by experience. In that case 'God' becomes a cipher for a deep valuable experience (for example 'love is God' or 'cosmic space is divine'). Then an image of God is very soon tailored to human measure, as sensual as possible and as open to human experience as possible. Vergote also points to another twist, namely the concern for a broad interfaith dialogue which points out essentially historical differences, and wants to preserve what all religions have in common or are thought to have in common. Of course a widespread opposition to the numerous restrictions that the institutional church lays on the religious sphere comes in here. And finally he points to the tendency to prefer the eternal movement of evolution to the firm roots of religious traditions. Incontrovertibly 'Christianity' is engaged in an evacuation of 'Christendom', with all its institutional, almost timeless, forms. Over against this he emphasizes that belief in the Christian revelation means that one takes a step which it is impossible for human beings to take by themselves. One must 'come out' in order to say 'yes' to a personal Reality which asks for an answer and which has communicated itself in the historical Jesus Christ:

> God is on the other side of the psychological element that human beings can bring to religion ... Knowing God is not an experience; it is something which comes to them ... Getting to God involves a leap.[28]

But Vergote tries to avoid an absolute dualism of experience and faith: 'The sign which addresses us calls for a leap of faith and this requires us to let go.' This leap of faith requires us to go further; it calls for an ongoing commitment in which both faith and experience are harmonized, but are harmonized by the faith which expresses itself in symbols (as is also the case with deep human love). To achieve this synthesis requires more than a cultural faith, namely a culture of faith.

There have been reactions to this view. Some find in Vergote an exaggerated dualism where a tension threatens to develop into a separation. J. Vandenbulcke[29] thinks that more positive things can be said about the experience of faith, among other things by seeing religious experience more broadly than Vergote does. Here an analysis of the term revelation is the way: understood properly, revelation is essentially connected with experience. Can truths of faith have the intrinsic authority of truth without being critically tested by the experience of reality, certainly when they are understood in broader terms? Cannot the depth dimension (of security, love, suffering and so on) be illuminated so that it becomes an encounter with a personal God?

> It seems to me that such illlumination can happen apart from any positive revelation whatever, though this does not mean that it can come about unless the personal God offers himself in experience.

Vandenbulcke then defends his position, as follows:

> However, if faith wants to be authentic and thus related to reality, then it must be able to indicate its roots in the experience of reality indicated above. This anchoring in reality is essential for the authentic content of faith to come into being.

But what is revelation? Revelation

> . . . illuminates unsuspected perspectives on the ultimate concerns of life within deep human experience. And for me this also includes the God who offers himself.

Furthermore,

> ... the most universal human nature – not necessarily, but in actual fact – always already has to do with the God who offers himself in experience but who is so difficult to point to. God is part of the milieu of human reality; but this assertion does not relieve us of the difficult task of pointing to him. Should we fail to do that in a satisfactory human way, our faith would lose its accountability. The Bible can be a great help in pointing to God in this way – but only to the degree that existential truths which can be intimated inter-personally are expressed in it, i.e. to the degree that God *really* speaks in it.

In my view Vandenbulcke is right to point out that Vergote threatens to make too great a division between the Christian and the universally human.[30] Indeed God must in some way touch human beings as God, and human beings must experience this, although the experience is given from God. And in view of God's universal will for salvation – certainly in the light of theology after the Second Vatican Council – this possible experience must go beyond the frontiers of Christianity as a concrete historical event. Should that not be the case, it seems impossible to point to authentic mystical experiences before or outside Christianity. Here J. Maréchal refers to the Muslim mystic al-Hallâj, who was terribly tortured and killed on 26 March 922 by an Islamic court because of his mystical views: according to Maréchal these views come very close to those of Ruusbroec. Of course al-Hallâj was much struck by the verses in the Qur'an which refer to Jesus, although he remained a Muslim until his cruel death.[31]

Taking the figure of al-Hallâj as his background, Maréchal writes the following:[32]

> From the perspective of monotheism the basic reality of mystical experiences cannot consist in the pure deployment of the soul on itself, as if this return of the soul into its own being already had any intrinsic religious value. If a monotheist is consistent with himself he can understand the mystical union

only in two ways: *either* within the limits of natural religion and without any direct experience of a transcendent order, as an intense higher degree of positive asceticism, which leads, by means of creatures seen *sub specie aeternitatis*, to an ever more perfect knowledge and love of God the creator; *or* as the coming into a soul which offers no hindrance to it of a transcendent gift from outside, which in the end is none other than God himself, who communicates himself freely to his creature.

In other words, non-Christians too can experience God – the God who is also the God of Christians – through their symbols as a free self-giving of God. And since God wills to communicate himself to anyone who is open to him, anyone can name him as such in one way or another even without calling him God as such.[33] However, Christians remain doubly privileged: they know the 'way' of Jesus Christ and they have the support of a long church tradition which emphasizes without interruption the bonds between both immanence and transcendence and 'creation' and 'redemption'. At the same time dualism is rejected, and both the freedom of God's self-communication and the universality of his will to communicate are affirmed. God's will for salvation goes beyond all limits of concrete historical religions, although Christianity holds that God offers himself in a unique way through Jesus Christ.[34] Any religious experience of light can communicate experience of God.

Openness to God or to the void?

The above remarks do not represent a conclusion to the quest from experience. The great question remains whether the experience of the mysterious Space which human beings open above themselves reveals God or reduces one to silence before a wide void. Does, for example, the symbolism of light open up on an authentic and unfathomably rich personal reality,[35] or does it bring us merely to the edge of the void? This is certainly not an idle question in the dialogue with the mystics, with Buddhism and with atheistic religious feeling.

As Cornelius Verhoeven emphasized in a prophetic essay entitled 'Around the Void',[36] more and more people feel that they must come clean about a kind of essential lostness. When in 1982 the International Catholic Childhood Bureau held a worldwide enquiry among affiliated national organizations about key questions asked by children, the main concern seemed to be their increasing experience of the spiritual void. The younger generation simply reflects what is being experienced more sharply in society. Gilles Lipovetsky, the French philosopher of culture, expressed this in a book which attracted much attention called *The Era of the Void*.[37] Nowhere does Lipovetsky give a precise description of the void. For him it is the consequence of narcissism: the 'I' becomes a floating sphere where there are no definitive ties; it is prepared to adapt constantly by means of fleeting systems and relationships, never structured by a firm attitude to the Other, whoever this may be. He calls the void *the* characteristic of postmodernism: 'postmodern desubstantialization' is increasingly removing the core from reality. He recognizes that the death of God has opened up an abyss of 'meaninglessness', but he also sees this concealed: 'everywhere there is indifference, no metaphysical anxiety'. He agrees with Christopher Lasch, who makes the void result in the narcissistic choice expressed by Jerry Rubin, 'to love myself enough so that I never need anyone to make me happy'.[38] It is not surprising that Lipovetsky ends up in a kind of philosophy of fashion, the expression of a 'humoristic, ludistic society'[39] in which people cannot or will not encounter the 'true' other and limit themselves to 'a playful parody', to a colourful and constantly changing kaleidoscope in which they pass the time in ever new and unique encounters with the 'appearance' of the other. Moreover he is opposed to any holistic approach which would again imprison the individual in collective rituals or thought-patterns. Desocialization makes further humanization possible. The state must encourage this difference, for in so far as there is meaning, it is found exclusively in the individual.

Marcel Gauchet goes far deeper than Lipovetsky. He describes the dying out of Christianity as the last phase of the development of humankind towards freedom, though this is an empty freedom. He leaves far behind the optimism of Hegel, but also of the current process theologies and of what often passes for liberation theology. The discussion which arose over his book entitled *The Disenchantment of the World*,[40] borrowed from Max Weber, and its significance for the current discussion about the meaning of existence, justifies a close inspection of his analysis. Gauchet sees the whole of human history as one great social and cultural process of liberation through which the world is gradually disenchanted by the forcing back of religion. It was initially all-embracing; it provided order and at the same time brought slavery. He recognizes the enormous significance of religion: 'With good reason religion has a central place in the lives of our ancestors and it is not fortuitous that it has dominated almost all history.'

Its disenchantment was brought about above all by three forces:

(*a*) the rise of the state with the growing autonomy of 'politics';[41]

(*b*) critical discourse;

(*c*) Christian belief, above all Catholicism, which sharpened the tension between church and state (this in opposition to Max Weber, who emphasized the role of Protestantism).

The stimulus towards liberation was monotheism, to which Christianity gave able support. Jean-Philippe Domecq sums up Gauchet's position like this:

> In the first place Christianity refined and universalized monotheistic religion. So the many gods became the One who becomes the wholly Other. But in this transition from the gods to God we have lost the mediators between nature and ourselves. God has withdrawn into the invisible, far away from this earth which he had created.[42]

This monotheism itself has a political origin. Moses is opposed to Egyptian oppression: our Yahweh cannot be compared with the gods of Egypt. Yahweh is not the greatest of all; he is the only God.

Jesus goes further along this line. Among other things Gauchet refers to Jesus' sayings 'My kingdom is not of this world' and 'Render to Caesar that which is Caesar's'. Religion is internalized and society slowly takes on political autonomy. It becomes areligious. Thus Christianity proves to be 'the religion of the exodus from religion'; Gauchet claims 'that Christianity bore within itself the seed both of the development of the states and of human rights' and thus of tolerance of both religions and atheism.

Meanwhile, he says, the whole of society has been completely entrusted to human beings. From now on religion is becoming memory, a dead weight or a hindrance to meaningful insight. He sees Vatican II as a last great convulsion of religion. Even as the church proclaims God more as God, it seems to be digging both its own grave and that of God: 'Perhaps the church needs to be more afraid of its perfection than of its corruption.' Religion can live on only in art (André Malraux's idea). However, a shadow side is that people are thrown back on their ultimate solitude, which is radical. The last pages of the book describe the pain of this:

> From now on we are forced to live naked and in anxiety – something that by the favour of the gods has been more or less spared us since the beginning of the human adventure . . . Now we must all work out our own answers. That is the nagging pain . . . which no sacral opium can make us forget: the inexplicable contradiction which is essentially bound up with the longing to be authentically subject.

And further:

> Society after religion is also the society where the problem of madness and of any personal confusion is developing in an

unknown direction. That is because it is a society which psychologically exhausts individuals, in which nothing helps or supports them when they constantly and everywhere experience the question: why me now?

Moreover in an extended review J.-P.Domecq raises the question:

> If the fundamental lack is so great in each of us, will the collectivity be able to keep this hidden for a long time? Will not this lack, as an abyss, take the place of the religious views which were formerly necessary for society?

Nowhere does one get away from this. We are equipped with a freedom which is directed only towards our own fragile selves, with only the night of nothingness as a perspective.[43]

Where Gauchet ends, Nietzsche – the most contemporary of the great classical masters of doubt – could begin again.[44] For Nietzsche, history is not a linear journey of liberation. He rejects any belief in progress. It is now that counts, not the future. He resolves, as he says in the preface to *Ecce Homo*, 'voluntarily to live in the midst of ice and high mountains'. His famous second innocence comes after 'mistrust', after his criticism of conscious thought, after anguish at its loss, and leads to the courage to recognize, to accept and to say 'yes' to the Abyss. He rejects any mysticism which is a flight to God, but he has intimations of the mysticism of life which is incomprehensible even to reason. However, he also rejects any authentic otherness with his great 'yes' to the 'eternal return' in successive reincarnations. Here vitalism and individualism are two facets of one basic vision. He makes Zarathustra say, 'Sing, speak no more', which by many after him can now be translated as, 'Interpret. Think no more.'

As an illustration, here is a kind of 'anti-sun hymn', so strangely different from that of Francis of Assisi. In *Thus Spoke Zarathustra*, Nietzsche writes:

> O sky above me! O pure, deep sky! You abyss of light!
> Gazing into you I tremble with divine desires.
> To cast myself into your height – that is my depth . . .
> Light, that is my being! O, if only I were night . . .
> for that is my solitude, this girdle of light!
> O, if only I were shadow and darkness . . .
> what should I drink from the wells of light
> and sing of you, you too, stars, sparks and glow worms in the sky!
> I would enjoy the light that you give!
> But I live in my own light, I gulp the flames which flare from me.

In this context, of course, there is no longer a place for the Jesus whom Nietzsche once admired and afterwards jealously mocked. Nietzsche called himself 'the Antichrist', out of an unclarified love-hate relationship, when on 5 January 1889 he signed his last letters in Turin before his fatal breakdown.

And yet Nietzsche is the one who, like Dostoevsky and Kierkegaard, pointed to the enormous importance of the individual, which cannot be reduced to a social product of the current categories of knowledge and morality. All three showed that science as such does not bring liberation. All three also fought against the nihilism of which Nietzsche was to be the tragic prophet.[45]

Lipovetsky, Gauchet and Nietzsche express one of the important components of our Western *Zeitgeist*. Of course there are others; one need only refer to the distinguished and much-respected agnostic Leo Apostel in a dialogue with Edward Schillebeeckx in Ghent in October 1987 which has become famous. On (a)theistic spirituality he remarked:

> At this time there is a general despair in Europe. That is my impression. People do not believe that there can be a future . . . That is the greatest danger: despair.[46]

Indeed, many people in the West no longer know how to deal with their lostness in the endless space of the void. Some at least – and this is a relatively new phenomenon – interpret the experience of the void in a very different way. They take counsel from the old tradition of Buddhism. Although Buddhism assumes a great many forms, many Westerners are intrigued by the way in which the great Eastern teaching deals with the experience of the void.

Romano Guardini cannot escape comparing Buddha and Jesus:

> There is only one whom we might be inclined to compare with Jesus: Buddha. This man is a great mystery. He lived in an awful, almost superhuman freedom, yet his kindness was as powerful as a cosmic force. Perhaps Buddha will be the last religious genius to be explained by Christianity. As yet no one has really uncovered his Christian significance. Perhaps Christ had not only one precursor, John, last of the prophets, but three: John the Baptist for the Chosen People, Socrates from the heart of antiquity, and Buddha, who spoke the ultimate word in Eastern religious cognition. Buddha is free, but his freedom is not that of Christ. Possibly Buddha's freedom is only the ultimate and supremely liberating knowledge of the vanity of this fallen world.[47]

And later he puts the question of Buddha's significance for Christians in an even more evocative way:

> Only one person ever seriously attempted . . . to lay hands on being – Buddha. He desired more than mere moral progress or peace outside the world. He attempted the inconceivable: himself part of existence, he tried to lift all existence by its 'bootstraps'. So far no Christian has succeeded in comprehending and evaluating Buddha's conception of Nirvana, the ultimate awakening, cessation of illusion and being . . .[48]

Buddha gave himself the name 'the Enlightened One'. When

he was dying, his disciples stood in a circle around him, and at the moment he thought good he broke the ties which bound him to this life: 'There is no more.' His disciples were aware that here a great mystery had taken place.

Buddhism, which puts a strong emphasis on wisdom, enlightenment and also on compassion, has never given positive content to liberation and enlightenment by Nirvana (not to be confused with Western nihilism). On this H. Waldenfels notes:

> Liberation is primarily about a being freed from, which leads into an openness to everything which cannot be described further. Moreover in content enlightenment means no more than that everything appears as it is.[49]

However attractive a comparison between the two great figures, Buddha and Jesus, might seem at first sight, differences between Judaism, Islam and Christianity on the one hand and Buddhism on the other seem unbridgable. Buddhism does not recognize a personal God, or indeed God at all. And in contrast to the three Abrahamic religions the problem of evil is largely avoided. Some see a possible bridge to the teaching of nirvana in Buddhism in Paul's teaching about kenosis, emptying (Phil. 2.6–11). However, here Waldenfels sees an impasse for those who want to compare both views.[50] Westerners, with their personalistic view of life which cannot imagine the abolition of the self as a liberation, face an enigma at this point. And for Western mystics, too, the one who sees does not disappear without remainder into One who is seen: a person experiences a Person. The Christian mystic will always be inclined to say of Buddhism what Ruusbroec wrote about the one who turns within himself but is not united with God's own self:

> They have united themselves with the blind, dark emptiness of their own being, and then they have the impression that they are of one being with God, and they take that to be their eternal bliss.[51]

Even in 'the abyss of darkness, where the loving spirit has died to itself', it remains the person who has been filled with light.

On the basis of his Eastern experience, J. S. O'Leary, a professor at the Sophia University in Tokyo, goes more deeply into the Buddhist challenge of the interpretation of the void.[52] According to the first Buddhism, nothing is created out of nothing, but nothing remains either; everything is always in movement. Not a single being has its own consistency. Thus the difference from Western personalism is radical. Samsara (eternal movement) is really no different from nirvana: both escape the categories of being or non-being. Language too, including religious language, which tries to grasp this, is inevitably fleeting (and thus in a sense related to Derrida's deconstructionism). There is no firm ground for concepts like those in Plato's theory of ideas. The best language is silence. A synthesis between Buddhism and Christianity, the religion of the Word, seems impossible. Certainly the two world-views can put critical questions to each other. Thus Buddhism too teaches that one cannot get any hold on the ultimate (we might think of Pseudo-Dionysius and Eckhart), while a personal relationship with this ultimate in which one is finally taken up is inconceivable.[53]

Buddhism can never be dogmatic, but it does not lapse into scepticism. Although 'all things are empty' and this is their identity, people try to 'understand' this. However, it is inconceivable that God should be thought of a as a firm 'rock'. Buddhists are serenely 'a-theistic' but not agnostic.[54] The void does not become absolutely sublime (which would lead to monism); however, it does indicate the radical impotence of a metaphysical theodicy.

Against the background briefly sketched out here, O'Leary wants to 'deconstruct' the traditional view of God which has grown up in history, something that is in fact already done by central texts of the Old Testament (Deuteronomy) and the New Testament (John). The God of Jesus is not an empty metaphysical God. For Christians he is encountered in someone, through his historical dealing with Jesus. He cannot be reduced to a concept. When, for example, it is said of him that he is 'light', it is because he is experienced in his icon Jesus, not because he is thought of in concepts. Any language embedded in a historical culture is contingent. Human beings themselves 'are' also there; they have their fixed position because they know that they are addressed concretely, not because they see themselves as something 'in themselves'.

But what about the uniqueness of Christ in this cultural historical interfaith context? Here O'Leary argues for a thorough reinterpretation of the incarnation – which we cannot go into in more detail within the framework of this book. He points to the enormous difference between Buddha, the wise Eastern prince with his undisrupted, harmonious life, into which all history is taken up, and Jesus crucified by an unjust environment in a unique moment of history and through his resurrection giving history an abiding perspective. Even the Word (Jesus) expresses this ultimate reality only as a horizon which is present in him, but through which Jesus' distinctiveness somehow remains untouchable,[55] just as his kingdom of God and his return also remain incomprehensible, surrounded as they are 'by clouds' (Mark 13.26). With a view to the uniqueness of Jesus and his universality O'Leary argues here for an 'empty christology', namely one which does not put Jesus in a particular cultural language. What is central for Christians continues to be the hope in faith of a universal breakthrough of the Light (Rom. 8.19–20), a hope which is concrete in all cultures and which must be communicated through commitment – among other things by a credible commitment to justice.

What I have just said has at least made it clear that even for believing Christians the journey through the void to the hoped-for light is a difficult one and requires much courage and hope. One cannot escape it: guided by the 'Spirit', one must chose from one's poverty. Hans Urs von Balthasar has written a brave and inspiring paragraph about this:

> Only in faith can we get away from the word as a support, and

tread the sphere of freedom without hesitation; only in trusting surrender may we venture outside the ship with Peter on the infinite waves of the Spirit of God. However, there is no longer a formula which the Other who stands before us would understand or could use. He requires of us something else that is unknown both to him and to us, but which can be given to both of us only through the creative Spirit of love. This Spirit is breath, not structure and outline. So this Spirit wants to breathe through us and not objectify us. He does not want to be seen, but to be the seeing eye of grace in us. It does not trouble the Spirit much whether we pray to him as long as with him we pray 'Abba, Father' and so enter into his inexpressible sighing from the ground of our soul. He is the light which can only be seen in that which is illuminated, and which is the love between Father and Son that has appeared in Jesus.[56]

We cannot escape the fact that when it comes to the experience of the void reasoning is of little help. The experience of meaninglessness makes a total theoretical scheme of meaning impossible. Only a practical trust that there is a total meaning gives perspective, despite the theoretical doubt that remains.[57] The only existential answer is another experience, that of hope, hope not as an abstract 'divine virtue' nor as a naive or blind and undirected expectation. For believing Christians it is a matter of waiting: not in resignation but in actively looking towards a horizon which is already present. We experience this horizon in ourselves, but it is unfolded by a Jesus experience in which the whole person recognizes how it becomes open to a light which gives trust. This is the beginning of 'seeing' an all-supporting reality which at the same time is love, in the midst of one's own life and great historical events, yet transcending them. This seeing is supported by a Christian tradition of experience, and recognized as in principle providing meaning for everyone.[58] It amounts to falling silent before a horizon of kindly Light within, perhaps symbolized by the golden light which the northern midsummer-night sun spreads over the lakes of Finland. That Light appears as the biblical expression of the strong and vulnerable mystery which holds people above the void. Christians are then the people – and all the people – who dare to live by this. They cannot then do other than bear witness by powerfully and vulnerably committing themselves so that all is inbreathed by it.

Meanwhile, many people only reach the firm ground of the light, on the basis of a hidden but ineradicable trust in the light, after they have experienced deep down the abyss of the mystery of evil as a terrifying reality. Gertrud le Fort has described this on the basis of her own German experience of the war:

> Just as only the night discloses the light, just as only life in the midst of an un-Christian people teaches the whole glory of Christ, so the experience of boundless evil indicates a new relationship to love, I would want to say a whole new love of love . . . For not only the shining day but also the night has wonders of its own. There are flowers which flourish only in the wilderness, stars which appear only on the horizon of the desert. There are experiences of the divine love which are given to us only in the most extreme forsakenness, indeed on the edge of despair.[59]

Here the symbol of light, not the coolness but the softness that expresses tenderness, has a whole attraction of its own. It points forward to a future, to a space where one can be expected. It touches the heart of consciousness, the specifically human consummation of the evolution of life, and heals anxiety, since it blots it out above the abyss of empty nothingness. It never compels, but remains challenging. It can become lasting or even transparent in people. It unlocks us from what the vicious circle which can be within our own selves. It can only be 'understood' (which is not to be confused with 'grasped') within a community in which the same direction is experienced in many forms as the prism of the same horizon of light. Here Christians are both 'other' and wholly co-human, with all those who look for a morning beyond the frontier of the now.

6

Towards a More Transparent Society

'The people that walked in darkness . . .' (Isaiah 9.1)

The history of the West can be written from different perspectives: as a chronicle of tribal wars, as a story of progress from alchemy to biotechnology, as a journey of discovery which leads to the 'global village', as a long process of general urbanization, and so on. It can also be (re)written from the perspective of the dialectic between church and state, which then in part coincides with the tension between Christianity and Christendom. But it is always about the passage of large groups through time.

Judaism and Christianity have never only envisaged individual salvation. Jesus himself wept over Jerusalem (Luke 19.31). He always had the salvation of 'his people' in view (Matt. 15.25) . He saw his successors as 'a light on the lampstand' (Luke 11.33). And the Gospel of Matthew ends with the call, 'Go, make disciples of all nations' (Matt. 28.19). The Book of Revelation speaks of 'a holy city, shining with God's glory' (Rev. 21.10–11).

Around the year 200 a Christian wrote a letter to Diognetus. In it we read:

> For happiness does not consist in domination over neighbours, nor in wishing to have more than the weak, nor in wealth, and power to compel those who are poorer, nor can anyone be an imitator of God in doing these things, but these things are outside his majesty. But whoever takes up the burden of his neighbour, and wishes to help another, who is worse off in that in which he is the stronger, and by ministering to those in need the things which he has received and holds from God becomes

a god to those who receive them – this man is an imitator of God (X, 5–6).[1]

The emperor Constantine opened up the Roman empire for Christianity (c.313) and the emperor Theodosius definitively made this faith the state religion (380). From this time Christianity gradually became interwoven with the whole of European society in East and West (through education, care of the sick, legislation, architecture, and so on). Everywhere people tried to influence traditions and attitudes by the spirit of the gospel. Europe is inconceivable without abbeys and parishes.

However, at the same time an ambiguous course was adopted: papal states, prince bishoprics, simony, wars of religion, crusades, inquisition, trading in indulgences, misuse of the 'secular arm'. What needed to be transparent was corrupted in many ways.[2] But the pressure of the gospel did not stop: Francis, Catherine of Siena, Jan Hus, John Ruusbroec, Bartolomé de las Casas, Erasmus, Thomas More, Ignatius of Loyola, Martin Luther, Mary Ward: time after time they forced a degenerate Christianity to examine its conscience. The norm remained intact, namely the dream of the kingdom of God as presented by that strange Jesus.[3]

The previous chapters focussed almost exclusively on the 'way inwards', on the illumination of the heart. But the light must not disappear under the bushel (Luke 11.33). Even now there are Europeans who summon the secularized Christianity in East and West in one form or another to a return to the sources by being more receptive to the old light. This last chapter will reflect on this, not with a view to the restoration of Christendom, but as a challenge to continue the true calling of Christianity in society on the threshold of the third millennium. And here Christian faith will need to be far more inspiring than the Christian religion.

The democratizing of information and of the knowledge of history has led to deep disillusionment among many Europeans, almost to collective depression: human beings seem to be de-humanizing themselves. The lure of despondency threatens a rapidly ageing population, while young people are grappling with feelings of impotence and cling to short-term perspectives. Anyone who read the prison novels of Solzhenitsyn about the Soviet empire, or Jung Chang's *Wild Swans*, or the private life of Mao as disclosed by his physician Li Zshisui; anyone who is objectively informed about the Communist dictatorship in China, who follows the recent history of Cambodia, Colombia or El Salvador, or hears about the tragedies in Africa, knows how inhuman systems hold men, women and children prisoners in fear and offer only a perspective of biological survival.

Europe itself has not forgotten how in this century tens of millions of baptized Catholics, Protestants and Orthodox Christians killed tens of millions of Christians and exterminated almost the whole Jewish people in Europe. The horizon of many millions who have to live below the poverty level in Western Europe – mostly as a result of long-term unemployment or precarious employment – remains sombre. And the fear of fundamentalist outbursts, whether Muslim or nationalistic, slumbers everywhere.

The desire for harmony through honesty

It is not the first time that this continent has been afraid of the darker side of history.[4] Thus at the beginning of the sixteenth century Thomas More was struck by the injustice and corruption which plagued Western Europe. This Chancellor of England wanted a transparent society and formulated his dream in his famous *Utopia*, written partly in Bruges and Antwerp and published for the first time in Louvain. More was still writing in the period of Christendom. However, the proportion of practising Christians at that time was no greater than in present-day society. Even now families, base communities, pressure groups are fighting for more transparency and honesty in every sphere, above all in social, economic and political life. Here believers also meet up with those of other views as pioneers in the wilderness. In fact they express what the mostly silent majority wants,[5] but they are held back by the pressure of what they think is the general opinion. The facts indicate an undiminished continuation of the demand everywhere for more transparency.

According to the 1981 European Values Study, when people were asked what characteristic they wanted to encourage children to adopt at home, throughout Western Europe honesty came out in first place by a long way (out of seventeen characteristics suggested).

Thomas More's dream lives on, as does the reality of his time. If we investigate the evolution of tolerance according to the findings of the European Values Study mentioned, we can note for most countries an increasing decline in actual attitudes to honesty.

Is the following behaviour justified?
(on a ten-point scale)

		Great Britain	France	Belgium
Accepting bribes at work	1981	1.61	2.49	2.27
	1990	1.52	2.11	2.36
Trying to get a free ride on	1981	2.05	2.47	2.11
public transport	1990	2.00	2.26	2.45
Asking for social security money	1981	1.67	3.25	2.09
to which one has no right	1990	1.79	3.47	2.68
Lying out of self-interest	1981	2.72	3.32	3.27
	1990	2.83	3.74	3.96
Avoiding taxes	1981	2.69	3.22	3.30
	1990	2.52	3.08	4.09
Keeping for yourself money	1981	2.42	2.98	3.02
that you've found	1990	2.59	3.85	4.24

No one can predict what the results of the new survey planned for 1999 will be. But in any event a considerable part of public opinion all over Europe feels that a counter-movement is necessary if we are to prevent a further decline. Different government representatives indicate that it is impossible to introduce yet more control and police activities to prevent the dykes breaking: in the long run one half of society would have to control the other, and who would control the controllers?

A society which does not take the value of honesty seriously will shift towards a climate of untrustworthiness at every level: in the family, in teaching, in businesses and political parties, and even in scientific investigations. In the long run the whole collective consciousness will then stand under a negative pressure – as in pre- and post-Stalinist Russia. For the moment there is no danger of a return to a Calvinist or Jansenist Puritanism, which moreover is often hypocritical. But history teaches that too great a threat of ethical chaos leads to totalitarianism, whether left-wing or right-wing. This is how the whole of society punishes itself for having allowed the pendulum of permissiveness to swing too far.

This and the following views will not lead to a moralizing plea; far less will they lapse into a summary of all too concrete therapies. However, they are meant to indicate some ways of clearing the atmosphere generally.

Honesty in public life is one aspect of the deeper value of 'truthfulness'. Truthfulness relates to the authenticity of the person itself, to how we deal with the truth. On the one hand this truthfulness is more important than ever in a world in which everyone increasingly depends on everyone else (the safety of cars and aeroplanes; reliable medicine; scientific studies; legislation and administration). On the other hand truthfulness is also increasingly threatened: no one is sufficiently well equipped to investigate truth and trustworthiness at every level. Anonymity in social relations follows mobility. The media can manipulate information. Every day we experience the tension between the 'children of the light' (and the truth) and the 'children of darkness' (and lies).[6] It is not enough to emphasize the truth at home and at school if this is constantly contradicted by public life as it actually is; the result is that mutual trust, even between family members and partners, declines.[7]

All who confess Jesus Christ, in whom 'there is no lie' (Mark 12.14), and who revealed God as love and truth, are here called to critical and constructive action. In this action believers know how much the historical and actual lack of truthfulness among many fellow-believers at every level can provoke the suspicion of those who are not members of the church. Their witness can only seem credible if it is modest and – despite all personal convictions – understanding and tolerant. Any form of language that suggests fundamentalism undermines the truth of the gospel. Moreover the ethical implications of a conviction of faith can usually be offered in the public forum only in secular packaging, and then with arguments which possibly do not allay the doubts that arise. This is not cowardice, but the humility of honesty, for Christians, too, usually seek new answers to new questions, although disinterestedness and detachment could improve lucidity.

Dostoievsky again warns where in *The Brothers Karamazov* he makes starets Zossima say to Alyosha:

> Above all be careful not to lie to yourself. Those who lie to themselves and listen to their own lies end up no longer being able to discern the truth in themselves or others. Then they lose respect for themselves and others. Respecting no one, they cease to love.

Transparent government

In our culture, democracy is the only form of constitution which guarantees essential human rights. However, democracy remains a tender plant. The export of it to the East and South shows how vulnerable it is. In the West it is threatened from within. J.-M. Guéhenno sounded the alarm, perhaps rather too loudly, but he pointed to the writing on the wall:

> We are heirs of the Enlightenment, but we no longer know what this legacy implies: laws have degenerated into recipes, justice into a method and the nation states into juridical spheres. Is this sufficient to ensure the continuation of the democratic ideology? Can a democracy exist without a nation?[8]

Here he touches on the question of putting responsibility on the intermediary social web which often has the specific general interest rather than that of the alienating and rival corporate macro-groups. These last rapidly lose trust because of their anonymity. There is a need for a counterbalance not only from the nations but also from the regions and communities. Regulations have become impossible to take in, and as a result the conscience, which always presupposes insight, is alienated. The truth then quickly becomes a question of correct procedure. Lofty guidelines which aim at the general well-being need to be made concrete through a greater sense of responsibility. The old saying *Quid leges sine moribus*, 'What use are laws without good morals', is truer than ever. A good society needs to be built up on the quality of all the groups which form it.[9]

Of course politics is a question of power, both in parties and in the larger institutions. In many cases the concentration of power leads to corruption – it is rare for those in authority to be so detached from the power that they need that they remain inwardly free. And only this freedom guarantees ethically good decisions.

Compromises are part of the political game. They are unavoidable and ethically responsible. However, they lead to horse-trading. The old proverb, 'the fish begins to rot at the head', remains all too true. The consequence is that people at the lower levels follow 'the good example'. The negative pressure on public opinion is not a fable. Billions of dollars in taxation disappear in such compromises. And there is a reaction: the taxpayers themselves broaden their readiness to compromise.

The same negative spiral characterizes the rise of an exaggerated nationalism, which is a threat not only for Europe but also for national societies themselves. Fifty years after the Second World War the need for reconciliation between the nations continues to be great. Many people in the churches have seen this, as is evident from the 1989 ecumenical congress in Basel (on 'Peace, Justice and the Preservation of Creation') and the second congress in Graz in 1997 (on Reconciliation).[10] The difficult growth of the churches towards unity-in-difference is beyond doubt a contribution to an ethically responsible European political federalism, one of the greatest challenges to keeping open a horizon of hope.

Precisely because confessing Christians need to have a great spiritual freedom by virtue of their calling, they have a political role of their own to play, even apart from any party-political association. The great Socialist Catholic politician Jacques Delors has recognized this. When asked by D. Wolton, 'What does faith basically mean for your commitment in public life?', he replied:

> What is most important? If I come up against limits or fail, I don't get downhearted. I begin with self-criticism, indeed an examination of my conscience, and I try to see whether the direction proposed is good or the method adequate... If there is a drama or any moment of failure, faith plays the most important role for me, a healing role.[11]

Given the presence of the 'powers of darkness' in the political struggle, even the best people time and again have to relativize a temporary success. Here the following reflection by Thomas More in his *Utopia* applies:

> If you cannot radically eradicate wrong ideas and remedy ingrown abuses as you would wish them, you cannot abandon affairs in your own country. That is like leaving a ship in a storm because you cannot control the storm! Of course you need not try to impress any completely new or revolutionary-sounding ideas on those who cannot follow you, since you know in advance that they have authority over people who think otherwise. No, try to tack and thus – as far as possible – bring them into the mainstream. If in this way you cannot produce general improvement, then at least make sure that there is the least possible evil. Ideally that will never happen as long as the human race is not ideal; and I still cannot see it becoming so.

More had to pay for his idealism and his impotence with his head, however soberly he tried to recognize the dialectic between Christianity and politics.

In a clear if typically Protestant book, Harry Kuitert rightly points to a real danger, namely that people may try to apply the Sermon on the Mount and other texts from scripture directly to politics. He puts it strongly:

> ... 1. no one observes the Sermon on the Mount in politics, not even Christian politicians, whether left-wing or right-wing; 2. no one can observe the Sermon on the Mount in politics; 3. no one need observe the Sermon on the Mount while in politics.[12]

Even he has to recognize that not only Christians but also the church must speak clearly in extreme cases (for example on racism). However, he thinks – in my view wrongly – that such situations occur rarely. In fact the whole of world history is one extreme situation. But do Christians (and the churches) see this sufficiently clearly? And shouldn't they, without giving detailed directives (which they seldom can and may do), constantly appeal for the blind to see? Otherwise they become the priest who doesn't stop on the road to Jericho and leaves the care of the 'poor' to the 'stranger' in order to entrench himself in the temple, in the sacral that has become sterile, away from the 'God in our midst'.

And it is not because they will not succeed completely that people should not try. As Reinhold Schneider wrote, even an unsuccessful initiative can bring light:

> Christians must go where there is no light; there they must be light. Christians win when, by offering themselves, they lose.[13]

Without the non-violent resistance of countless martyrs to Nazism, Communism and a graceless capitalism, the world today would have become even less habitable. This critical resistance is an ongoing task.

In his verdict on the Ceausescu regime the old Romanian professor Virgil Candea asked:

Become pure again! Away with the falsification at every level (political, cultural, religious), for we have never known hope.

All dictatorships are built on secrecy, on making files and people disappear. But for a long time democratic regimes, too, have not always been transparent. From top to bottom an appeal is made to 'reasons of state', always rightly and often wrongly. Tension between truthfulness and secrecy in politics is inevitable.

In his criticism of C. Schmitt's defence of the arcanum,[14] W. Palaver asks for a 'political theology of public life'.[15] He rejects Elias Canetti's view that 'secrecy belongs in the innermost core of power',[16] and finds support in Dostoievsky's parable of the Grand Inquisitor. For him, Jesus' declaration to the high priest Caiaphas continues to point the way:

> I have spoken openly to the world; I have always taught in synagogues and in the temple, where all Jews come together; I have said nothing secretly (John 18.20).

However, Palaver forgets that even holy politicians are never confronted with a holy population and that even Jesus did not say everything to everyone.[17]

In fact there are far more limits to transparency in politics than in interpersonal relations. Excessive clarity (not to be confused with dishonesty) can lead to catastrophes for the general welfare (for example in premature disclosures of devaluations or criminal offences). Twilight zones are part of political ethics, but they remain dangerous for politicians with little or no ethical standards.

A transparent economy

In contrast to the period before the Second World War, when the term 'business ethics' was used only by moralists, now big businesses, business schools and universities throughout the West have woken up to the need to present a number of rules of the game or codes of 'business ethics', at least as guidelines. They have learned that more ethical sensitivity in a company, in professional life and in relations with the trade unions can have positive economic results. Although no one would deny the truth of the saying 'business is business', opinion has grown stronger. The relaxation of the almost sacred banking system in Switzerland is one example.

But disconcerting challenges remain here. The globalization of the economy at the same time requires a globalization of the rules of the game. If major rivals elsewhere evade even a minimum of fair play – not least because there is no freedom of opinion (e.g. in China or Saudi Arabia) – everyone will be forced to more 'compromises', with negative consequences for the labour market and with severe abuse of workers' rights. The social market economy is an ideal,[18] but what if this is not recognized outside a few Western European countries? The United Nations, and above all the International Labour Bureau in Geneva and the GATT negotiations, are trying to create some order. Meanwhile starvation wages, child labour, arms production, powerful drug cartels, commercial and financial mafias continue to put a heavy burden on international trade. Only constructive and critical pressure groups everywhere can do something in a wilderness of lawlessness.

Vatican II, taking up a number of great social encyclicals, made a stand in principle in the 1965 Pastoral Constitution *Gaudium et spes*. After the Council, a papal commission was set up, named 'Justice and Peace', followed in many countries by national commissions. Anyone who follows the statements in its numerous publications will recognize its courage and thoroughness, but will also have to concede how little it was heeded. Even countless Christians, among both employers and employees, limited themselves to lip service. But there are remarkable initiatives which are producing practical results.[19] Universities have established networks of ethical centres. Thus for example the Centre for the Study of Christian Ethics in Louvain forms the spearhead of a group of Catholic and Protestant universities in Europe inspired by Christianity, with networks elsewhere.[20] There is also interfaith zeal for more transparency: in 1994 the InterFaith Foundation established in London published a *Code of Ethics on International Business for Christians, Muslims and Jews*.

Meanwhile the Commission of the European Union has pushed through a number of guidelines aimed at more honest competition. It is striking that in continental Europe, above all the sociologically Protestant countries observe the rules of the economic game more scrupulously, while the sociologically Catholic and Orthodox countries in the south and east all too often remain entangled in old traditions of dishonest competition. The European Values Study also shows that the former are less permissive in public ethics generally.

In this century social legislation has markedly humanized and clarified relations between employers and employees. Meanwhile from northern Europe, concern about another relationship has become increasingly important, that with nature. People want a beautiful environment. Not only is the 'health' of water, air, earth and forests part of human health, but people also recognize a reservoir of symbols there which are indispensable for their psychosomatic balance. Moreover of course the population is putting pressure on politicians and employers to deal more carefully with humankind's cosmic body.

According to the European Values Study, in Western Europe 93% of the population support environmental movements, which is more even than those who support human rights movements (91%), and markedly more than supporters of peace movements (74%) or women's movements (60%). Another fact from a whole series of questions points in the same direction: 69% of those between eighteen and twenty-four (as compared with 54% of those between sixty-five and seventy-four) agree with the following statement: 'I would be ready to give up part of my income if I could be sure that the money would be used to prevent environmental pollution.' And 80% of the youngest age-group (as compared with 46% of the oldest) disagree with the statement: 'If we want to combat unemployment in this country we have to ignore environmental problems.'

Of course such a mentality leads to goods which are produced with more ethical responsibility and to an improvement in the quality of what is produced. Consumer associations are on the increase. In a short time the transparency of the economy is becoming very important for all concerned. Perhaps never before have non-material values scored so high in business life. H. van Luijk rightly concludes:

> The market, ethics and spirituality (religious or secular) need one another more than ever. In the market, ethics without spirituality has no roots and spirituality without ethics has no purpose, but together both are capable of changing the appearance of the market.[21]

Transparent sexuality

For every child, adolescent, married or unmarried adult and for the elderly, discovering, maintaining and developing their sexual identity is a difficult task. Anyone who is honest will recognize here a very mysterious reality of light and dark forces which both liberate and imprison, which promise happiness and cause much pain. A variety of statistical investigations show how many people, often all their lives, stumble along the way (we might think of the numerous multiple relationships of teenagers, the increasing number of divorces – between 50% and 70% in the large cities of Western Europe – paedophilia, incest, AIDS and the discussions about homosexuality). There is much suffering under apparently attractive façades. Eros and thanatos often remain close together. Much possible tenderness is harmed by the bestiality of so-called civilized human beings. All over the world women and children are the principal victims here. Jesus' remarks about those who cause offence, above all to the most vulnerable, remain just as true.

At least it cannot be claimed that the humanization of sexuality has regressed. Historical investigations provide extensive information about former times: power was much more important than love,[22] even in the age of Christendom. A 1992 investigation by the French survey organization Panorama CSA shows that every age-group, all social classes and both men and women think the values of mutual respect and fidelity very important, and that by far the great majority of French people also say that they are faithful (fidelity in marriage scores much higher than sticking to an ideology or a party).[23] But younger people and those who live in great cities are markedly more permissive than average here. The pressure of the environment is becoming increasingly more threatening. Many who would like things to be different are facing a disorientating public opinion.

All religions have wrestled with the meaning of human sexuality,[24] and all legislations have tried to order the chaotic aspects of the life of the senses with a view to guaranteeing a degree of security in interpersonal relations. Scripture – both the Old and the New Testaments – teaches how often attempts must be made to guard good sexuality and to stem the egotistical pretensions of the most powerful. From Genesis on (God saw that the creation of man and woman was good), sexuality is seen as a blessing. The Song of Songs is an impressive love song and several times Jesus used the symbolism of the wedding feast to illuminate the kingdom of God. And although the whole of Western history is stamped by Manicheanism and – later – by Jansenism, many great mystics have used the symbol of the man-woman relationship to signify their union with God. Explicitly or implicitly they have seen sexuality as a liberating combination of transparency and tenderness. This combination heals men and women so that they are whole. In all Western churches the failure to recognize the saving significance of sexuality has led to a suppression and to an often ambiguous culture of purity and virginity, which has of course had explosive boomerang effects. A particular interpretation of purity becomes more important than true love.

The negative consequence of this is the devaluation of sexual transparency. Sexuality, eros and love get uncoupled. This then results in a levelling out of the deeper possibilities of encounter between men and women and ultimately in an alienation. But the longing for a deep, lasting and clear relationship which touches all levels of humanity has not been stilled. That is evident from the great majority of wedding celebrations. More than in previous centuries,[25] mutual dedication – the word is appropriate here – is sought in fresh and open respect. It can even be said that here a new and more refined meaning for purity emerges, namely that of transparency in dealing with one another.[26] Partners do not want to appropriate each other as possessions;[27] they do not want to lay hands on the mystery of the other, but remain open to a tactful mutual deciphering of the heart and the spirit through the body. And along with union this calls for acceptance of distance, of underivability, of the attraction of difference in equality. For the believer this underivability points to the marvellous unfathomability of a deeper presence in the other loved one, which the Bible calls 'the temple of the Holy Spirit'. Only such a clear tenderness, which excludes any fierceness, becomes the horizon to eternity [28] and confirms hope beyond death.

Nor is it surprising that in all the investigations, committed Christians put a significantly stronger emphasis on trust and respect. The Christian family movements which blossomed from France around the middle of the twentieth century brought about and reflected the recent development towards more openness and more depth in the collective conscience of Christians.[29] Of course the task is never-ending. Every individual, every family, every generation will have to row here against a particular stream. Families and groups of friends can provide support here by developing a style of their own, and at the same time pay creative attention to those who have to live with the shadow of failure.

Abstract ideals of love and family can perplex people. For too long people whose love has come to grief have been banished to a twilight zone and refused opportunities to allow honest openness to blossom again. Then everything can become dark and the heart bitter. Here too a way must remain open towards the light, when friendship offers patient support so that it is possible gradually to grow into a deeper serenity. In this way two will o' the wisps can be avoided: emotional chaos and solitude without expectation. The believer can (it has long been inappropriate to use 'must') learn to listen quietly to this inner light on the way of the cross. By themselves dying to a great deal (the parable of the grain of corn in the earth), individuals can find the strength to support those around them. We may hope that the church itself will also rapidly find the way towards the transparency of the mercy of the Lord, without doing violence to the invitation to trust. Let whoever is without sin – against love – throw the first stone . . .

Transparent dealings with life and death

Almost inevitably, medicalization, the organization of health care, new insights into biology, the ageing of the population and anonymity have led to a more subtle approach to life and death and to a trivialization of them. Whereas on the one hand there is a fight to keep a premature baby alive or to hold on to a beloved terminally ill patient a few days longer, on the other hand techniques and deviant views lead to the use and misuse of embryos and a (premature) application of active euthanasia. The terrain is complex and constantly shifting. There is a pluralism of attitudes even among serious persons. If fundamental honesty and transparency is required anywhere, it is in this situation; otherwise we shall find ourselves in the twilight zone of a negative, dark spiral as a result of makeshift solutions. Then doubt about the trustworthiness of members of the family and of the medical staff can gain the upper hand and increase anxiety about both living and dying. More than anywhere else, in this sphere people expect a combination of clarity and tenderness, two values which far surpass all technology. And here too almost everything depends on a particular climate that the mentality influences.

Of course legislation is required to preserve respect for the values mentioned, but at the same time the influence of pressure groups which can help to avoid abortion in appropriate ways and stimulate palliative care of the sick have a role.[29] A positive climate of this kind does not come about automatically. A specific view can prove undermining here, as is shown by the great regional differences in attitudes, for example between Western and Eastern Europe. These regional differences are partly caused by the absence of such provisions, and also by ethical indifference. Thus in the former Soviet Union abortion was so trivialized that a woman could have six to eight abortions; or in China and India because girls were killed before or after birth a baneful imbalance between the numbers of boys and girls can be noted (according to the *International Herald Tribune* of 14 May 1991, in a number of countries there was a ratio of 114 boys to 100 girls, which indicates millions of 'lost' girls).

Jewish-Christian ethics has always emphasized the fifth commandment ('you shall not kill') towards countries with other views. According to surveys in Western Europe this commandment still scores the highest of the ten commandments.[30] Beyond the boundaries of the confessions here Christians can form a permanent pressure group – internationally as well – and so themselves preserve other cultures from a downward slope. Many church leaders have rightly spoken of the need to be quite unambiguous here.

Meanwhile we must live with much powerlessness. An understanding of human tragedies does not exclude an emphasis on clear choices. Many people bravely opt for life. In the face of the brutal treatment of human life in many parts of the world the Red Cross, Médecins sans Frontières and other medical aid organizations are often helpless. But their commitment remains indispensable as a horizon for hope in the future. It is significant that they are Western in origin. They are based on an age-old tradition of Christian compassion which believes that suffering people too are made for the abiding light.

Those who respect the worth of the human person in the abstract or avoid the concrete implications of general principles run the risk of reducing this worth to what is valuable and worthless by their own standards and thus failing to recognize the abiding uniqueness of the other who asks for compassion. Perhaps in the end only those who believe and hope that even the 'socially worthless' are called to enter an abidingly other dimension will find the strength to take the way of support to the end. For them the light that goes out here will shine again beyond the night.

Transparent churches

The increasing difference between Christendom and Christianity and between state and church gives believers and churches new opportunities for more transparency both inwardly and outwardly and above all more freedom to illuminate the nucleus of the message of the gospel. Not only the collapse of some great ideologies (like Marxism, Fascism, and, compared with the situation before the Second World War, also nationalism), but also the abiding quest for religion that characterizes the secularized West has uncovered a need for meaning. Attempts are being made to provide roots which will feed the concern for norms and values. Although Sunday observance is declining year after year, by far the majority of Europeans still want a meaningful religious accompaniment to birth, marriage and death. Bibles continue to sell in large numbers. Millions of people go on pilgrimage every year. The esoteric literature, too, indicates a widespread longing for an 'inner side'. Even medicine is beginning to discover the healing power of religion and prayer, now that the psychosomatic nature of human beings is being given more attention.[31]

Down the centuries the churches have been the bed in which this broad stream was able to run. Yet trust in the churches has long crumbled among Europeans and has almost disappeared among the youngest generations. The reasons for this are numerous, complex and different, depending on the particular history of the country concerned. Of course much of the blame is to be put on the culture of 'bread and circuses', on the dictatorship of economism and even on fundamentalist Islam, which makes 'religion' as such suspect. But it would be dishonest to close one's eyes to our own shortcomings, which have weakened credibility.

Most believers may have given up the old triumphalism which E. de Smedt, Bishop of Bruges, identified at the time of the Second Vatican Council as one of the main evils of the church. They know that both church history with its light and shadow sides (and their grievous consequences down to the present day) and present happenings in the church with their encouraging and disillusioning aspects compel humility. A variety of synods of bishops and even John Paul II have recognized this. The task of putting one's own house in order is never-ending.

Perhaps the most important reason why the churches do not look sufficiently transparent from the outside is that they do not look sufficiently transparent to their own members. Christians who want to be real believers are aware that the gap between the gospel and conscience on the one hand and a number of views and practices in the church on the other remains too great. Here I shall limit myself to the largest church, the Catholic Church, though much of what I say applies to other churches.

The faithful still note that with no convincing arguments to the contrary, many good proposals from national synods and pastoral councils remain blocked. One example may suffice. When an important church, like that of Germany, holds an imposing synod (1972–1975) at which ten final proposals fall outside the competence of its own episcopate (and thus are presented to the Holy See), they have to wait ten years to see that only one of them is allowed, namely the right to hold a synod every ten years. The malaise which stems from this does not go away. In October 1991 the influential 'Central Committee of German Catholics' published a dossier which aroused considerable attention, entitled 'Dialogue instead of the Rejection of Dialogue – How is this to be dealt with in the Church?'. The subtitles are eloquent: 'Farewell to patriarchalism – women ask for a say'; 'Farewell to clericalism – the laity ask for a say'; 'Farewell to centralism – the parishes ask for a say.' In conclusion there is a request for more than mere consultation, for real attention to change by the faithful, the bishops and Rome. Bishops have also expressed their discontent. Already during the 1985 Roman synod in which the two decades after Vatican II were evaluated, the report of the Canadian bishops expressed their desire for change:

> It seems all too easy to set against any form of collegiality or democracy the fact that the church is a divine institution. The synod must quite clearly confirm its support for collegiality and establish the consequences of that for church life . . . We accept far too much that the one holy catholic and apostolic church is the church which is governed universally by the pope and that the dioceses are no more than administrative divisions, governed by the bishops.[32]

If not only laity and priests but also bishops are denied a real say, this has an effect on credibility both inside and outside the church. Honest dialogue takes place all too rarely. Nevertheless, during the autumn assembly of the German episcopate in 1994, Bishop Karl Lehmann, the president, made a long plea for 'dialogue as a form of finding the truth' and stated that 'dialogue is a central term for the renewal of the church'.[33]

In France, too, at the time of the autumn assembly of the episcopate in 1994, Bishop C. Dagens pleaded for 'a voice from the laity'. In the Netherlands, after a great deal of tension, people have become aware that things cannot go forward without honest dialogue. In September 1994 the Dialogue Commission appointed by the bishops published an extended recommendation[34] which among other things mentioned 'the readiness and the capacity to put oneself, at least for a while, in the perspective of the dialogue partner: a change of perspective'. It also mentioned 'the sense on the part of the dialogue partner that not all the questions about which the magisterium has spoken are part of the unalienable treasury of the church'.

The referenda which were organized in 1996–1997 in many European countries and in North America, though controversial in some respects, indicate that the crisis is continuing. One can only hope that dialogue will become more transparent at all levels, including dialogue between the church and science and dialogue about human rights in the church.[35] The way in which the place of women in the church is being treated – nuntii are trying to stifle the discussion about this by putting pressure on bishops and the large women's organizations – bears witness to dishonesty and blindness. It remains depressing to have to note how fragile is the dialogue between biblical scholars and dogmatic theologians, and the dialogue of both of them with the official church leaders. There are some dangerous time bombs for the near future here. We have to note that Jacques Stewart, President of the Protestant Federation of France, met with no disagreement when in an interview in *Le Monde* on 2 July 1996 he called for more simplicity in the Catholic Church:

I would like the Catholic Church to show more simplicity.

And isn't it time for the European Synod planned for October 1999 to be really ecumenical, with the complete and active participation of the other churches, as proposed by Konrad Raiser, General Secretary of the World Council of Churches? Then Vatican II will be thirty-five years behind us, and after all this council was primarily intended by Pope John XXIII to further ecumenism. Meanwhile a spokesman of the Papal Council for Unity has already reacted positively. The church has a great need for more imagination, and more space for the working of the Spirit.

Jesus and his first disciples appeared as a sphere in which the spirit could move. They made some very firm statements, but they did not hide behind dogmatic definitions and detailed legal texts. Yet they asked a great deal, at both a personal and a collective level. They offered an open ideal, not a system. They did not make an idol of the truth but emphasized the call of the beatitudes. Therefore they were persecuted by all those who were concerned for power.

Vatican II represented a refreshing return to the sources, though in many respects the Council was only a stage. The acceleration of history calls for an accelerated reform. And this can only come about through a more open dialogue in faith in which trust replaces anxiety and transparent government calls for an honest evaluation. Only in this way can disciples write a new 'Acts of the Apostles' for our time.

Meanwhile there is more and more talk about the magical year 2000. We may doubt whether the pressure around the dawn of the third millennium will further the work of the Holy Spirit. The visionary Karl Rahner already had his doubts about this at a very early stage. In 1981, in an interview about 'Christianity on the Threshold of the Third Millennium', he said:

> It is obvious that the whole church apparatus, the pope and all the sacraments and all the Roman authorities, with all the bishops and the church tax, only serves to awaken a very tiny bit of faith, hope and love in the human heart. In a lecture at the end of the Council I once said that this whole apparatus of the church and the council with all the bishops, etc., is rather like a great pile of ore from which only a few grams of authentic uranium can be extracted. If that happens, the whole thing has some meaning; if not, then all the rest is in vain. The main thing is for a person ultimately to give himself, his life, to God unconditionally in responsibility and in love of neighbour. Everything else is merely a means to that end.[36]

The 'holy remnant' (Isaiah 4.2–6)

In society the light can shine only when the consciences of individuals influence behaviour, customs, laws and attitudes.[37] Only where conscience speaks is there trustworthiness and thus the possibility of transparency. Then fear of falsification and lies gives way. For believers who are conscious of their weakness, the trustworthiness of the conscience is ultimately based on the trustworthiness of the God of Jesus Christ. For them the basis for 'doing the truth' remains here, however solitary it may sometimes be.

Hans Urs von Balthasar put it like this:

> In the sphere of human trust, which is constantly threatened and broken, the trustworthy trust of God can only maintain

itself in the form of judgment, of ever new decisions and divisions. As the trustworthy God increasingly intervenes, this division becomes all the more inexorable, as it calls for the rejection of all those who do not agree, precisely so that through the catastrophe the 'holy remnant' is in a position to recognize God's lightning as the last revelation of his truth and trust and accept their being struck by it as vicarious expiation: by allowing the judgment to happen completely, the 'holy remnant' collaborates.[38]

The innocent Jesus, with his totally conscious trust in his calling, remains the prototype of this 'holy remnant'.

The complexity of present-day society, in which almost everyone is affected by one or another ambiguity of a legal, economic or political nature, can lead to a paralysing sense of ethical impotence: the web of determinisms is all too embracing. Children experience the pressure of family, school or sports club, positive or negative; businesses have to combine profitability, concern for the environment and employment; doctors have to survive in the tensions between hospital control, syndicates of doctors and health funds; and for governments and community authorities all that is left is often only the norm of 'the least evil'. Moreover the vivisection of the spirit and heart by philosophers and psychologists makes even the most ethically disposed people wonder about the authenticity of the motives which govern their dedication. And yet the way has to be continued through the minefield. We cannot give way to the hydra of necessity. A. Gesché rightly called for 'a liberation of history from fate'.[39] The time of deserting this 'earthly vale of tears' to 'earn heaven' on one's own is over.

Those who are free – however limited their recognition of this freedom – know the value of inescapable honest dedication. The ambiguity of the context cannot prevent them from doing what they recognize as their duty to a world which is better to live in. The issue here is finally a fundamentally ethical realism, the basis for what Édouard Mounier calls a responsible 'tragic optimism'. Mysticism must aim to further justice. Without institutional order and legal protection true love continues to be threatened not only by the weak but also by the so-called strong man, too rapidly lured by 'the right of the strongest'.

Emanuel Levinas recognizes the challenge posed by 'the face of the other' which calls for an acceptance of committed solidarity, above all when that face is sad, vulnerable or wounded. In this one face one sees the face of all humankind. *Ecce Homo*. And one of Pascal's best-known *Pensées* is: 'Jesus will be in agony until the end of the world: until then we must not sleep' (553).

We must purge all relations and institutions which structure relationships in order to achieve this transparency, which removes as much fear, suspicion and injustice as possible. The task is gigantic, but the future of the humanity of humankind depends on it. However, the individual is not up to this task. Only realistic group prophecy is in a position to put right structures which have gone wrong and to break through the a prioris of traditions and opinions. Everywhere clear alliances are needed. By virtue of their gospel freedom, which implies detachment from their own prejudices, confessing Christians have a kind of spearhead function here. It depends on their honesty whether their critical and constructive dedication can help a creative transparency to develop in all organizations and movements. Here I believe that new forms of gospel life which come about in the midst of the mire of reality are indispensable: groups of friends who can provide the imagination to open up a horizon behind the constraints of necessity. They know that the dream of God's kingdom is entrusted to them and that only dedication to this dream makes sense.[40]

Of course, the age-old struggle between light and darkness, between chaos and cosmos in society and in the human heart will continue to the end of time. And another of Pascal's *Pensées* will not lose its significance:

> There is enough light for those who only want to see and enough darkness for those who are of a contrary disposition (530).

Notes

Introduction

1. M.-M. Davy, *Traversée en solitaire*, Paris 1989, 20: 'When a child receives the grace to love nature and integrates it into itself, one day, in the fullness of an acquired freedom, it will discover a way of light.'
2. *L'oeil écoute* is the title of a book by Paul Claudel.
3. E. Levinas, *Totalité et Infini*, The Hague 1961, 81: 'The miracle of creation consists in the creation of a moral being.'
4. P. Tillich, 'The Significance of the History of Religions', in J. M. Kitagawa, *The History of Religions. Essays on the Problem of Understanding*, Chicago 1967, 254.
5. M. Meslin, *L'expérience humaine du divin*, Paris 1988, 234.
6. L. Dupré and J. A. Wiseman OSB, *Light from Light. An Anthology of Christian Mysticism*, New York 1988.
7. H. M. M. Fortmann, *Als ziende de onzienlijke. Een cultuurpsychologische studie over de religieuze waarneming en de zogenaamde religieuze projectie* (4 vols), Hilversum and Antwerp 1964–1968.
8. M. M. Davy and J.-P. Renneteau, *La lumière dans le christianisme*, Paris 1989.
9. K. Rahner, *Vom Glauben inmitten der Welt*, Freiburg 1981, 135: 'To be able to stammer about God is in the end far more important than to speak precisely about the world.'

1. In Search of the Light

1. L. Dupré, *The Other Dimension. A Search for the Meaning of Religious Attitudes*, New York 1972, 164–5.
2. J. Mirsky, *Houses of God*, New York 1965.

3. M. Eliade, 'Significations de la "lumière intérieure"', *Eranos-Jahrbuch* XXVI, 1957, 241.

4. Egyptian (and Eastern) influence on Israel is unmistakable. Thus reference is made to the so-called Sumerian Job: 'My God, your day shines gloriously over the land. For me the day is dark' (inscription from Nippur, c.1700 BCE).

5. Full text in e.g. W. Beyerlin (ed.), *Near Eastern Texts Relating to the Old Testament*, London and Philadelphia 1978, 16ff. E. Hornung, *Echnaton. Die Religion des Lichtes*, Zurich 1995, is critical of Akhenaten.

6. 'Farbenlehre', in J. W. Goethe, *Sämtliche Werke* 21, 10.

7. Heliogabalus (218–222), the fourteen-year-old archpriest of the sun god of Emesa, became Roman emperor and made his sun god the centre of the state religion with the official name '*Sol invictus*' (the unconquered sun). From Aurelian onwards (270–275), the sun cult and the emperor cult were united. Thus these two emperors became the first divine sun kings of the West. The day of the foundation of Aurelian's temple to the sun fell on 25 December, which was regarded as the day of the birth of the sun god (W. Wili, 'Die Römische Sonnengottheiten und Mithras', *Eranos-Jahrbuch* X, 1943, 125–68).

8. P. Schmitt, '*Sol invictus*. Betrachtungen zu spätrömischer Religion und Politik', *Eranos-Jahrbuch* X, 1954, 169–252.

9. W. Callewaert, *India-Goden als mensen*, Leuven 1991, Chapter 4 ('The Sun is Worshipped'). In the first half of the seventeenth century an Indian 'Francis', Toukârâm, wrote in his psalms on the deity: 'Royal and with childlike grace, a living image of love, he overshadows sun and moon with his light' (Toukârâm, *Psaumes du Pélerin*, UNESCO, Paris 1956, 60).

10. See Richard Kraut (ed.), *The Cambridge Companion to Plato*, Cambridge 1993.

11. The human being is imagined as a charioteer who has to try to get to the heavenly banquet with a pair of winged horses (soul and body).

12. Plato, *Republic*, 514a–517c.

13. For texts see e.g. Plotinus, *Enneads*, trans. Stephen MacKenna revised B. S. Page, London 1956.

14. Plotinus, *Treatise* 38.

15. G. Quispel defines Gnosticism as 'an independent religion

which is characterized by the mythical expression of personal experience deriving from the awareness that a tragic split has taken place in the deity'. As a result of this, human beings are alienated from their 'selves'; however, the deity also hungers for the light, scattered in the darkness. Quispel is a pupil of Jung and is himself a Gnostic. G. Quispel, 'Gnosticism and the New Testament', in *The Bible in Modern Scholarship*, ed. J. P. Hyatt, 1965, 259.

16. A confused and at the same time profound search for redemption characterizes a good deal of the Mediterranean area at the rise of Christianity. Against this background the cry for help made to Paul by a Macedonian in a dream when Paul is on the coast at Troas and about to cross to Greece (and Europe for the first time) has a quite special significance: 'Come over to Macedonia and help us' (Acts 16.9).

17. H. Conzelmann, *TDNT* 9, *phos*, 343. See now G. Lüdemann and M. Janssen, *Suppressed Prayers*, London 1998.

18. H. C. Puech, *Le manichéisme, son fondateur, sa doctrine*, Paris 1949. Amin Maalouf wrote a historical novel about Mani, *Les jardins de lumière*, Paris 1991.

19. H. Jonas, *The Gnostic Religion*, Boston ²1963, 73.

20. L. Van Bladel, 'Te veel flauwekul over religie?', *Streven* 63, 1996, 116–22 (prompted by some publications by the Leuven philosopher P. Moyaert).

21. S. van Wersch, *De gnostisch-occulte vloedgolf. Van Simon de Tovenaar tot New Age, een kritische beoordeling*, Kampen ²1990.

22. Gnosticism in its many forms, but always with some kind of cult of light, is widespread. Without moving too far from the heading one might think of the Rosicrucians, Freemasonry, of the teaching and initiatives of Rudolf Steiner, and of C. G. Jung. A Gnostic thread runs through Romanticism (Keats, Shelley, De Chateaubriand, Novalis and – earlier – Goethe).

23. Pascal, *Pensées*, 72.

24. *Lettres choisies de Voltaire*, ed. R. Naves, Paris 1920, 351.

25. P. Chaunu, *La civilisation de l'Europe des Lumières*, Paris 1971, 252.

26. Id., 289: 'A central affirmation of the Enlightenment is that of regularity and comprehensibility. It is not in contradiction with that of revelation, which points inwards. It is paradoxical that the insistence on total comprehensibility leads to a practical agnosticism, with

a modest retreat.' For the beginning of this whole period see P. Hazard, *The European Mind, 1680–1715*, London 1953, and for the Enlightenment and its consequences, J. Byrne, *Glory, Jest and Riddle. Religious Thought in the Enlightenment*, London 1996.

27. It is striking that two creative thinkers of great stature, diametrically opposed, namely G. W. F. Hegel and F. Nietzsche, could both be regarded as expressions of Gnosticism. For the former, as a philosopher of absolute 'holism', God was ultimately everything; for the latter, God was nothing.

28. J. B. Bullen (ed.), *The Sun is God. Painting, Literature and Mythology in the Nineteenth Century*, Oxford 1989, on Shelley, Byron, Turner, Ruskin, etc.

29. The Jesuit order, which was still capable of doing some bridge-building, was first abolished in Portugal in 1759 and then by Pope Clement XIV in 1773, also elsewhere, with the exception of Russia.

30. The following works give an extensive illustration of the poverty of this period: *The Christian Centuries*, Vol.2, *The Middle Ages*, ed. D. Knowles and D. Obolensky, London 1969; *The History of the Church*, Vols. 3–5, ed. H. Jedin and J. Dolan, New York 1980.

31. N. Berdyaev, *L'ésprit de Dostoievski*, Paris and Liège 1929, 12.

32. M. A. Lathouwers, *F. M. Dostoievsky*, Bruges and Utrecht 1968; P. Evodokimov, *Gogol et Dostoïevsky. La déscente aux enfers*, Paris 1961; id., *Dostoïevsky et le problème du mal*, Paris 1978; R. Guardini, *Der Mensch und der Glaube, Versuche über die religiöse Existenz in Dostoiewskijs grossen Romanen*, Leipzig 1932.

33. Berdyaev, *L'esprit de Dostoievsky* (n.31), 266: 'It is through the darkness that people come to the light; and it is the greatness of Dostoievsky that he has shown how the light arises out of darkness.'

34. Lathouwers, *F. M. Dostoïevski* (n.32), sums up his view in his short study as follows (138): 'Thus Dostoievsky sees human beings and humankind going the difficult way to the light; to that infinite and absolute light by comparison with which the light that we kindle will always prove to be a sorry light, but which, because it is before everything grace, will also time and again have pity on our dishonour.'

35. H. Troyat, *Dostoievsky*, Paris 1940, 591–625.

36. O. Clement, *L'ésprit de Soljenitsyne*, Paris 1974, 141.

37. Ibid., 57.

38. Solzhenistyn, *Cancer Ward*, Harmondsworth 1971, 459f.
39. Ibid., 517.
40. A. Solzhenitsyn, *The First Circle*, London 1988, 252.
41. Ibid., 258f.
42. Solzhenitsyn, *A Candle in the Wind*, London 1973.
43. Solzhenitsyn, *The First Circle* (n.40), 235.
44. P. Lippert, *Aus dem Engadin*, Munich 1929.
45. J. van der Vegt, 'Tussen Empedokles en Einstein, De poëzie van Hans Andreus', *Ons Erfdeel* 20, 1977, 49–66.
46. A. M. Greeley, *Ecstasy*, New York 1974. According to a random sample in the USA, 25% had a similar experience. For 47%, natural phenomena, like a sunset, were a stimulus; 14% had 'the feeling that I was bathed in light' (127–9).
47. D. Hay, *Asking Questions about Religious Experience*, Oxford 1987.
48. I. Hölscher, 'Der Schrei des Falkes', in W. Dahlberg (ed.), *Wege in ein neues Bewusstsein*, Frankfurt 1987, 30ff.

2. The Light of Revelation

1. The same experience is also echoed elsewhere, e.g. in the prophet Micah (7.8–9): 'When I sit in darkness, the Lord will be a light to me. I will bear the indignation of the Lord because I have sinned against him.' Similarly in Ps. 27.1: 'The Lord is my light and my salvation – whom then shall I fear?'
2. In the Septuagint, the Hebrew word *kabod* (= glory) is translated by the Greek *doxa*. However, in the Septuagint *doxa* is almost exclusively applied to God. This is the meaning in which it is used by all the New Testament authors; it refers to the manifestation of God's being. When the term is applied to Jesus, it almost always refers to the glorified Jesus after Easter. In Luke's infancy gospel it refers to Jesus' coming into the world from God.
3. F. Stier, *Vielleicht ist irgendwo Tag, Aufzeichnungen*, Freiburg im Breisgau 1981, 194.
4. After the Flood, God makes a covenant with Noah: 'I set my bow in the clouds; this shall be the sign of the covenant between me and the earth.'
5. In Judaism there are trends which run through the symbolism of light, associated with that of darkness, in a dualistic direction.

Thus the Qumran texts accentuate the tension between the world as 'the kingdom of darkness' and 'the kingdom of light'. The members of the Qumran sect are then 'children of light' who stand over against the 'children of darkness'. The fascination of this dualism was later to remain virulent throughout the history of the church.

6. J. P. Meier, *A Marginal Jew. Rethinking the Historical Jesus*, Vols I and II, New York and London 1991, 1994.

7. L. de Grandmaison ends his commentary on the person of Jesus with the word which Catharine of Genoa thought the best description of what she experienced in her contemplation of God, *'nettezza'*, i.e. the 'incomparable limpidity' of Jesus (L. de Grandmaison, *Jésus-Christ*, Paris ^{23}1941, II, 121). In all Kafka's writing there is only one sentence about Jesus: 'He is an abyss of light. You have to close your eyes not to be hurled into it.' D. Mollat, *Vocabulaire de théologie biblique*, 510.

8. The text refers to Ex. 33.9; 40.34-48, where God dwells in the tent with the glory in the cloud resting upon it. John is the only New Testament writer to use the term 'only-begotten'.

9. For the complex and still very unsatisfactory interpretation of the Prologue of the Gospel of John see 'Autour du Prologue de Jean', in a special issue of *Recherches de science religieuse* 83, 1995, 171-303.

10. L. Geysels, 'Kana: openbaring van Jezus' glorie', *VBS informatie* no.17, 1986, 74-80, and 18, 1987, 2-8 (here 77). This whole section is inspired by that article.

11. R. Brown, *The Community of the Beloved Disciple*, New York 1979.

12. X. Léon-Dufour, *Lecture de l'Evangile selon Jean II*, Paris 1990, 323-55; M. Rein, 'Die Heilung des Blindgeborenen', in *Wissenschaftliche Untersuchungen zum NT*, 2. Reihe, Tübingen 1995, 73; O. Schwankl, 'Licht und Finsternis. Ein metaphorisches Paradigma in den johanneischen Schriften', *Herders Biblische Studien* 5, 1995, 223ff.; also J. Delobel, 'De genezing van de blindgeborene', in *Ziende blind? Bijbelse wonderverhalen*, Antwerp 1976, 176ff.

13. John 5.17, 'My Father is working still and I am working', is said by Jesus after the healing of the lame man, also on a sabbath.

14. Léon-Dufour, *Jean II* (n.12), 332.

15. F. J. Steinmetz, 'Wandelt im Licht, nicht in der Finsternis. Versuch einer Antwort auf I Joh 1, 5-2, 11', *Geist und Leben* 58, 1985, 440-5.

16. The Gnostics claimed to be better 'spirituals'. Supposing themselves to be directly linked to the divine light, they felt themselves to be above ordinary people who were not enlightened. They followed only a 'spiritual' Jesus, passing over the concrete everyday world, which essentialy belongs to the way of life of a disciple of Jesus (see L. Geysels, 'Licht en liefde', *Die Nieuwe Boodschap* no.117, 1990, 335).

17. R. E. Brown is more critical: it follows, for example, from the end of the first letter, that the author of the letters of John could encourage Gnosticism (and in fact a number of communities which appealed to John were lost to Gnosticism): 'We know that any one born of God does not sin, but he who was born of God keeps him, and the evil one does not touch him. We know that we are of God, and the whole world is in the power of the evil one' (I John 5.18–19). The 'children of light' are here so radically separated from the 'children of darkness' that they must feel themselves predestined above all evil, even ethical evil (something that the many kinds of Cathars – the 'pure' – were later to repeat). Moreover, what then remains of the love for all those who do not (yet) believe in Christ (cf. Matt. 25) and of love of enemies? Brown rightly says that Matthew and Luke are more balanced, and that John exaggerates (see Chapter 7). See id., *The Epistles of John*, The Anchor Bible 30, New York 1982, e.g. 636f.

18. 'In the Old Latin manuscripts a and g[1] we find in Matt. 3.15 in connection with the baptism of Jesus that after being baptized in the Jordan he was bathed in a powerful light. We find the passage in all the Syrian baptismal liturgies' (A. Klijn, *Na het nieuwe Testament*, Baarn 1973, 15).

19. In an earlier pericope, Elymas the magician fared less well on the island of Cyprus. This 'Jewish magician and false prophet' (Acts 3.10) wanted to prevent the Roman proconsul from listening to Paul and Barnabas. Paul punished him: 'And now, behold the hand of the Lord is upon you, and you shall be blind and unable to see the sun for a time.' The result was: 'Immediately mist and darkness fell upon him and he went about seeking people to lead him by the hand. Then the proconsul believed, when he saw what had occurred, for he was astonished at the teaching of the Lord' (Acts 13.11–12).

20. The Greeks kept the Book of Revelation out of the canon until the end of the fourteenth century. Revelation is a visionary

commentary on human evil and on the glory of Christ and those who follow him. This glory is depicted on the face of the still John and the saints in Hans Memling's 'Apocalypse' in the Sint Janshospital in Bruges. Of this F. van der Meer writes: 'No one before him or after him has depicted so much so peacefully and yet so clearly with a somewhat unearthly sublimity' (F. van der Meer, *Apocalypse, visioenen uit het Boek der Openbaring in de kunst*, Antwerp 1978, 271).

21. J. Lambrecht, 'Tot steeds grotere glorie (2 Kor.3.18)', *Collationes* 13, 1983, 133.

22. R. Guardini, *The Lord*, London 1956.

23. R. Schneider, *Winter in Wien. Aus meinem Notizbüchern*, 1957/58, Freiburg 1958, 67, 79, 99. See the commentary in E. Biser, 'Die nichtgeladenen. Zur theologischen Relevanz gescheiterter Glaubensversuche', *Stimmen der Zeit* 200, 1982, 627–39.

24. J. S. O'Leary discusses this complicated theological problem urgently in *La vérité chrétienne à l'age du pluralisme religieux*, Paris 1995, above all 269ff., and hopes for a revision of traditional christology.

25. K. Rahner, *Wat is een christen? Motivierung van ons geloof*, Tielt 1977, 429.

3. Light in the Community of Faith

1. See H. Rahner, *Greek Myths and Christian Mystery*, New York 1971; id., 'Das Christliche Mysterium von Sonne und Mond', *Eranos-Jahrbuch* X, 1943, 305–404.

2. The Jews, too, were opposed to the idolatrous worship of the heavenly bodies.

3. Belief in astrology continues to the present day. According to a 1994 French CSA enquiry, 60% of the population claim to believe in astrology, 67% in the eighteen- to twenty-four-year-old age group. Millions of Europeans believe in the zodiac (horoscopes are 'in' everywhere).

4. For the 'Christmas moon' and the 'Easter moon' see H. Rahner, 'Das christliche Mysterium' (n.1), 380–404. Until the late Middle Ages moon symbolism was drawn on in relation to Mary and the church.

5. According to the Didache, Ignatius of Antioch, etc. Hence the Italian *domenica*, French *dimanche*.

6. J. P. Meier, *A Marginal Jew. Rethinking the Historical Jesus*, New York 1991, I, 205–19, does not place Jesus' birth in Bethlehem but in Nazareth.

7. See *The Apostolic Fathers*, ed. Kirsopp Lake, Loeb Classical Library 1913.

8. Ibid.

9. See the collection *Die Griechischen christlichen Schriftsteller der ersten Jahrhunderte*, Berlin; V.Lossky, *Essai sur la théologie mystique de l'Orient*, Paris 1944.

10. In a preface to a book written long after his conversion he remarks: 'The only reason, dear Horatius, why we fell into the hands of the Manichaeans was that they promised to lead us to God through pure insight, without relying on authority – something that we found "fearful"' (*De utilitate credendi*, 1,2).

11. Aurelius Augustine, *Confessions* VI, 5,7.

12. Ibid., VII, 10, 16.

13. *Sermon* 88.

14. V. Paronetto, *Augustinus, De Boodschap van een leven*, Kampen 1991,165; cf. also F.-J. Tonnard, 'La notion de lumière en philosophie augustinienne', *Revue augustinienne* 2, 1962, 62–72.

15. J. Vanneste, *Le mystère de Dieu. Essai sur la structure rationnelle de la doctrine mystique du Pseudo-Denys l'Areopagite*, Museum Lessianum sectio philosophica 45, Bruges 1959; P.-T. Camelot, 'Le corpus Dionysien', s.v. 'Lumière', in *Dictionnaire de spiritualité ascétique et mystique*, Paris 1976, 1154–8.

16. B. Rordorf, *Tu ne feras pas d'image. Prolégomènes à une théologie de l'amour de Dieu*, Cogitatio Fidei, Paris 1992, 167.

17. L. Bouyer, *Verité des Icônes*, Paris 1990, with a critical commentary on Rubliev's icon of the Trinity.

18. For the whole of this section I consulted the excellent work by E. Sendler S. J, *L'Icône. Image de l'Invisible. Éléments de théologie, ésthetique et technique*, Collectio Christus 54, Paris 1981 (the author himself paints icons).

19. L. Ouspensky and V. Lossky, *The Meaning of Icons*, Boston 1969, e.g.: 'The art of icons is a sacral art in the true sense of the word. It is wholly nurtured by the spiritual truth of which it seeks to give a pictorial expression . . . No one can interpret it better than the person whose heart is rooted in the same spirit.'

20. L. Ouspensky, *Essai sur la théologie de l'icône dans l'Eglise ortho-*

doxe I, Paris 1960, 190–1; id., *Théologie de l'Icône dans l'Eglise orthodoxe*, Paris 1980, in which the author speaks less disparagingly about the Western church than in his previous book; F. Tristan, *Les premières images chrétiennes du symbole à l'icône: IIe–VIe siècles*, Paris 1996.

21. Ouspensky, *Essai* (n.20), 194. There are attractive illustrations of icons in Sendler, *L'Icône* (n.18); Bouyer, *Verité des Icônes* (n.17); W. P. Theunissen, *Ikonen. Fascinatie en werkelijkheid*, Tielt and Kampen 1995. Icons can also be found as miniatures (as in the collection in the Topkapi Museum in Istanbul), as mosaics (like that of Christ between Mary and John the Baptist in Aya Sophia), or as frescoes (like the splendid fresco [1300–1320] which depicts the risen Christ leading Adam and Eve from limbo to heaven in the Church of the Redeemer at Chora, a suburb of Istanbul). The Orthodox celebrate the feast of the Sacred Countenance on 16 August and on the first Sunday of Lent the victory over the iconoclasts.

22. O. Clément, *Questions sur l'homme*, Paris 1962, 88–9; O. Gorianoff, *Serafim van Sarov*, Monastieke Cahiers 3, Bonheiden 1977; P. Evdokimov, *L'art de l'icône, Théologie de la Beauté*, Paris 1970, 31–3.

23. Gorianoff, *Serafim van Sarov* (n.22), 240.

24. A. Malraux, *Le musée imaginaire de la sculpture mondiale III, Le Monde Chrétien*, Paris 1952, 17.

25. J. Le Goff (ed.), *Time, Work and Culture in the Middle Ages*, Chicago 1982, 211.

26. G. Duby, T*he Age of the Cathedrals. Art and Society 980–1420*, London 1981, 114–15.

27. Ibid., 163.

28. Ibid., 141.

29. *Le monde de Chartres*, La-Pierre-qui-vire 1965, with the long poem by Charles Péguy; J. P. Deremble and C. Manhes, *Les vitraux légendaires de Chartres*, Paris 1988.

30. F. van der Meer, *Uit het oude Europa*, Baarn 1991, 69–71 (on the stained-glass windows of Chartres).

31. Later, Jan van Eyck, 'the painter of pious noon light', was to express the same idea in the lamb of God in St Baaf's Cathedral in Ghent. See P. Schmidt, *Het Lam Gods*, Leuven 1995.

32. E.Panofsky, *Les primitifs flamands*, Hazan 1992, 275–6.

33. 'She is more beautiful than the sun and stands above the whole order of the stars. Compared with the (natural) light she comes first.

She is the splendour of the eternal light and the unstained mirror of God's majesty.'

34. For a profound commentary see E. Leclerc, *Symbolen van de godservaring. Een analyse van het 'Zonnelied' van Franciscus*, Haarlem 1974. For Francis himself see C. Frugoni, *Francis of Assisi*, London 1997.

35. The quotations are taken from Dante Alighieri, *The Divine Comedy*, trans. H. F. Tozer, Oxford 1904.

36. Beatrice is clothed in the three divine virtues: faith (white), hope (green) and love (flaming red).

37. H. Urs von Balthasar comments on this: 'Nothing in the *Comedy* approaches the power of this scene: the centre lies here. Here the eros about the subjective has developed into the objective form of the sacrament; here conversely the sacramental form is unveiled and justified and made credible as love' (*The Glory of the Lord*, 2, Edinburgh 1985).

38. P. Mommaers, *Hadewych, Schrijfster, Begijn, Mystica*, Averbode 1989, 16ff.

39. Ibid., 112.: 'A good century later Jan van Ruusbroec was to call the heart of the soul a wilderness: "We must see our created being as a wild and desolate wilderness, in which the God who rules us dwells. And we must wander in this wilderness, removed from our own ways and manners. And he will imagine union with God as the endless play of the divine abyss which calls into it the human abyss that becomes ever deeper."' It needs to be noted here that Hadewijch, like Ruusbroec, seeks to experience the strange God very strongly in the humanity of Jesus, who must also enter the night and experience forsakenness. Superficially, the powerfully emotional language of Hadewijch gives the impression that she is over-emphasizing feelings. But 'enlightened discourse' is central for her.

40. The texts quoted here are all taken from *Hadewijch. The Complete Works*, Classics of Christian Spirituality, translated with an introduction by Mother Columba Hart OSB, New York 1980.

41. Of the travelling she says: 'The deep travelling which is so fearfully dark, that is the hidden storm of the divine pleasure.'

42. For the social and political context see J. B. Poujkens and L. Reypens, 'De eeuw van Ruusbroec', in *Jan van Ruusbroec. Leven en werken*, Mechelen and Amsterdam 1931, 18–41.

43. The texts quoted here are taken from John Ruusbroec, *The*

Spiritual Espousals and Other Works, The Classics of Western Spirituality, translated with an introduction by James A. Wiseman, New York 1985.

44. In the second book, Ruusbroec develops allegorical visions for which, strikingly, the zodiac provides the thread (172–220). In his symbolic masterpiece *The Book of the Spiritual Tabernacle*, among others he uses the images of the water lily, the sunflower, the gold coin and transfigured light.

45. The text is taken from Julian of Norwich, *Revelations of Divine Love*, Harmondsworth 1973.

46. J. Walsh, *The Revelations of Divine Love of Julian of Norwich*, St Meinrad, Indiana 1974, notes: 'Alongside Julian, the author of the *Cloud of Unknowing*, and even Walter Hilton are figures of the past' (7). For the *Cloud of Unknowing* see the translation and introduction by Clifton Wolters, Harmondsworth 1961. Walter Hilton (1396) is the author of the *Scale of Perfection*.

47. E. Meuthen, *Nikolaus von Kues (1401–1464), Skizze einer Biographie*, Münster 1992; L. Dupré points out the influence of Dionysius the Carthusian of Rijkel on Cusa ('The Mystical Theology of Cusanus' *De visione Dei*', in G. Cristianson and T. M. Izbicki, *Nicholas of Cusa on Christ and the Church*, Leiden 1996, 209).

48. There is a translation in now somewhat antiquated language by E. G. Salter with an introduction by Evelyn Underhill, Nicholas of Cusa, *The Vision of God*, London 1928.

49. See St John of the Cross, *Complete Works*, translated and edited by E. Allison Peers, London 1934–35, Vol. I.

50. For St Teresa see *The Complete Works of Saint Teresa of Jesus*, translated and edited by E. Allison Peers (3 vols.), London 1946.

51. For the *Pensées* see e.g. the translation by A. Krailsheimer, Harmondsworth 1995.

52. E. Leclerc, *Rencontre d'immensités. Une lecture de Pascal*, Paris 1993, is inspiring here. The figures in brackets refer to the numbering in the classic edition of Pascal's *Pensées* edited by L. Brunschvicg.

53. The text is included in the Brunschvicg edition. On Pascal's death, a small folded piece of parchment was found sewn into the lining of his jacket, and in it a sheet of paper. On both was written in his own hand approximately the same version of the text of the memorial. When he had a new jacket made, he himself sewed the two pages in.

54. R. Guardini wrote a profound book about Pascal, *Essays on Pascal*, Antwerp and Hilversum 1962.

55. In *Le mystère Jésus* he mediates on Jesus' abandonment. Here we also find the significant statement: 'Jesus will be in agony until the end of the world; during this time we must not sleep.'

56. *Pensée* 793 is a long meditation on love of neighbour.

57. J. Ker, *J. H. Newman*, Oxford 1988.

58. Newman was always sensitive to the theme of light. This is echoed in a note on his sister Mary, who had died young and whom he loved very much: 'Dear Mary seemed to me to be embodied in every tree, hidden behind every hill. What a veil, what a curtain is the world of the senses! A pretty curtain, but nothing but a curtain.' And in *The Dream of Gerontius* (no.7), the guardian angel takes the soul away to lay it gently in the waters (of purgatory) until its return 'when the morning dawns'.

59. People said that he had 'a silver voice' when he preached.

60. *Meditations and Devotions*, London 1953, 294.

61. Newman put the conscience above all things, as in his famous declaration: 'Quite certainly, should I be obliged to mention religion in an after-dinner toast (which does not seem very likely), if you wish I shall drink to the Pope, but first to the conscience, and then to the Pope' (Ker, *Newman* [n.61], 690).

62. *Grammar of Assent* (1870), London 1901, 107–8.

63. *Callista: A Tale of the Third Century*, London 1856, 314–15.

64. *Occasional Sermons* (1856), 67. Newman constantly drew a distinction between a rational approach to the mystery of existence ('notional') and an approach based on experience ('real'); 'intellectual ideas cannot compete in effectiveness with the experience of concrete facts' (*Grammar*, 13–14).

65. T. Merrigan, *Clear Heads and Holy Hearts*, Louvain Theological Pastoral Monographs 7, 1991, 39.

66. *Apologia pro Vita Sua* (1865), London 1959, 277f.

67. A century later Walter Kasper was to write: 'For scripture and for the Christian tradition there is no "answer to the question of evil". In the end, even for scripture, evil remains "a mystery of evil" (II Thess. 2.7).' Quotation from 'Das Böse in der Perspektive des christlichen Glaubens', *Christlicher Glaube in moderner Gesellschaft* 9, Freiburg 1981, 187.

68. J. F. Six, *La véritable enfance de Thérèse de Lisieux. Névrose et*

sainteté, Paris 1972, 21, 45, speaks of a 'univers de mort' and an 'atmosphère morne'.

69. Six calls her a 'prisoner of the Carmel' (ibid., 252).

70. *Manuscrits autobiographiques*, Paris 1995, 247. For the context see Thérèse de Lisieux, *Oeuvres complètes*, Paris 1992, 241–3 and J.-F. Six, *Light of the Night. The Last Eighteen Months of Thérèse of Lisieux*, London 1997. It was very difficult to investigate and publish these authentic texts. In *The Story of a Soul*, the Carmel had long since rewritten Thérèse's manuscripts to provide a sugary spirituality (Six, *Light of the Night*, 3, 184f.).

71. '. . . there is no longer a veil in front of me; it is a wall which reaches to the heaven and covers the firmament and all the stars . . .' (*Oeuvres complètes*, 244). On 3 June (?) 1897 she says to Mother Agnes of Jesus: 'I must go on to my last moment. That will put an end to my torture. Like the poor wandering Jew' (ibid., 597).

72. P. Teilhard de Chardin, *Science and Christ*, London and New York 1968, 51.

73. Id., *Man's Place in Nature*, London and New York 1966, 36.

74. Ibid., 115.

75. Ibid., 119.

76. Id., *The Phenomenon of Man*, London and New York 1959, 257–89, 307–9. There is a commentary in H. de Lubac, *La pensée religieuse de Père Teilhard de Chardin*, Paris 1962, 157–8.

77. Id., *The Heart of Matter*, London and New York 1978; see also 'The Christic', ibid., and 'The Mass on the World', in *Hymn of the Universe*, London and New York 1970.

78. For a detailed study see H. de Lubac, 'L'éternel féminin', preceded by the text of Teilhard de Chardin, Paris 1983, a reissue of *L'Éternel Féminin, Étude sur un texte du Père Teilhard de Chardin* (1968), with some additions.

79. *The Heart of Matter*, 21f.

80. In a letter to Léontine Zanta (10 January 1927) he wrote: 'May you be given deep in your heart the vision of the mysterious transparency . . . through which the universal Christ lightens the one and highest ground of things to work through them on us and to take us to their common peak' (quoted in de Lubac, *La pensée religieuse*, 84).

81. In an appendix, 'The Spiritual Power of Matter', written in Jersey in 1919 (in *Hymn to the Universe*, n.81, 59–71), which he added

to this text, he quotes and comments on II Kings 2.11: 'And as they still went on and talked, behold, a chariot of fire and horses of fire separated the two of them. And Elijah went up by a whirlwind into heaven.'

82. But his father was a friend of Archbishop Nathan Söderblom, and in his youth he himself thought that he would study theology. In 1930, with Sven Stolpe, he developed a plan for the defence of Christianity. The French Catholic revival attracted them both, as did the work of Martin Buber.

83. Dag Hammarskjöld, *Markings*, London 1964. Perhaps because of his Christian, mystical leanings, Hammarskjöld was never popular in Sweden.

4. Through the Night

1. 'Truly I say to you, unless you turn and become like children, you will never enter the kingdom of heaven.'

2. Dietrich Bonhoeffer, *Letters and Papers from Prison*, London 1971, 360. There is a parallel voice in Marguerite Yourcenar's novel *The Abyss*, London 1984: 'Perhaps God is just a tiny flame in our hand and it is our task to feed this and to see that it does not go out . . . How many unfortunates who are offended by the idea of God's omnipotence would rush from the depths of their despair if people helped them with their question about God's weakness?'

3. P. Teilhard de Chardin, *L'Energie spirituelle de la souffrance*, Paris 1951, 9. We find an echo of this in various letters: 'The more consciously life is lived, the more painful it becomes . . .' 'What a strange and painful thing life is, don't you think?' – 'I feel more and more that the world is a great and terrible thing.' (H. de Lubac, *La pensée religieuse du Père Teilhard de Chardin*, Paris 1962, 50–1).

4. According to the European Values Study of 1990, 91% of people in Western Europe say that they are 'very happy' or 'happy', 91% in northern Europe, 84% in southern Europe, 65% in eastern Europe, 89% in North America. The respective figures for those in Europe (total) and in the USA who believe in heaven are 31.5% and 81% (in hell 19% and 65%). 'Optimism' seems to be stronger everywhere, but is this out of conviction or out of fear?

5. K. Lehmann, *Jesus Christus ist auferstanden*, Freiburg 1957, 28; see H. Küng, 'meaningless suffering cannot be understood theoretic-

ally, but must be endured in trust', *Credo*, London and New York 1993, 91.

6. P. Ricoeur, *Evil and Liberation. Philosophy and Theology of Hope*, Rotterdam 1971; id., *Le mal. Un défi à la philosophie et à la théologie*, Geneva 1988; A. Gesché, *Le Mal. 1. Dieu pour penser*, Paris 1993.

7. Hell (*Hölle*) is a Germanic word which means hollow, pit, and later tomb, and therefore the realm of the dead, into which one tumbles from a bridge. It is the abode of 'lies'. The New Testament has no certain text about Jesus' 'descent into hell' (see perhaps I Peter 3.19–20; 4.6). From the second century on, the idea was developed in order to emphasize that Jesus also addresses those who have never met him, and presumably the phrase 'he descended into hell' was only incorporated into the Creed in the fourth century. See *Theologische Realenzyklopadie* 15, 1986, s.v. 'Hölle'; H. Kung, *Eternal Life?*, London and New York 1984, 124–37; H. U. von Balthasar, *L'enfer. Une question*, Paris 1988.

8. 'Devil' comes from the Greek *diabolos* (in Hebrew, *satan*), the adversary, who sows confusion. He personifies negative characteristics and is symbolized by 'negative' beasts (snake, goat, dragon). In the New Testament he is the 'murderer', the 'liar' *par excellence*, in II Cor. 4.4 even 'the god of this world', *TDNT* 2, 1–21, 70–81; cf. *Evangelisches Kirchenlexikon; Internationale Theologische Enzyklopädie* 4, 1995, s.v. 'Teufel'. The 'demons' are seen as 'fallen angels'. According to Augustine, the fall of the angels began with creation, when light and darkness were separated (*De Civ.Dei* IX, 1, 13). Popular imagination developed a whole demonology.

9. J. P. Meier, *A Marginal Jew. Rethinking the Historical Jesus*, II, New York 1994, 404ff.

10. L. Boff, *The Lord's Prayer*, Maryknoll 1984, opts for a metaphorical personification.

11. Meier, *Marginal Jew* (n.9), 648ff. (above all Mark).

12. R. E. Brown, *The Epistles of John*, New York 1982, 228.

13. J. A. Fitzmyer, *The Gospel according to Luke* 1, New York 1981, 187, 510.

14. For the complexity of the term 'Antichrist' see Brown, *Epistles* (n.12), 332ff.

15. Over against 'the lies' stands 'the Truthful One', as Ignatius of Antioch writes (Rom. 8): 'He, the mouth who cannot lie, through whom the Father has spoken the truth.'

16. Numerous examples in J. Delumeau, *La Peur en Occident*, Paris 1978; A. K. Turner, *A History of Hell*, London 1995.

17. J. Le Goff, *The Birth of Purgatory*, London 1984; J. Kerhofs, 'Reincarnation and Christian Belief', *Collationes* 20, 1990, 4.

18. As late as the 1950s in Norway there were discussions in the Storting (the parliament) about whether or not hell existed; a Lutheran bishop who denied that it did was exonerated.

19. 'Satan, who no longer has any reason to exist in nature and in history, also seems to have been robbed of his eschatological status. There is no freedom lucid enough in evil to suggest an eternal anti-kingdom. The figure of Satan has become metaphorical: with some diffidence it expresses the riddle of human evil (C.Duquoc, 'La liberté cristalline', in *Penser la foi. Recherches en théologie aujourd'hui. Mélanges offerts à Joseph Moingt*, Paris 1993, 1011). Gesché, *Le mal* (n.6), 71ff., does not go so far in his approach, but also argues for a position *etsi diabolus non daretur*. Similarly H.von Balthasar, *Espérer pour tous*, Paris 1987.

20. Archbishop C.Schönborn of Vienna lamented 'the declining belief in angels and demons among Christians' (CIP 63, 1996), a belief which is reinforced in the new Catechism.

21. Pascal, *Pensées*, 796: 'Jesus Christ said great things so simply that it seems as though he had not thought them great; and yet so clearly that we easily see what he thought of them. This clearness, joined to this simplicity, is wonderful.'

22. G.von le Fort, *Gedichte*, 24.

23. See in P. Ricoeur, *Finitude et Culpabilité, II. La symbolique du mal*, Paris 1960, 30ff. ('La souillure'). Here among other things he refers to 'the ambiguity of purity, which seeks a shaky balance between the physical and the ethical' (43). Here the complexity and the ambiguity of the symbolism of virginity is not to be underestimated.

24. 'And the Lord spoke to Aaron, saying, "Drink no wine nor strong drink, you nor your sons with you, when you go into the tent of meeting, lest you die; it shall be a statute for ever throughout your generations. You are to distinguish between the holy and the common, and between the unclean and the clean."'

25. Mary Douglas, *Purity and Danger. An Analysis of Pollution and Taboo*, London 1966.

26. M. Meslin, *L'expérience humaine du divin*, Paris 1988, 72–97.

27. See for example Matt. 5.17–48; 6.1–8; 7.1–29; 12.1–45, etc.
28. See Vaclav Havel's essay on Charta 77, *An Attempt to Live in the Truth*, and H. Bacht, 'Einfalt des Herzens – eine vergessene Tugend', in *Geist und Leben* 29, 1956, 423ff.
29. *The Vision of God*, ch.7.
30. 'No one is good, but God' (Mark 10.8).
31. J. Kerhofs, 'Our ambiguous memories', in *Rebuilding Societies in Crisis. Justice at the Core of Reconciliation*, Conference of European Justice and Peace Commissions, Brussels 1996, 13–20.
32. J. Delumeau, *Le péché et la peur. La culpabilisation en Occident, XIIIe–XVIIIe siècles*, Paris 1983.
33. A Gesché, *Le Mal* (n. 6), 129: 'I would not hesitate to say that one must to some degree "de-moralize" the theology of evil.'
34. Matt. 7.6: 'Do not give dogs what is holy; and do not throw your pearls before swine, let they trample them under foot and turn to attack you.'
35. A. Vanneste, *Het dogma van de erfzonde: zinloze mythe of openbaring van een grondstructuur van het menselijk bestaan?*, Tielt 1969.
36. A. Vergote, *Bekentenis en begeerte in de religie*, Kapellen 1978, 119.
37. T. S. Eliot, *Four Quartets*, London 1944, 59.
38. A. Grosser gives an impressive synthesis of this in 'La mémoire des peuples', *Études* 384, 1996, 503–12.
39. C. W. M. Verhoeven, *Symboliek van de sluier*, Amsterdam 1961, 31.
40. *Frankfurter Hefte* 23, 1968, 750.
41. M. Buber, *The Eclipse of God*, New York 1952.
42. According to the 1990 European Values Study in Western Europe 73% still believe in God (61% in the age group eighteen to twenty-four) but only 42% in a personal God (32% in the age-group eighteen to twenty-four).
43. B. Welte writes about this experience in *Das Licht des Nichts. Von der Möglichkeit neuer religiöser Erfahrung*, Düsseldorf 1985; the absolute limit experience of God's absence contains an experience of his presence. For this 'access to transcendence through the experience of nothingness' see H. Lenz, *Mut zum Nichts als Weg zu Gott. Bernhard Weltes religionsphilosophische Anstösse zur Erneuerung des Glaubens*, Freiburger Theologische Studien 139, 1989, 46.
44. H. de Lubac, *Affrontements mystiques*, Paris 1950, 160ff.

45. T. van den Hoogen, 'Duister licht. Het verlangen naar God en de mystiek van Nietzsche', *Tijdschrift voor Theologie* 34, 1994, 385–406.

46. Buber, *The Eclipse of God* (n. 41). Buber adds: 'It had become very light in the room. The light no longer flowed in, it was there. The old man stood up, came to me, put his hand on my shoulder and said, "Let's call each other by our first names." The conversation was completed. For where two are truly together they are there in the name of God.'

47. H. de Lubac, *Le mystère du surnaturel*, Paris 1965, 107.

48. H. Denzinger, *Enchiridion Symbolorum*, Freiburg 1991, no.3026.

49. E. Jüngel, *God as the Mystery of the World*, Edinburgh 1983, 155.

50. A. Gesché, *Dieu, Dieu pour penser*, III, Paris 1994, 37.

51. Y. Congar, 'Ecclesia ab Abel', in *Abhandlungen über Theologie und Kirche, Festschrift für Karl Adam*, Düsseldorf 1942, 79–108.

52. J. Delesalle, *Tran van Toan, Quand l'amour éclipse Dieu*, Paris 1984.

53. L. Bertsch and F. Schlösser (eds.), *Kirchliche und nichtkirchliche Religiosität*, Quaestiones Disputatae 81, Freiburg 1978.

54. H. Rahner, 'Erfahrungen eines katholischen Theologen', in K. Lehmann (ed.), *Vor dem Geheimnis Gottes den Menschen verstehen*, Munich 1984, 118ff.

5. Light, A Way to the Unnameable?

1. Above all the works by R. Moody (on the near-death experience) made an impression: *La Vie après la vie*, Paris 1977; *La Lumière de l'au-delà*, Paris 1988. An interview with Moody appeared in *Nouvelles Clés* 4, 1989, 45–8. There is an International Association for Near Death Studies (IANDS). See also J. Cornwell, 'Into Death and Back', *The Tablet*, 21 September 1991, 1140–1.

2. Karl Marx, *Critique of Hegel's Philosophy of Right*, ed. J. O'Malley, Cambridge 1970, 55.

3. M. Knoll, 'Die Welt der inneren Lichterscheinungen', *Eranos-Jahrbuch* XXXIV, 1965, 161–93.

4. For experts, consciousness is still 'an obscure matter'. See for example S. Blakeslee, 'The conscious mind is still baffling to experts of all stripes', *The New York Times*, Science, 15 April 1996, 89.

5. M. Eliade, 'Significations de la "lumière intérieure"', *Eranos-Jahrbuch* XXXVI, 1967, especially 189–90.

6. K. Rahner, 'Christian Living Formerly and Today', in *Theological Investigations* 7, London and New York 1971, 15.

7. *Faith in a Wintry Season, Conversations and Interviews with Karl Rahner from the Last Years of his Life*, edited by Paul Imhof and Hubert Biallowons, New York 1989.

8. J. B. Lotz, *Transzendentale Erfahrung*, Freiburg 1978, especially Ch.VII, 'Die religiöse Erfahrung', 267–8.

9. Ibid., 285: 'The objective truth of reflection always needs to be embedded in the subjective to prevent it losing itself in empty rationality; but the subjective truth of the experience is just as dependent on the objective if it is not to slip away into a vague irrationality. Therefore experience is still there in reflection and the beginning of reflection in experience.' Of course this is true of the experience of e.g. love, beauty, light, guilt. The tension between experience and reflection on experience explains the difficulty of putting an experience into 'language', above all in the case of the deepest experiences, affecting the basis of one's self. Mystics speak of the 'language' of silence. Emotional experiences can make people speechless.

10. See for example J. Kerkhofs, 'Changing Values and Lasting Identity – Europe's Identity and Cultural Diversity', in L. Bekemans and R. Picht (eds.), *European Societies between Diversity and Convergence* II, College of Europe, Brussels 1996, 21–34.

11. See for example Jung Chang, *Wild Swans. Three Daughters of China*, London 1991; Li Zhisui, *The Private Life of Chairman Mao*, London 1994.

12. *Grammar of Assent*, 13–14. This aspect of Newman's philosophy has been discussed in the standard work by I. Ker, *J. H. Newman. A Biography*, Oxford 1988, 538–42. Dag Hammarskjöld had felt this in his own way in the following note from *Markings*: 'Landscape: only your immediate experience of the detail can provide the soil in your soul where the beauty of the whole can grow' (90).

13. Avery Dulles, *Models of Revelation*, New York 1992, 131ff.

14. T. Fawcett, *The Symbolic Language of Religion*, London 1970, especially Part IV, 'The Erosion of Symbolism in Western Thought'.

15. P. L. Berger, *A Rumour of Angels. Modern Society and the Rediscovery of the Supernatural*, New York 1969.

16. Lotz, *Transzendentale Erfahrung* (n.8), 267f.

17. K. Rahner, 'The Theology of the Religious Meaning of Images', in *Theological Investigations* 23, London and New York 1992, 158. We find this made concrete in Paul Claudel, *Feuilles des Saints*: '... In human eyes they have seen a kind of passage of the eternal light and on an authentic face the tenderness of reality which we feel beyond the frontiers of life, which makes our suffering here below great and makes us die of pain and boredom' (66). Cf. also: '... Had you not first seen him in my eyes, would you then need heaven so strongly?' (187). See also B. Chenu, *La Trace d'un visage. De la parole au regard*, Paris 1992.

18. According to the 1990 European Values Study the percentages of those who call themselves 'religious' are: Western Europe 54%, Northern Europe 50%, Eastern Europe, 65%, Southern Europe 74%, United States 82%.

19. R. Otto, *The Idea of the Holy*, London ²1950. Henri Bergson follows this closely in his great works *Essai sur les données immédiates de la conscience*, Paris 1889, and *Les deux sources de la morale et de la religion*, Paris 1932.

20. For this section I am indebted, among other works, to M. Meslin, *L'expérience humaine du divin*, Paris 1988.

21. See the criticism by A. Vergote, *Explorations de l'espace théologique*, no.12, 'Equivoques et articulation du sacré', *BiblEph-TheolLov* 90, 1990, 229–50, where he distinguishes between the human sacral and the religious sacral and in this last the specifically Christian element which among other things essentially implies the absolute otherness of God. See also his *Religie, geloof en ongeloof*, Kapellen 1984.

22. Y. Congar, *I Believe in the Holy Spirit*, London 1983.

23. W. Kasper and G. Sauter, *Kirche – Ort des Geistes*, Freiburg 1976.

24. R. M. Rilke, *Werke II.1, Gedichte und Übertragungen*, Frankfurt 1980, 222.

25. K. Rahner, 'Justifying Faith in an Agnostic World', *Theological Investigations* 21, 1991, 130–6.

26. H. U. von Balthasar, *The Glory of the Lord* I, Edinburgh 1983, where among other things he says that 'innate light of faith and extensive historical revelation meet, recognize and strengthen each other'.

27. P. Rousselot wrote an article about this which attracted attention at the time: 'Les yeux de la foi', *Recherches de Science Religieuse* I, 1910, 241–59, 444–75. Newman offers a partial parallel with his illative sense (insight comes suddenly from the convergence of indications). Similarly R. Guardini, *Die Sinne und die religiöse Erkenntnis*, 1950, sees different levels of experiences coming together in a Gestalt, as in the 'seeing' of a 'rose'.

28. A. Vergote, 'Ervaringsgeloof en geloofservaring', *Streven* 52, 1985, 891–903; id., *Cultuur, Religie, Geloof*, Leuven 1989.

29. J. Vandenbulcke, 'Geloof op basis van ervaring', *Tijdschrift voor Theologie* 29, 1989, 170–8. Here he refers to Langdon Gilkey, 'Ervaring en interpretatie van de religieuze dimensie', *Tijdschrift voor Theologie* 11, 1971, 293–302.

30. It is not surprising that Vergote distances himself here from writers like J. Maréchal, H. De Lubac and K. Rahner, who point to the transcendent in the thinking of the mind.

31. Here Maréchal quotes L. Massignon, the great expert on Islam, *La Passion d'al Hosayn-ibn-Mansoûr al Hallâj, martyr mystique de l'islam* (2 vols), Paris 1922. 'In the long and always tragic history of the mystical callings in Islam, we do not find such superhuman accents either before him or after him, where the whole passion of love casts itself down before God, personally present, with childlike veneration and surrender.'

32. J. Maréchal, *Études sur la Psychologie des Mystiques* II, Paris 1937, 452.

33. Vatican II expresses this still very cautiously, but already very differently from earlier conciliar texts: 'The Catholic Church rejects nothing of what is true and holy in these [other] religions. She has a high regard for the manner of life and conduct, the precepts and doctrines which, although differing in many ways from what she herself teaches, often reflect a ray of that truth which enlightens all men', *Nostra Aetate* 2. The Decree on Missionary Activity makes the same statement: 'Although in ways known to himself, God can lead those who, through no fault of their own, are ignorant of the Gospel to that faith without which it is impossible to please him . . .' (*Ad gentes*, 7).

34. Karl Rahner has often spelt out this view explicitly, for example: 'For in fact in its true meaning it (Christianity) is not one particular religion among others but rather the sheer objectivation in

history of that experience of God which exists *everywhere*'; quotation from 'The Experience of God Today', in *Theological Investigations* 11, London and New York 1974, 164.

35. Meslin says: 'Any inner experience of the divine, i.e any spiritual life, has its roots and expresses itself in a psychological activity, conscious or not', even if this 'divine' cannot as yet be recognized as a personal God. Here it must be pointed out that one cannot emphasize sufficiently that all concepts of person fall short when applied to God. God is not an 'individual', but we cannot imagine any person who was not an individual, hence the symbolism of 'Father' (296). Public opinion is also vaguely aware of this. Thus in the 1990 European Values Study for ten West European countries only 42% replied positively to the question 'Is there a personal God?' (54% of Catholics and 32% of Protestants), but when asked 'How often do you pray to God, outside religious services?', 25% replied 'often', 26% sometimes, 11% 'very rarely', 11% 'only in times of crisis', and 26% 'never'. The differences between a concept and an attitude are striking.

36. C. Verhoeven, *Rondom de leegte*, Utrecht nd.

37. G. Lipovetsky, *L'ère du vide. Essai sur l'individualisme contemporain*, Paris 1983.

38. C. Lasch, *The Culture of Narcissism*, New York 1979, 44. Two important sociological studies indicate the progressive individualization in Europe and North America: P. Ester, L. Halman and R. de Moor, *The Individualizing Society. Value Change in Europe and North America*, European Values Study, Tilburg 1993; R. N. Bellah et al., *Habits of the Heart. Individualism and Commitment in American Life*, New York 1985.

39. G. Lipovetsky, *L'empire de l'éphémère. La mode et son destin dans les sociétés modernes*, Paris 1987.

40. M. Gauchet, *Le désenchantement du monde (une histoire politique de la religion)*, Paris 1985.

41. 'With the state one enters the time of opposition between the social structure and the essence of the religious.'

42. J.-P. Domecq, *Le Monde*, 7 June 1986. On Gauchet, see also J.-L. Schlegel, 'La gnose ou le réenchantement du monde', *Études* 386, 1986, 389–404; P. Colin and O. Mongin (eds.), *Un monde désenchanté? Débat avec Marcel Gauchet*, Paris 1988.

43. J. Kerkhofs, 'Omgaan met de leegte. Pastoraltheologie als

een bevrijdingstheologie', *Collationes* 19, 1989, 156–74. Of course Gauchet's book is open to criticism; thus for example many historical facts do not fit into his philosophy of history. But alongside that of many others like Foucault, Lacan, Derrida, his thesis illustrates the impasse of the void for which humankind has 'freed' itself.

44. See *Nietzsche and Christianity*, ed. C. Geffré and J.-P. Jossua, *Concilium* 145, 1981; P. Valadier, *Nietzsche et la critique du christianisme*, Paris 1974.

45. 'Do we not wander as through an endless nothingness?', F. Nietzsche, *The Joyful Wisdom*, Edinburgh 1910.

46. E. Schillebeeckx and L. Apostel, '(A)theistische spirtualiteit', special number of *Tijdschrift voor Geestelijk Leven*, April 1988, 12–13.

47. R. Guardini, *The Lord*, London 1956, 305.

48. Ibid., 305f.; H. de Lubac acknowledged how much this remark of Guardini's influenced him (*La rencontre du bouddhisme et de l'occident*, Collection Théologie 24, Paris 1952).

49. H. Waldenfels, 'Boeddhisme en christendom in dialoog', *Communio* 13, 1988, 301.

50. Id., *Manuel de théologie fondamentale*, Paris 1990, 41–4, 354–8; 'De ontmoeting tussen boeddhisten en christenen', in *Pro Mundi Vita Bulletin* 67, 1977; P.Magnin, 'Le vrai défi du bouddhisme à l'Occident chrétien', in *Études* 376, 1992, 683–93.

51. *Opera omnia* I, 134–6, quoted with commentary in P. Mommaers and J. van Bragt, *Ruusbroec in gesprek met het Oosten. Mystiek in boeddhisme en christendom*, Averbode and Kampen 1995, 385, 223.

52. J. S. O'Leary, *La vérité chrétienne à l'âge du pluralisme religieux*, Cogitatio Fidei 181, Paris 1994, above all ch.5, 'La vacuité'; ch.6, '"Dieu" déconstruit'; cf. ch.7, 'Le Christ vide' – very significant titles.

53. Ibid., 173: '"The void" is the supreme concept in this philosophy, but as a name, as a concept, it is still on the level of a superfluous truth; the ultimate truth remains ineffable.' We might think of the great discretion among theologians in speaking of Christian eschatology.

54. O'Leary refers here to the Jewish thinker R. L. Rubenstein, who sees God as 'the Holy Nothingness, the fullness from which emerged the totality of all that has existence, exists and shall exist' (198).

55. Ibid., 285: 'The figure of the Crucified is directed towards an

unknown future, but indicates the way of life which most fits with the expectation of this future. Immediate simplicity, but at the same time an unfathomable riddle. The distance between the historical figure of Christ and an eschatological figure which surpasses any imagination leads to a great difference of interpretations.'

56. H. Urs von Balthasar, 'Der Unbekannte jenseits des Wortes', *Spiritus Creator. Skizzen zur Theologie* III, Einsiedeln 1967, 100.

57. E. Schillebeeckx, 'Erfahrung und Glaube', in *Christlicher Glaube in moderner Gesellschaft* 25, Freiburg 1981, above all 103–12; also id., *The Church*, London 1990; H. Küng, *Does God Exist?*, New York and London 1979, 457–60, 571–5.

58. J. B. Metz, *Glaube in Geschichte und Gesellschaft. Studien zu einer praktischen Fundamentaltheologie*, Mainz 1977, 57, correctly writes, 'Where is what is relevant for all subjects – including the dead and the defeated?'

59. With a commentary by E. Biser, 'Der Weg durch die Nacht. Die aktuelle Zeitdeutung Gertrud von Le Forts', *Stimmen der Zeit* 116, 1991, 735–49.

6. Towards a More Transparent Society

1. *The Apostolic Fathers*, ed Kirsopp Lake, LCL, Vol.II, London and New York 1913, 373.

2. C. Duquoc, 'The Ambiguous Role of Memory in the Church', *Concilium* 1990/1, 39–53.

3. Developed at length in E.Schillebeeckx, *Christ*, London and New York 1980.

4. J. Delumeau, *La Peur en Occident, XIVe–XVIIIe siècles. Une cité assiegée*, Paris 1976.

5. E. Noelle-Neumann, *Die Schweigespirale. Öffentliche Meinung – unsere soziale Haut*, Munich and Zurich 1980.

6. Karl Rahner, 'On Truthfulness', in *Theological Investigations* 7, 1971, 242, writes of the threat posed by new forms of untruthfulness by subtle brainwashing: 'It is not really that men have become more evil in God's eyes, but rather that the actual possibilities of lying have increased so much. And therefore lying is more prevalent than ever before. And this element of mendacity can become all-pervasive and extend to all departments of life, permeating everything from the officially fabricated ideologies to the cigarette advertisements . . .'

7. According to the European Values Study, in Western Europe 77% say that they have complete trust in their own family (in Northern Europe 83%, in Central Europe 75%, in Southern Europe 81%, in the USA 88%). To the question whether one can trust most people, the respective positive answers were: 33%, 57%, 25%, 33% and 49%.

8. J.-M. Guéhenno, *Het einde van de democratie*, Tielt 1994, 9.

9. A European version of the magisterial American work by R. Bellah et al., *The Good Society*, New York 1992, would be desirable.

10. *Rebuilding Societies in Crisis. Justice at the Core of Reconciliation*, Conference of European Justice and Peace Commissions, Brussels 1996; *Lumen Vitae*, 1995, 19–34, published a rich document, 'Faire face au sentiment d'impuissance' (by a theological team from Justice and Peace).

11. J. Delors, *L'unité d'un homme. Entretiens avec D. Wolton*, Paris 1994, cf. 320–1. In the same spirit see T. Mazowiecki, *Partei nehmen für die Hoffnung. Über die Moral in der Politik*, Freiburg 1990.

12. H. M. Kuitert, *Everything is Politics, but Politics is not Everything. A Theological Perspective on Faith and Politics*, London 1986, 103f. The book by the Bishop of Basel, K. Koch, *Verbindliches Christsein – verbindender Glaube. Spannungen und Herausforderungen eines zeitgemässen Christentums*, Fribourg CH 1995, is inspiring.

13. R. Schneider, *Schwert und Friede*, Suhrkamp Taschenbuch 1987, 40.

14. C. H. Schmitt, *Römischer Katholizismus und politische Form*, Munich ²1925, 58.

15. W. Palaver, 'Das Arkanum in der Politik. Carl Schmitts Verteidigung der Geheimpolitik', *Theologisch-Praktische Quartalschrift* 114, 1996, 152–67.

16. E. Canetti, *Crowds and Power*, London 1962, 343.

17. See e.g. Mark 10.32; Matt. 10.27; 13.10ff.; 16.20; Luke 8.56; 9.36; John 7.1–13; 16.25 (he spoke in 'veiled language').

18. M. Albert, *Capitalism against Capitalism*, London 1991; J. Müller, W. Kerber et al., *Soziales Denken in einer zerrissenen Welt*, Quaestiones Disputatae 136, Freiburg 1991.

19. Thus UNIAPAC, the International Christian Union of Business Executives, together with the thirty associated national associations, regularly organizes congresses on ethical aspects of economic life, including symposia for multinationals and church leaders.

The French association CFPC has taken a series of initiatives to put a stop to corruption under the motto: 'It's enough, let's clarify our relations and make our actions transparent.'

20. This think-tank publishes two journals, *Ethische Perspektieven* and *Ethical Perspectives*, which also discuss topics like biomedical ethics and law, and peace and environmental ethics.

21. H. van Luijk, 'Markt, ethiek en spiritualiteit', in a special number of *Speling*, 45, 1993, 4, 19, on 'Business and Spirituality'.

22. G. Duby, *The Knight, the Lady and the Priest. The Making of Modern Marriage in Mediaeval France*, Harmondsworth 1985.

23. *Panorama*, January 1993.

24. For the wrestling of Catholics with their church see F. Mounier, *L'amour, le sexe et les catholiques*, Paris 1994; the author points to the difference between 'sense' and 'norm' (230).

25. P. Aries and G. Duby (eds.), *Histoire de la vie privée* (5 vols), Paris 1985–87.

26. Mary Patricia Barth Fourqurean wrote an open letter to the students about her eleven years' efforts at the university parish of Georgetown University, Washington, DC, in which she shared the discovery of this refined meaning: 'Chastity as Shared Strength. An Open Letter to Students', *America*, 6 November 1993, 10–15.

27. A quotation from a letter dated 16 October 1862 from a Jesuit to his niece on the eve of her marriage: 'Now that you are going to marry X, do not think that from now on you will be freer. The contrary will happen. Your husband will be your master, your ruler, your true lord. You must obey him completely, and show eternal submission and respect. You must never again have your own will, his will will be yours. You will be a possession of X.'

28. J. Kerkhofs, *Het gezin in goede en kwade dagen*, Tielt 1982, ch.5, 'Called to Clarity'.

29. P. M. Zulehner and H. Denz, *Wie Europa lebt und glaubt. Europäischer Wertestudie*, Tabellenband, Vienna 1993, 139–40.

30. J. Stoetzel, *Les valeurs du temps présent: une enquête européenne*, Paris 1983, 98–102, 118.

31. In its issue of 24 June 1996, *Time Magazine* published an extended dossier on 'Faith and Healing'.

32. J. Kerkhofs, 'The Laity and the Extraordinary Synod 1985', *Pro Mundi Vita, Bulletin* 107, 1986, 37. See also Y. Congar, *Église et papauté. Regards historiques*, Paris 1994. Already four years after

Vatican II, Cardinal L. Suenens published a strong demand for the freeing up of the council by the Roman Curia and complained about the secrecy: *Informations Catholiques Internationales*, 15 May 1969.

33. 'Eine Lebensfrage für die Kirche. Bischof Karl Lehmann zum Dialog als Form der Wahrheitsfindung', *Herder Korrespondenz* 49, 1995, 29–35.

34. Advice from the Dialogue Commission, *Kerkelijke Documentatie* 22,1994, 3–23.

35. B.-J. Declerq and J. Kerkhofs (eds), *Human Rights in the Church*, Justice and Peace, Brussels 1986; C. Vander Stichele (ed.), *Disciples and Discipline. European Debate on Human Rights in the Roman Catholic Church*, Leuven 1993.

36. *Civitas* 36, 1981, 5–6, 307.

37. P. Valadier, *Inévitable morale*, Paris 1990; id., *Eloge de la conscience*, Paris 1994.

38. H. Urs von Balthasar, 'Truth and Life', *Concilium* 1/3, 1967, 43–6.

39. A. Gesché, *La Destinée. Dieu pour penser* V, Paris 1995, 163.

40. T. W. Adorno – an unexpected source – wrote in his *Minima Moralia*, Frankfurt 1970, 333: 'Philosophy – in the only way in which one can recommend it in the face of despair – will be the attempt to look at all things as they continue from the perspective of redemption. Knowledge has no other light than that which shines on the world from redemption; all the rest gets lost in restructuring and is only a fragment of technology' (quoted by Gesché, *La Destinée* [n.39], 9f.)